Social Courts in Theory and Practice

University of Pennsylvania Press
Law in Social Context Series

Keith Hawkins and John M. Thomas, Series Editors

A complete listing of the books in this series appears at the back of this volume

Social Courts in Theory and Practice

Yugoslav Workers' Courts in Comparative Perspective

Robert M. Hayden

upp

UNIVERSITY OF PENNSYLVANIA PRESS / Philadelphia

Permission to reproduce the jacket illustration granted by *Start*, Zagreb, Yugoslavia.

Printed in the United States of America

Library of Congress Cataloging-in-Publication Data

Hayden, Robert M.
Social courts in theory and practice: Yugoslav workers' courts in comparative perspective / Robert M. Hayden.
p. cm. — (Law in social context series)
Includes bibliographical references and index.
ISBN 0-8122-8259-0
1. Social courts—Yugoslavia. 2. Social courts. I. Title.
II. Series.
KKZ1552.H39 1991
347'.01—dc20
[342.71] 90-40821
CIP

for Milica

Contents

Preface

This book is both interdisciplinary and comparative, drawing on the literatures and techniques of anthropology and academic law, and on data and concepts developed in the social study of law in the United States and India as well as in its primary locus of study, Yugoslavia. These characteristics may occasionally make parts of the book heavy going for those who suddenly find themselves reading outside of their accustomed disciplinary or area boundaries, but I hope that such readers will make the effort to handle the unfamiliar material. In the social study of legal phenomena, understanding of the formal structures of the institutions in question and of the ideological constructs that inform them is essential if the social analysis is to succeed. At the same time, it is also necessary to avoid the trap of seeing as unique phenomena that in fact have close parallels in other societies and settings. The wide scope of this book is meant to meet both of these tasks, and thus to give general meaning to the study of a particular manifestation of Yugoslav socialist legality.

This general orientation is even more necessary as this Preface is written, since the phenomenon of "actually existing socialism" in Europe seems to be coming to an abrupt end, and its Yugoslav variant of self-management is also unlikely to survive in the form that it exhibited when the research for this book was undertaken. Yet the institutions of socialist law, and particularly the Yugoslav self-management court systems, will continue to hold more than a historical interest for those who study law as a social phenomenon, since many of the ideals of socialist legality are found in other legal and social systems, including that of modern America.

In view of the potential for major changes in Yugoslav society and law, however, it is necessary to state that this study represents an "ethnographic present" of the early to mid-1980s. The ethnographic fieldwork was conducted in 1982–83, with some follow-up in 1984, and developments in self-management law were followed through 1986. For later years, only the most important developments in Yugoslav law are discussed, generally as notes to the text on events in 1982–86. Thus the book cannot claim to be up to date on current Yugoslav law; but it is, I believe, accurate in its depiction of legal institutions and rules in the period during which the study was undertaken, as well as in its reflection of the ethos of fieldwork by an American social scientist in Yugoslavia at that time.

* * *

I have been very fortunate in the help that I received while researching and writing this book. The project began as the subject of a Fulbright research fellowship for 1981–83, a period during which I was affiliated with the Institute for Comparative Law in Belgrade. I am grateful to the Fulbright program with Yugoslavia for its financial and logistical support, and for the help and friendship offered by the staff of the Fulbright Commission in Belgrade and by the director and staff of the institute. I am also extremely grateful to the staff of the Court of Associated Labor in Belgrade, who let me observe their activities, answered my questions and, by their general friendliness, made the observational part of the study and some of the documentary research not only possible but also enjoyable.

Research trips in other years were supported by the National Science Foundation Law and Social Science Program under grant number SES-8409554 (1984), the International Research and Exchanges Board (IREX; 1985–86), and the University of Pittsburgh (1988). The Law Faculty of Belgrade University provided a comfortable academic home in 1985–86, along with generous professional assistance. Support for analysis and writing was provided by the American Bar Foundation and by a grant from the Joint Committee on Eastern Europe of the American Council of Learned Societies and the Social Science Research Council (1985–86). All of this support is gratefully acknowledged.

In any research, however, the personal and collegial assistance of individuals is at least as important as the financial support offered by institutions. In 1982–83, Dr. Vladimir Jovanović, then Director of the Institute for Comparative Law, gave generously of his time and expertise to train a very rank novice in the intricacies of Yugoslav self-management law and smoothed the path of research in more ways than I am probably even aware of. His collegial support has continued since those days, and I am very grateful for his help over the years. More recently, I have benefitted from the assistance of Professor Veroljub Rajović, and particularly that of Professors Vlajko Brajić and Stevan Lilić, all of the Law Faculty of Belgrade University. In Chicago, Kathy Rosich provided expert data analysis, and Jack Heinz gave crucial moral and political support at the American Bar Foundation.

My deepest gratitude, however, must go to my wife, Milica, for her love and comfort, and for making phone calls when my Serbo-Croatian was deficient, translating odd terms at odder moments, raising my sometimes flagging spirits, short-circuiting my culture shock, and otherwise aiding in the research enterprise in so many ways that they cannot be recounted.

Pittsburgh
March 1990

Part I

The Problem and the Research

Chapter 1
Introduction

Comparative Studies: Law and Anthropology

Comparative is a rather slippery term in American academic writing, and particularly in legal scholarship. The ordinary-language use of the word would indicate that a comparative study is one in which the attributes of one subject are examined in tandem with those of another in order to determine their likenesses and dissimilarities. Yet a quick look at most of what is generally viewed as "comparative law" in American legal scholarship would show that such simultaneous examination of two or more subjects is not usually to be found. Instead, "comparative" legal studies tend to be those that concentrate on a legal system that is not American, making at most a few tentative suggestions as to how the features of this other system might illuminate a problem in American law. Often explicit comparisons in the ordinary-language sense are not even attempted, although there may be implicit contrasts with commonly held understandings of American phenomena in the structure or wording of an argument.

Of course, academic lawyers are not alone in using *comparative* as a code for "other," non-American subjects of study. Political scientists, sociologists, and literary critics who study foreign materials are often described as comparativists, even when they concentrate all of their efforts on one foreign culture, country, or region and do not essay explicit comparisons with American or English-language phenomena. And many of these scholars do not in fact make such comparisons. Those who study other cultures and societies are likely to belong to area-studies associations and to see their main intellectual audience as others studying the same part of the world, an attitude that can only be reinforced by the low status that is generally given to area-studies specialists in the traditional disciplines (see Pletsch 1981:582–585). Thus a political scientist who studies Eastern Europe may be more likely to attend the annual meetings of the American Association for the Advancement of Slavic Studies than those of the American Political Science Association, while an economist or sociologist who studies India may feel more at home at the annual meetings of the Association for Asian Studies or the annual Wisconsin Conference on South Asia than at the gatherings of his or her home discipline. The result of this alienation of those who engage in "comparative" studies is the isolation of their work from the mainstream of their disciplines. Indianists write for fellow Indianists, East Europeanists for their Slavicist comrades, and little notice of their work is taken by "mainstream" practitioners of the writers' disciplines.[1]

A further problem with the isolation of "comparative" scholars in their respective area-studies communities is their insulation from each other. Frequently, area-studies specialists are as parochial as their mainstream colleagues, but attentive to different parishes. This dispersion of knowledge generated along geographic lines also hinders comparisons of phenomena found in the various areas.

This intellectual isolation is perhaps particularly pronounced in the case of comparative lawyers, since legal education in America is usually viewed as predominantly a matter of professional training for practice. Legal knowledge is intensely local, and awareness of the rules, traditions, and practices of lawyers in another society is generally perceived as being of little practical value to a lawyer who has no expectation of working there. This is not to deny the intellectual respectability of comparative lawyers in American academic legal scholarship, of course, but rather to recognize that their skills and interests are generally regarded as marginal to the primary role of the law school.

Yet truly comparative studies, in the ordinary-language sense, can be invaluable. In sociology, Weber argued that comparative research is necessary to determine the parameters of general phenomena and distinguish them from those that are contingent on particular social or cultural structures (see Roth 1968:xxix–xxxix). And even if one is skeptical about the ability of the social sciences to generate laws of the same level of generality as the natural sciences, comparative research still serves as a control over viewing the structures of one's own society as necessarily representative of the range of human experience. Quite simply, the experience of looking closely at a foreign social structure can force one to look at one's own society from a different perspective.

In regard to law, comparative research can be particularly enlightening, precisely because so many of the traditional concerns of lawyers seem so connected with the particulars of time and place, here and now. If it can be shown that phenomena that are generally considered to be unique to modern American society, for example, are in fact more widespread, then the appropriate legal response to them may be rethought. One way to conduct such a study would be to test generally accepted views of modern American law and society against data from other times and places (see, e.g., Galanter 1983). If the comparative data are similar to the American information, then the general perception of the uniqueness of the latter should change.[2] This type of study, which is likely to be limited in scope to one or a few empirical questions, devotes most of its effort to the domestic phenomenon, drawing on comparative data primarily for contrast. It is thus primarily a form of hypothesis-testing which can be illuminating of narrow issues, but does not of itself raise many larger questions.

A different kind of comparative study can raise the larger questions. Such work takes its problematic from issues in the study of modern industrial society and looks elsewhere for phenomena that, by their contrast with those from which the analysis starts, and with which the analyst and his or her readers presume familiarity, lead one to perceive the supposedly familiar in a new way. In this kind of study, more emphasis is placed on the analysis of the foreign data than on those from the domestic setting, once a problem has been set up involving the latter. The most grand-scale comparative enterprise of this second kind (and perhaps the most widely misunderstood and misrepresented; see Buss 1985) was undoubtedly that of Weber, while major current efforts at such comparison are exemplified by the work of Dumont (1978; 1980; 1985).

The present study is of this second type, although much more modest in scope than Weber's or Dumont's. Rather than comparing and contrasting cultural or ideological systems writ large, I am concerned with understanding a set of ideas concerning legal institutions that seems to crop up in widely varied political-legal environments. The ideas are expressed in different idioms, each reflecting the particular cultural setting, but the underlying concepts seem similar despite the differences in specific context.

The ideas under consideration are those concerning the desirability and feasibility of creating alternatives to the regular system of formal courts in several countries. This is an idea that has had great currency in the United States since the late 1970s, where a movement for alternative dispute resolution (ADR) has produced a large scholarly and semischolarly literature on the topic and many practical attempts to implement it. While some of this literature does make reference to supposedly similar phenomena in other countries, there has been little effort to look seriously at these comparative materials. Instead, too often the virtues of supposedly informal institutions in other cultures are assumed, and then it is proposed that these features should be recreated in America.

Such an approach may suffer from several inadequacies. One is that the foreign institution may not function in fact in the manner assumed, and thus the comparison would be false empirically.[3] But perhaps more important, the presence of supposedly alternative, nonformal dispute institutions in other societies is often accompanied by a literature within those societies asserting their desirability or necessity, or both; and this indigenous literature is often ignored. Yet the arguments given for the creation or maintenance of legal institutions in different societies may be valuable in several ways. First, they provide crucial criteria for evaluating the performance of the particular institution. Perhaps more important for comparative scholarship, however, is the possibility that the rationales expressed for creating nonformal courts in different societies may exhibit similarities in structure despite the differences in particular context.

This book considers both of these possibilities. The heart of the work is a detailed study of the ways in which cases are handled by a workers' court in Yugoslavia, the Court of Associated Labor (CAL) in Belgrade, and of the indigenous Yugoslav literature that centers on this kind of court. The book is thus a study in comparative law in the most narrow, traditional sense of the term, since it encompasses a detailed study of this foreign legal institution and the indigenous literature surrounding it. It is also a comparative work in a wider sense, however, because the Yugoslav data are expressly compared with ideas and positions that are found in the American literature on informal courts and ADR.

While the study is thus one in comparative law, it is also one in the anthropology of law. Methodologically, the work is based in large part on an ethnographic study of the CAL in Belgrade, thus drawing on the traditional methods of anthropological research. The design and intent of the work reflect one of the traditional goals of anthropological research (see Marcus and Fischer 1986:128–131), that of comparing a foreign phenomenon with a domestic one, with a view toward furthering understanding of the latter.[4] Yet I hope that something further can be gained as well. In this study, the foreign subject will be assessed, initially, largely on its own terms; that is, in reference to an indigenous Yugoslav literature on the courts of associated labor and the ways that they should or should not function. The study cannot stop there, however. What is to me most interesting are the similarities between that Yugoslav literature and the American one, and between both of them and the political and legal arguments from other times and places, American and foreign. One of the goals of this study is to compare these literatures, with each other and with empirical research on the subjects of some of the separate polemics, in order to explore their commonalities, differences, and the potential reasons for both. The ultimate aim of the work is to generate some hypotheses concerning the workings of social courts and their political representation in any political culture. It will be seen that the idea of social courts will likely be always attractive in complex societies, but is never likely to be achieved, for it contains within itself an inherent and inevitable flaw of political logic and structure. Yet the idea will continue to be promoted because it can easily be made to fit the interests of conservative elements within complex societies, those who are in power and wish to preserve their positions; even, ironically, as it is promoted by people who would rather transform the established power structure.

The Concept of Social Courts

The Unpopularity of Regular Courts

Modern America

Regular courts seem to be frequent targets of discontent. In the United States since the early 1970s, a great deal of professional and scholarly attention has been devoted to the idea that there is a need to create alternatives to the regular courts for many kinds of disputes (see Abel 1982, vol. 1; Tomasic and Feeley 1982; Harrington 1985; this literature is itself surveyed by Merry [1987] and Yngvesson [1988]). The need has been seen to lie in many flaws of the regular courts, but one dominant theme has been that they are too costly and inefficient for many small cases. The Chief Justice of the United States stated in 1976 that it was often no longer economically feasible to take many small cases to court, and questioned the appropriateness of the adversary system in such cases (Burger 1976), thereby giving support to the idea that the system was indeed flawed.

In 1976, the Chief Justice organized the National Conference on the Causes of Popular Dissatisfaction with the Administration of Justice (see *Federal Rules Decisions* 1976), known as the "Pound Conference," named after a famous 1906 address by Roscoe Pound on the same topic. This conference, which was attended by judges, lawyers, law professors, and social scientists, mainly concentrated on the issues of cost and efficiency of the courts. However, some of the participants questioned whether courts and litigation were appropriate for some kinds of disputes, particularly those involving parties with multiple ties and complex interrelationships (Sander 1976). The adversary nature of courts and their tendency to reduce the complicated relationships of social life to inflexible legal categories were thought to make them disruptive of such relationships. It would be better to have institutions that would foster communication and compromise between the parties in minor disputes, rather than stress rights and assign blame for wrongs (Danzig 1973).

This idea reflected the early stages of the development of what Marc Galanter (1985a; cf. Galanter 1985b) has called a "second kind of learning about law," focusing on the social contexts in which disputes arise and the varieties of institutions used to process them (see Abel 1974). The argument drew heavily on the literature of legal anthropology, which was devising typologies of dispute institutions reflecting the presence or absence of a third party and the amount of power the third party had to decide the case (see, e.g., Nader 1969; Nader and Todd 1978). These typologies typically ran from negotiation, in which there was no third party, through mediation and arbitration (in which the third party has no power to impose a solution [mediation] or only so much authority as the parties might voluntarily grant [arbitration]), to adjudication (in which the third party has the power to impose a decision on the disputants).

Mediation, in which a third party tries to facilitate the disputants in arriving at a resolution to their conflict but has no power of his or her own to impose a solution, has proven exceptionally attractive as a noncoercive alternative to courts. When it is contrasted with adjudication, mediation is generally seen as "softer" (Greenhouse 1985b:90–91), flexible (Nader 1969), conciliatory (Gulliver 1969), even therapeutic (Gibbs 1963). Although there has been some questioning of the supposed noncoerciveness of mediation (Merry 1982) and of the relevance of models of institutions in tribal societies to the problems of disputants in industrial societies (Felstiner 1974), the desirability of mediation has remained a basic assumption of the alternatives movement. The idea that mediation could be used in industrial societies has received some support from a rather impressionistic literature on the "success" of alternative, lay courts in socialist countries (see, e.g., Berman 1969).[5] By the time of the Pound Conference, the view that procedures other than adjudication might be preferable for many kinds of disputes in modern societies was current in scholarship concerning law and society (see, e.g., Danzig 1973; Danzig and Lowy 1975; Johnson, Kantor, and Schwartz 1977; Aaronson et al. 1977).[6]

In 1977 the American Bar Association (ABA) sponsored the National Conference on Minor Disputes Resolution. In addition to the considerations of cost and efficiency raised at the Pound Conference, the ABA conference noted that informal alternatives to the judicial process may be most appropriate for resolving disputes between people involved in interdependent relationships, saying that

> in such cases there is a particular need for a noncoercive process (such as mediation) that has the capacity of reorienting the basic relationship between the disputants, rather than simply dealing with the surface symptoms of their relationship, as a court typically would. (American Bar Association 1977:13)

This statement marked the adoption of the critique of regular, formal courts as inappropriate mechanisms for handling certain kinds of disputes expressed in the literature of the "second learning about law." The argument is not only that courts may not be suitable for the kinds of issues that cases between related parties present, but also that they may, through the adversariness they foster, even disrupt further relations that would be better off continuing. It is becoming axiomatic that lawyers and law professors put too much emphasis on courtroom combat, instead of negotiation and reconciliation (see, e.g., Bok 1983). This view was graphically stated by Chief Justice Burger in his 1983 report to the American Bar Association on the state of justice:

> [W]e must move away from total reliance on the adversary contest for resolving all disputes. For some disputes, trials will be the only means, but for many, trials by the adversary process must in time go by the way of the ancient trial by battle and blood. Our system is too costly, too painful, too destructive, too inefficient for a truly civilized people. (Burger 1984:66)

The Chief Justice thought that there must be a better way. It is clear that much scholarly and professional opinion in the United States also feels that there must be.

Other Places, Other Times

Dissatisfaction with formal legality is not new in America. Earlier efforts to render justice more accessible and fair by making it less formal were made as far back as the early nineteenth century (Steele 1981) and include such specific innovations as the creation of small claims courts, domestic relations courts, and juvenile courts (Steele 1981; Harrington 1985). As Harrington notes (1982:36), there are striking parallels between the rhetoric of informal justice used in the 1970s' arguments for informal justice and those found in the first three decades of this century: that the formal legality of the courts hinders the attainment of substantively just or equitable results (cf. Abel 1979), and that for many kinds of cases, it would be better to create institutions to foster reconciliation or prevention of disputes rather than allow them to go through the formal process of adversarial litigation (Harrington 1985:53–63).

Neither have such arguments been limited to the United States. Dissatisfaction with the regular courts has been a feature of some third world countries both during their colonial periods and after independence. Thus India, for example, has seen arguments that the formal, British-derived courts were unsuited for many kinds of disputes between Indians almost since the courts were created (Galanter 1968 and 1972; Baxi and Galanter 1978; Meschievitz and Galanter 1982). As in America, arguments were made that the formal courts were disruptive of ongoing relations as they were not sensitive to the complexities of Indian social life, while the informal native *panchayats* (councils, or village courts) were said to foster compromise. This position was taken by early British administrators who wished to preserve the traditional system of *panchayats* for native cases (e.g., Elphinstone 1973 [1821]), although these attempts proved unsuccessful in that Indians refused to use them (Ballhatchet 1957:105–115, 192–201). Later, when British judges were confronted with Indian cases, they often complained that the judicial process was not up to the task of fairly deciding them, and that it in fact encouraged litigation by undermining local norms (see Rudolph and Rudolph 1965:31–32). The argument was again that judges could not adequately know the context of a dispute, and so could not render justice. These sentiments were echoed by Mohandas K. Gandhi, who believed that the formal court system prompted the disruption of social relations, while the traditional *panchayat* system maintained harmony (Gandhi 1939:54–57). Similar criticisms of formal justice have been made in Sri Lanka (see Tiruchelvam 1984), and the distinction between conciliatory, informal customary procedures and the rigidity of the formal courts has been a staple of the literature on law in Africa (e.g., Bush 1979; but cf. Van Velsen 1969).

Other kinds of criticism of formal legality have been developed in the socialist countries. In postrevolutionary societies there frequently has been mistrust of lawyers and other legal professionals of the previous regime, who were seen as adherents to antirevolutionary attitudes (see, e.g., Salas 1983 [Cuba]; Sachs 1985 [Mozambique]; Huszar 1978 and Kulcsar 1984:112–115 [Hungary]). For this reason, the abilities of formal courts to render decisions appropriate to the new social order have been questioned. A second socialist idea has been that there should be greater participation of ordinary people in the administration of justice as a means of achieving true socialist democracy (see Tiruchelvam 1984:2–8).[7] This view has been linked with the classical Marxist ideal of the withering of state and law with the development of socialist society (Tiruchelvam 1984:6).[8] However, it has also been associated with the idea that the most appropriate way of handling many kinds of conflicts would be by the education of the parties or through some other method of repairing disrupted social relations and preventing further disruptions and that regular courts are not well-suited for this purpose (Ramundo 1965). This last view reconnects some of the socialist criticisms with those from other times and places, including modern America.

Alternatives to Regular Courts

The Common Response: Social or Lay Courts

The various arguments recalled above have often led to rather similar proposals for the creation of alternatives to the regular courts for certain kinds of disputes. These proposals center on the socialization or laicization of some aspects of the judicial function, generally through the creation of special institutions to handle minor disputes or those between people in ongoing relationships. Thus India has seen attempts to create officially sponsored versions of the supposedly traditional village *panchayat* system,[9] staffed by nonlawyers, since at least the mid-nineteenth century and continuing up to the present (Baxi and Galanter 1978; Meschievitz and Galanter 1982; Galanter 1968). Similarly, attempts were made in colonial and independent Sri Lanka (formerly Ceylon) to institute conciliation boards and other forms of informal, lay judicial institutions for minor village disputes (Tiruchelvam 1984). In Africa, separate lay judicial institutions have been maintained in many countries (Bush 1979). And "comrades' courts" and other lay, socialist judicial institutions have been created in the Soviet Union (Berman and Spindler 1963; Butler 1977), many of the East European socialist countries (Butler 1972), Cuba (Salas 1983), and Mozambique (Isaacman and Isaacman 1982).

A common element of all of these alternatives to regular courts is that the judicial function is supposed to be executed by laymen rather than legal professionals. Further, the alternative courts are often meant to be within the social settings in which the disputes arise and are, therefore, located apart from the regular courts. Thus the Soviet comrades' courts, for example, are located in housing units or within factories, while in India the government-sponsored *nyaya panchayats* are located in villages.[10] In all of these institutions, the idea is that judges familiar with local conditions and with the parties will render more appropriate decisions than could be obtained in regular courts. We might, then, define *social courts* as institutions for handling disputes that are embedded in a social field, in which the parties themselves take an active role in the proceedings, and in which the third-party intervener (analogous to a judge, but ideally more of a mediator) is not a legal professional, but rather a member (or members) of the local community.

Attempts at socializing justice have not been limited to third world and socialist countries. Access to justice was a major concern of European legal scholars in the 1970s (see Cappelletti 1978–79). Alternative dispute institutions have been created in Australia (see Ray 1983, Appendix 3) and West Germany (Strempel 1983), as well as in other countries (see Cappelletti and Garth 1978).

In America, too, the advocates of alternative courts have proposed the creation of lay institutions that would draw their staff and their cases from the communities or the neighborhoods in which they are located (Danzig 1973; Fisher 1975; Sander 1976). These advocates have drawn their inspiration from the anthropological studies and the writings on socialist courts cited above. Chief Justice Burger proposed in a speech to the American Bar Association in 1977 that America has much to learn from both underdeveloped societies and those that are highly advanced (E. Moore 1985:5), and his keynote speech at the Pound Conference suggested that Americans could learn from less litigious societies such as Japan (Burger 1976:94). He also suggested that panels of nonlawyers, perhaps guided by a lawyer or paralegal, might be given "unreviewable authority to decide certain kinds of minor claims," saying that such an approach had "a background in other countries" (Burger 1976:93–94). A proposal at the same conference by Frank Sander of the Harvard Law School for the creation of "multi-door justice centers" that would contain mediation and arbitration services as well as regular courts was explicitly a combination of Danzig's (1973) idea of noncoercive neighborhood moots, which was based on the anthropological literature, and Fisher's model (1975) of coercive but informal, lay neighborhood courts, which had been derived from the literature on socialist comrades' courts. The latter institutions have obtained approval from some rather unlikely allies, including the *Wall Street Journal* (Morgenthaler 1979, cited in E. Moore 1985:4) and emissaries of the American Bar Association (Snyder 1980).

These advocates of alternative dispute institutions in America have had some success. In 1976 the American Bar Association formed a Special Committee on Alternative Means of Dispute Resolution, which has organized conferences on alternatives to courts, publishes a quarterly newsletter and a variety of other materials on the subject, and has assisted some states in developing legislation on informal dispute resolution (see Ray 1983). In 1980 the United States Congress passed the

Dispute Resolution Act (PL 96-190), which was supposed to establish a national resource center on dispute resolution, and under which ten million dollars were to be granted to organizations that sought to develop community or neighborhood models for the improvement of dispute resolution institutions. No money has been allocated for this purpose by Congress, however, so the passage of the act may turn out to have been primarily a symbolic action.

In the 1970s the U.S. Department of Justice did take some concrete steps toward the creation of alternative courts. Even before the Pound Conference, the department had published materials on "exemplary projects," innovative attempts at improving the administration of justice by improving local access to and participation in it, such as the Night Prosecutor Program of Columbus, Ohio (U.S. Department of Justice 1974), and community-based corrections in Des Moines (Boorkman et al. 1976). The Pound Conference recommended the creation of Neighborhood Justice Centers (NJCs), and the Justice Department responded by commissioning an analysis of potential models for such a program (McGillis and Mullen 1977) and then by funding three experimental NJCs in Atlanta, Kansas City, and Los Angeles (see Cook et al. 1980). The department also supported other research on alternative means of processing disputes (e.g., Johnson and Schwartz 1978), including the survey and analysis "European Alternatives to Criminal Trials and Their Applicability in the United States" (Felstiner and Drew 1978).

Despite the absence of funding under the federal Dispute Resolution Act, alternative dispute resolution (ADR) has become a growth industry in American law on the state level. As of 1982, more than 170 communities in forty states had created some kind of "alternative dispute center" (Ray 1983), and by 1984 seventeen states had enacted laws relating to mediation (Freedman 1984:i). ADR has been particularly attractive to judges and others concerned with court administration, as evidenced by special issues on the subject in the *Justice System Journal* (1984) and *Judicature* (1986). Teaching materials have been prepared for law schools (e.g., Goldberg et al. 1985; Kanowitz 1985; see *Journal of Legal Education* 1984). At least two new journals devoted to alternative approaches to dispute resolution have recently appeared, *Negotiation Journal* and the *Missouri Journal of Dispute Resolution*. And one may participate in professional seminars on ADR on tax-deductible cruises.[11]

Not all of the ADR innovations are meant to be social or lay alternatives to regular courts. For example, recent experiments have drawn on legal professionals and court personnel for programs of "neutral evaluation" of a case by a court-appointed lawyer (Brazil et al.

1986) or "summary jury trials," and a Society of Professionals in Dispute Resolution has also been formed. Further, ADR is now meant to encompass disputes ranging from family altercations or those between neighbors to environmental issues and even international conflicts. Nevertheless, the provision of community-based dispute institutions is still cited as a desirable goal of ADR (see, e.g., Alfini 1986:252), and the figures noted above on the creation of alternative dispute centers indicate that this goal of the ADR movement still remains. In addition, theoretical arguments in favor of instituting community justice as a partial means of transforming wider social structures continue to be made (e.g., Barber 1984:280–281; Henry 1985). Clearly, the idea of alternative, social justice maintains vitality.

The Problem of Voluntary Participation

The experimental NJCs funded by the Department of Justice were evaluated favorably by the department's own study team (Cook et al. 1980), which found that the centers were successful in attracting cases; that they processed them quickly and efficiently; that parties were satisfied with the mediation services provided by the centers; and that a large majority of the agreements reached through mediation were holding six months later (Cook et al. 1980:103–104). However, as the authors of the report themselves noted (p. 103), their work was policy-oriented and hence had to provide firm conclusions and recommendations. Other studies have been less sanguine about the success of mediation centers in achieving such goals as getting to the roots of problems and thus restoring relationships (Tomasic 1982; Felstiner and Williams 1978; Merry 1982). Nevertheless, there is substantial research support for the proposition that mediation is more satisfying than litigation for disputants who experience it (Merry and Silbey 1984:152; Pearson 1982:432–433) and that compliance with mediated outcomes is higher than with court orders in similar cases (Pearson 1982:433–434; McEwan and Maiman 1984, but cf. Vidmar 1984).

Despite these favorable features of mediation, NJCs and other alternative dispute centers have consistently had difficulty generating substantial voluntary caseloads (Pearson 1982; Merry and Silbey 1984; Benoit 1984; Harrington 1985).[12] This problem was, in fact, noted by the Department of Justice's evaluation of the experimental NJCs: overall, only 17 percent of the cases at the three NJCs were the result of self-referral (Cook et al. 1980:29). The caseload of most NJCs is mainly derived from referrals by the formal legal system, particularly the criminal courts, and by social agencies.[13] The authors of the evaluation attributed this lack of voluntary use to insufficient public awareness of the availability of the NJCs' services and recommended that ways be developed to rectify this situation (ibid., pp. 104–105). Others have suggested that lawyers discourage the use of these alternatives (see Pearson 1982:428), either because of lack of understanding of them or because of antipathy to deprofessionalized justice.

There is some empirical evidence indicating that the lack of public awareness argument is weak. Sally E. Merry and Susan Silbey (1984), who studied mediation and court use in the Boston area, found that even disputants who knew about the availability of mediation did not usually use it. Merry and Silbey make a cultural argument, saying that

> [p]articularly in interpersonal disputes, conflict behavior is hedged with judgments about appropriate or virtuous ways of behaving generally. Rules about how to fight or whether to fight, how to respond to insults and grievances, how to live with one's neighbors, are parts of elaborate and complex belief systems. . . . In other words, dispute behavior reflects community evaluations, moral codes and cultural notions, learned but not entirely chosen, of the way people of virtue and integrity live. (Merry and Silbey 1984:176–177)

Their data indicate Americans feel that disputes should in general not be taken to outsiders and that negotiation is preferred to litigation, but that litigation may be chosen when a situation seems irresolvable without an authoritative decision by a third party. Further, disputes that are taken this far are phrased in moral terms, as conflicts over rights, to counter the general view that going to court is improper.[14] They use this cultural argument to challenge the view that use of a dispute forum or institution is based on a rational evaluation of the costs and benefits of alternative choices, which underlies much of the literature on alternatives to courts. By their reasoning, even though mediation is likely to be superior to litigation on many grounds, litigants in America will not use it because it does not fit in with American cultural patterns.

Attribution of the lack of voluntary use of alternative courts in the United States to the specifics of American culture seems unwarranted, however, as the same pattern is observed in other societies, including those cited as inspirations for mediation centers and NJCs. In India, for example, none of the attempts at instituting alternatives to the regular courts has ever succeeded in attracting voluntary use. The most recent effort, the post-independence *nyaya panchayats*, attracted a substantial number of cases when they were first created, but their use dwindled quickly to the point where they are now moribund (Meschievitz and Galanter 1982). Similarly, the attempts at creating village courts in Sri Lanka failed because few would use them (Tiruchelvam 1984). In Africa, Abel has noted that the introduction of modern courts leads to a decline in the use of tribal dispute institutions: "[T]he mere availability of modern courts seems to undermine tribal dispute processing elsewhere in society" (Abel 1979:196).

In the European socialist countries, the same pattern of lack of voluntary use is exhibited by the comrades' courts. In Hungary, lay labor courts were introduced into work organizations in the early 1960s, but they have never attracted much use.[15] In East Germany, the Soviet Union, and Poland, comrades' courts are infrequently used voluntarily by workers; instead, more than 90 percent of their cases are brought *against* individual workers by their employers or on referral from prosecutors or other state agencies (Berg 1983 [USSR]; Markovits 1984 [E. Germany]; Los 1978 [Poland]). The literature on these courts, like that on American alternatives, treats this lack of voluntary use as rather puzzling. A Polish scholar, for example, says that while the Polish workers' courts "have several attractive features, such as their educational and prophylactic character, their informal, inexpensive and fast procedure, and their democratic premises. . . . unfortunately, these courts do not work very well in practice" as few workers bring cases to them (Los 1978:814). The general pattern is thus that alternative courts are rarely used voluntarily; indeed, we are hard pressed to find alternative courts that do generate substantial voluntary caseloads.

The Apparent Exception: The Yugoslav Courts of Associated Labor

The only social, alternative courts that have managed to generate substantial numbers of cases voluntarily brought by ordinary citizens seem to be the Yugoslav courts of associated labor (*sudovi udruženog rada*) (hereafter, CALs). As will be explained in chapter 3, these courts came into existence in 1974 as part of the system set up by the new constitution of that year, which was based on the concept of socialist self-management and mandated that justice would be administered by "regular courts as agencies of state power, and by self-management courts" (Constitution, Article 217).[16] The CALs were meant to be an important step toward the socialization (*podruštvlavanje*) of the judicial function (Perović 1980:145; Djordjević 1982:815): staffed by nonlawyers, with informal procedures, the courts' task was not to be the determination of legal rights, but rather the resolution of disputes (*rešavanje sporova*) and the resolution of disrupted relations (*uredjivanje odnose*) between the parties (Trifunović 1975:25). As with mediation, their authority was not to rest on their ability to impose sanctions, but rather on their capacity to assist the disputants through their internal moral authority (Matović 1974:974).

The CALs were created in the Yugoslav republics and provinces[17] in 1974 and 1975, and almost immediately developed substantial caseloads. By the end of 1976, forty-eight CALs of first instance (trial level) had been established throughout Yugoslavia, with 2,618 judges, and they attracted nearly 26,000 cases (Mandić 1978). By the end of 1978 the number of courts had not changed, but there were then 4,024 judges handling 50,594 cases (Perović 1980:180–183). In 1980 the CALs received more than 80,000 new cases (Korać 1981:8). From the start, more than 90 percent of the cases in the CAL were initiated by individuals (Korać 1981:8).

The difference in voluntary court use between the CALs and other social courts in socialist countries may become more clear if we compare per capita use rates. The CALs are labor courts, and although subject-matter jurisdiction is almost certain to vary between courts in different countries,[18] it is most appropriate to compare them with labor courts in other countries, using individually initiated cases per 10,000 workers as a measure. In East Germany in 1982, 20.7 such cases per 10,000 workers were initiated in the social labor courts,[19] and similar figures can be found for labor disputes in the comrades' courts in the Soviet Union (Berg 1983:145). The same measure for the CALs in Serbia in 1981 was 87.1 cases per 10,000 workers. By way of comparison with a nonsocialist European country, for the labor courts in West Germany, the comparable measure was 149.[20]

The immediate question raised by these figures is why these Yugoslav courts attract use by individual plaintiffs when other social alternative courts do not do so. The ethnographic research on which this book is based was designed to answer this question, as described in the next chapter. However, the purpose of engaging in empirical research on this question was not simply due to its interest as a possible exception to the usual pattern of nonuse of alternative courts. Instead, the Yugoslav case offered an opportunity to explore the adequacy and coherence of the theoretical and political arguments made in favor of social courts in a wide variety of socioeconomic and cultural settings, which are surprisingly similar. This opportunity arose not only because of the phenomena of the CALs themselves, but also because of the theoretical literature concerning them within Yugoslavia, which resonated in interesting ways with political and scholarly debates from these other places and times. The implications of the commonalities of these similar arguments, from such disparate settings as modern America, colonial India, and socialist Yugoslavia, form the wider problematic of this study, and are addressed in the concluding chapter.

Chapter 2

The Question of Method: An Ethnographic Study of a Court of Associated Labor

To answer the question of why the CALs attract so many voluntary users, we need to know much more about the activities of the CALs: detailed information on who uses the courts, for what kinds of cases, how cases are handled by the courts, what other options are available to the potential plaintiffs, and the political and legal environment in which the courts operate. The research reported in this book was aimed at answering those questions, using data gathered from many sources and by several methods. The analysis centers on an observational study of the CAL in Belgrade, done in accordance with traditional ethnographic methods. This observational study was complemented by documentary and statistical data on the work of the CALs in Belgrade, in Serbia and, when available, in other parts of Yugoslavia and in the country as a whole. Finally, I have drawn on discussions of the CALs in both the scholarly and popular Yugoslav press, in regard to the concepts behind the CALs and some of the political arguments that have been made concerning these courts, particularly in the years 1982–86.

This multiple-method approach to research is desirable, in part because of the possibilities it affords for cross-checking data obtained by each method (see Konečni and Ebbeson 1979). Further, it is only through knowledge of the general patterns of court use, as revealed through figures on, for example, case types, outcomes, and party configurations, that the particular cases observed can be evaluated. For obvious reasons, participant observation cannot be based on a statistically random sample of cases; one never knows when access will be afforded or cut off, or particular cases identified by a randomizing procedure may be missed because of scheduling problems, illness, or other factors. Thus while one engaged in observational research must try to view some kind of reasonably representative selection of cases, in the end one is left with the cases that were actually observed. An analysis of documentary and interview materials provides the best way to both plan one's observations and assess the representativeness of the observational data finally obtained.

If observational research has so many uncertainties, the question might be raised as to whether the effort of undertaking it is worthwhile. Of course the value of observational research is well recognized, even in such determinedly positivistic fields as political science (see Fenno 1986). But the case study is inevitably and irreconcilably at odds with most of the generalizing principles of science (see Lijphart 1971), and in regard to the study of legal institutions the question is, at first glance, a valid one: if observations cannot be considered representative in the formal sense, then what is their value?

Ethnographic Studies of Legal Institutions

Part of the answer to the question of the value of observational research lies in the peculiar nature of legal institutions. Law inevitably deals with normative topics—with what is right, proper, or correct; more particularly, law deals with what F. G. Bailey has called the "public face of politics," the principles and rules that can be used to publicly justify a course of action (Bailey 1969:5). What may be peculiar to modern law is the way in which the legal field has claimed to be self-contained and self-referential (see Bourdieu 1987), and at the same time the sole legitimate determinant of the application of physical force to people subject to the law's jurisdiction. In this conjunction of values and power, it is difficult to obtain an accurate view of the ways that the legal system actually functions, because any depiction not in accordance with the self-representation dominant within the legal field will be branded incorrect, possibly illegitimate, perhaps treasonous.[1] For this reason, scholarly work within the dominant tradition of law is not likely to provide accurate representations of the ways in which legal institutions actually function. What is needed instead is research that attempts to view the operation of the legal system directly, and as objectively as possible.

In the United States, observational research has been crucial to the development of knowledge concerning the functioning of the legal system and particularly of the courts. The best-developed body of work has been done on the workings of criminal courts, especially on the process of negotiating the conclusions of these cases through the offering of a guilty plea in exchange for a specific sentence, usually to less than the maximum charge, a process generally known as plea bargaining. It has long been known from figures on case dispositions that relatively few criminal cases are actually tried in the United States and that most convictions are obtained by guilty plea. Impressionistic studies in law journals[2] argued that defendants' rights were being undermined by collusion between prosecutors and defense attorneys (Alschuler 1968). One writer went so far as to call criminal trials a "confidence game" worked on defendants (Blumberg 1967). However, careful observational research on the processes through which criminal cases are handled in various jurisdictions indicate that: (1) negotiation is a tactical move which can favor defendants as well as prosecutors (Mather 1979); (2) "bargaining" is frequently truly adversarial (Utz 1978); (3) plea negotiation is usually structured around "going rates" for different kinds of crimes and thus is not an abdication of (legal) certainty for the chance of the market (Utz 1978; Mather 1979).

The effect of this more detailed understanding of criminal court processes in America can be seen by comparing the comments on plea-bargaining in two editions of a well known text on the American criminal justice system, Herbert Jacobs's *Justice in America*. In the 1972 edition, Jacobs (1972:226) stated that "[b]argaining with defendants over their punishment rather than determining their guilt by trial is a perversion of the adversary process." By the 1978 edition, however, this condemnation had been replaced by a much more sophisticated view based on the observational studies mentioned above:

> Although critics focus on plea bargains, bench and jury trials continue to constitute an essential part of the criminal justice process. It is true that only a very small proportion of cases go to trial, particularly a trial by jury. But the possibility of going to trial constrains the plea-bargaining process. (Jacobs 1978:191)

This more sophisticated view of plea bargaining is now accepted by virtually all scholars who have engaged in careful observational research on the criminal courts. It could not have been developed without such research, since the workings of the criminal courts were presumed to be more along the lines of legal theory. Thus the model of the criminal justice process now accepted by most scholars involved in empirical research on law in its social context[3] is dependent on observational data.

It is, in fact, largely for reasons of ensuring reliable data that for the last forty years anthropologists interested in law have focused on the analysis of trouble cases. As Llewellyn and Hoebel noted in their classic study of Cheyenne law (1941), such cases are the most certain source of data on the ways that legal processes operate, since they present the researcher with what actually did happen[4] rather than with what should, ideally, have been done.

Research findings are not necessarily reliable just because they are based on real cases, however, even when these have been observed at firsthand. There are several potential complications. First, it is necessary to try to insure that the particular cases or activities observed are not overly unrepresentative of the general phenomenon. One way of controlling for this problem is to gather other kinds of data on the subject of investigation, such as survey or documentary materials. Even with such materials at hand, however, it is necessary to spend a substantial amount of time actually observing the subject of study, and over a protracted period of time. It is only through such long-term observation that one can control for such factors as seasonal variations in the use of the courts for particular kinds of cases (see Scaglion 1976), or for the natural tendency of informants to attempt either to create a good impression or to give the researcher what they think that he or she wants to see.

This is, of course, an old problem in anthropology, and generally accepted standards of ethnographic research call for observations over a year or more by a researcher who has a good command of the local language and who takes part as much as possible in the mundane practices of everyday life (see Naroll 1962, but cf. Heider 1988). It is particularly important that these strictures be observed in studies of legal institutions, however. As a social field that is particularly subject to narrow ideological self-representation as well as a tendency toward a certain theatricality in its day-to-day functioning, a court is especially prone to present a mask to those not part of its regular personnel (see Mather 1979; an abject lesson in the dangers of unsophisticated, short-term observations in courts can be found in Schulhofer 1984).

The present study of the CALs was designed to address and compensate for these problems. Details of the conduct of the research will be reserved for a later chapter,[5] but, briefly, the work involved more than four hundred hours of observation in the CAL in Belgrade over a period of fourteen months, with additional observations undertaken in the regular courts in the city. This observational research was augmented by interviews with lawyers, court personnel, academics, and others, as well as by documentary research in the records of the CAL in Belgrade and doctrinal research in Yugoslav legal publications. This supplementary research was undertaken before, during, and after the observational study, and afforded me some opportunities to clear up questions that had developed during the initial analysis of the observational data by checking with informants, as well as to learn of developments since that time.

The Problem of Generalization

> *the case study is presented because the relationship between behavior and structure may be generalizeable, not the behavior or structure itself.*
> —*Comisso 1979:139*

As mentioned earlier, a conceptual problem with case studies is that they violate the generalizing ideals of science. All cases are unique, so how can the lessons of one be generalized to address problems raised by others?

There are several possible answers to this question. At the level of the philosophy of science, it is necessary to recognize that there is a difference between sciences like chemistry, which deal with "repeatable unit phenomena and with actions that, once carefully described, are known forever" and those like evolutionary biology, which deal with "unique phenomena, with intricate interactions and with balances of selection pressures—in short, with phenomena of such complexity that an exhaustive description is beyond our power" (Mayr 1965:vi). Anthropology, of course, is of the latter variety, even in its closest attempts to approximate the former (see Aberle 1987). Yet this does not render the enterprise invalid, since carefully designed case studies are critical to advancing understanding of the complexities of social life and social action.

The most interesting case studies are those that may be seen as "crucial experiments," in which variables of interest are present in an interesting way (Naroll 1966:336). In such cases, the detailed analysis possible in the case study permits examination of the interactions of these variables. This kind of study is often useful for building theory, as hypothesis-generating case studies, which "start out with a more or less vague notion of possible hypotheses, and attempt to formulate definite hypotheses to be tested subsequently among a large number of cases" (Lijphart 1971:692). The generation of such hypotheses is one of the goals of the present study.

The Yugoslav CAL qualifies as a "crucial experiment" because, as will be seen in the next two chapters, the self-management ideology of both society and law that was dominant at the time the study was done[6] was meant to embody many of the ideals of decentralization, public participation, and informalism that underlie the concept of social courts. If any system could institutionalize such courts, it should have been Yugoslavia in the 1970s and early 1980s. Conversely, if the CALs at that time did not attain the goals of the proponents of social courts, this failure should also be of interest. Either way, the analysis of the experience of the CALs should be illuminating in regard to the general prospects for implementing social courts. Thus the case study is presented so that the connections between the different aspects of informalism and lay justice can be explored in a context that should have been most favorable for their implementation.

There is one more consideration in regard to the general utility of a case study: comparison with other such studies. Since no one works in a total intellectual vacuum, any case study constitutes an implied comparison, at least, to other works. It is important to recognize the hazards of comparison, however, and to try to control for them.

One potential pitfall is to compare a foreign institution, as revealed by a case study, with a superficial or impressionistic depiction of a domestic one. This problem has been recognized by anthropologists of law for years (see Van Velsen 1969), yet the error is still often made. Much of the literature on alternatives to formal courts, for example, rests on this kind of false comparison, between an ideal of Western judicial process and the specifics of a non-Western one (see Hayden 1987:264–265).

A rather different kind of false comparison is made when a domestic institution is compared with a superficial or impressionistic depiction of a foreign one. Again, the ADR literature is marred by this kind of work (e.g., Sander 1976; see Merry 1987:2060–2062), and there is a large set of references to the supposed peaceable kingdom of the nonlitigious Japanese that makes the same error (see Kidder 1987). In another realm, there are a number of less than critical assessments of the workings of social courts in socialist countries which do not seem to be based on long-term fieldwork. The *locus classicus* of this kind of work is the literature on the popular tribunals of Cuba (see Salas 1983). Part of the problem here may be due to the overly optimistic assessments of writers sympathetic to socialism, a matter of scholarly politics to which we will return in the next section.

The present study aims to avoid these problems by making comparisons only between institutions that have been the subjects of intensive empirical study. Thus the comparisons made between the workings of the CALs and, for example, those of American courts will be based on the empirical studies of the latter, rather than on some idealized or impressionistic model of them. It is only through such comparisons that accurate generalizations can be made.

The Scholarship of Politics: Objectivity and the Ethnography of Actually Existing Socialism

Much as we might wish it were otherwise, few would now hold to the position that scholarship in the social sciences can be truly objective. When the research in question is being done in an East European socialist society by a Western scholar, however, particularly an American, the problem of the politics of scholarship (or the scholarship of politics?) raises its head. In the early 1980s, after all, the dominant American political attitude toward Eastern Europe was to view it as part of an "evil empire." Furthermore, much of the American-based research in Soviet and East European studies is funded by special agencies that channel money from the federal government, among other bodies, and are generally considered to be part of an area studies enterprise that has obvious political import.[7]

The problem is compounded by the inherently political nature of scholarship on socialism, wherever practiced. Despite official and semi-official hostility to socialism, there are a number of Western scholars who are expressly committed to socialism and view their work as a tool for bringing it about (see, e.g., Abel 1982; Henry 1985). On the other hand, there are East European writers who view the practice of actually existing socialism with misgivings or worse, even when they favor the ideals of socialism (see Feher et al. 1983, particularly chapter 1). It is possible that the gap between Western leftists and East European intellectuals is unbridgeable: as three of the latter put it,

> the problem of being a Marxist in practical terms means different things in the East and the West: in the latter, it is a question of whether the critical theory offered by Marxism is still actual or sufficient, while within the framework of "really existing" socialism it is a question of whether Marxism can fulfill the functions of a critical theory at all. (Feher et al. 1983:7)

Although some writers may be safely classed as political extremists, uncritically for or against socialism, most are likely to try to maintain as objective a stance as possible. Anthropologists are especially prone to adopting this position; from our close experience with the societies of Eastern Europe, most of us recognize that it is not an evil empire, yet most also recognize that there are aspects of East European political life that are in contradiction to the ideals of both liberal democracy and all but the most tendentious and dogmatic theories of socialism.[8] It may be that anthropologists, like East Europeans themselves, are frequently prompted by their experiences to question the mechanisms of actually exisiting socialism even when they still hold many of the ideals of socialist theory.

My own position is firmly in this middle ground. Certainly I am neither antisocialist, nor, in particular, anti-Yugoslav (see Hayden 1989c). As far as the research on the CALs goes, a primary goal of my analysis is to assess these courts in terms of the *Yugoslav* theory concerning them; I then try to put both the courts and the debates about them into a broader theoretical context. In this way I believe that my analysis is as objective as possible, despite the inherent politicization of the topic.

Part II

Courts and Law in Modern Yugoslavia

Chapter 3
Yugoslav Self-Management and Law

The Uncommon State[1]

Geopolitical Position: "Something in Between"

All countries are different, of course, but Yugoslavia is a most unusual state. For more than fifteen hundred years, the territory of modern Yugoslavia contained one of the basic cultural borders of Europe. The original division of the Roman Empire into eastern and western administrative areas, which met in the center of what is now Yugoslavia, led to an enduring political and cultural division between the Roman world and the Byzantine, Roman Catholicism and Eastern Orthodoxy, Latin script and Cyrillic, the (Islamic) Ottoman Empire and the (Christian) West. We may recall that while the term "the Near East" has become obsolete in American English, at least, it used to be seen as beginning in the Balkans with some of the lands now part of Yugoslavia, including Serbia, Bosnia, Macedonia, and Montenegro.[2]

The cultural, religious, and orthographic divisions from these earlier times are still apparent in Yugoslavia,[3] but the country no longer contains a political border between East and West. Rather, Yugoslavia as a nation has come to occupy a geopolitical position between the Western Europe of NATO and the Common Market, and the Eastern Europe of the Warsaw Pact and COMECON. It is bordered by two NATO countries (Italy and Greece), three members of the Warsaw Pact (Hungary, Rumania, Bulgaria), one Western-oriented neutral country (Austria), and perhaps the most xenophobic country on earth, the totally unaligned Albania. Rather than joining the competing European military, political, and economic alliances, Yugoslavia has become one of the only European members of a third-world club, the

Conference of Nonaligned Nations (Albania is so unaligned as to not even be a member of the nonaligned).

Politically, the Yugoslav state is also different from those of the rest of Europe. While Yugoslavia is a socialist state governed by a communist party[4] endowed with a monopoly on power, Yugoslavs enjoy substantially more personal and political freedoms than the citizens of other one-party (communist) socialist states. Since the mid-1960s, for example, crossing the Yugoslav border has been little different from crossing those of Western European countries, for both Yugoslavs and foreigners. In the early 1980s, exits by Yugoslav citizens were made at the rate of about twenty million a year (on a population base of 22 million),[5] while tourism for foreigners is now a major component of the Yugoslav economy. Similarly, the Yugoslav press has long had a reputation for greater independence than those of the Warsaw Pact countries (see Robinson 1977), and its autonomy is generally thought to have increased in recent years, although there is still occasionally censorship of books and journals. Newspapers and magazines from both East and West are widely available in Yugoslav cities.

In the period since the death of President Tito (1980), Yugoslavia has been undergoing a period of economic stagnation, coupled with rising ethnic tensions and increasing questioning of the political structures created during the postwar period of rule by the communist party (see Burg 1986; Rusinow 1988). At the same time, many of the restrictions on political debate that had been traditional under Tito have loosened, leading to increasingly open and assertive political debates. At the time the present study was undertaken, however, the economic and social crises were just beginning, and the criticisms of the political structure were muted. Thus in the early 1980s, Yugoslavia was a country in which the political strictures usually found in one-party socialist states were loosening, in striking contrast with the situations then prevailing in most of the other socialist countries in Europe.

In regard to its socioeconomic system, Yugoslavia is also "something in between" the categories generally used to describe most countries. As a socialist country ruled by a communist party holding a monopoly on power, Yugoslavia could belong to the second world. Yet the republic of Slovenia, in the northwestern part of the country, has a standard of living comparable to that of parts of Western Europe and one of the lowest unemployment rates in the world, and considers itself to be part of the first world. And the province of Kosovo in the southeast has an economic structure and standard of living reminiscent of the third world. The differences in economic development and standard of living in different regions have put great stress on the national political structure, and have contributed greatly to the ethnic tensions that have been heightened in 1987–89 (see Rusinow 1988).

In light of Yugoslavia's singular political and economic position in Europe and, indeed, in the world, it is hardly surprising that its leaders have worked to create a distinctive political and economic system. At least since the break with Stalin and Soviet-style communism in 1948, the Yugoslavs have developed a separate philosophical and structural variant of socialism based on the principles of "self-management" by the working class and all working people. This effort has led to the creation of new legal categories and institutions, including the concept of self-management law and the institutions of self-management courts. These innovations will be discussed in the last section of this chapter, but first the conceptual and organizational bases of self-management must be explored.

The Self-Managed Society

The Idea of Self-Management[6]

The essential goal of self-management as an ideology was to provide an outline for a social system that avoided the excesses of both statist societies (such as the Soviet Union) and capitalist ones. Since capitalism was considered to be unproblematical as an ideal type, we will be more concerned with the Yugoslav effort to develop a socialist structure that differed from that of the Soviet-style system. The flaw with the latter was seen in its authoritarian nature, due to the concentration of power at the top of the political system:

> Statist socialism results from the identification of revolutionary authority—"dictatorship of the proletariat" . . . —with the state organization of authority, that is, with that organization of authority characteristic of *representative* democracy, modified so that political pluralism in the legislative arena has been exchanged for a political monopoly that has been extended from the executive branch to all other areas of social and political relationships. (Supek 1973:295; emphasis in original)

This was the pattern to be avoided, since it is excessively hierarchical and even alienating, driving many people from participation in public matters into purely private pursuits (Supek 1973:301–302).

Self-management, on the other hand, is meant to be a matter of participation, an egalitarian system rather than a hierarchical one, with great scope for discourse, little for command. This facilitation of participation was meant to avoid the problems of hierarchy and alienation through the mechanisms of self-government. Assuming the continued ideological hegemony of the Communist Party, a basic idea of the formulators of self-management was the separation of the Party from the direct exercise of power, through the transfer of power to the legislative rather than the executive branch of government. This ideal of participatory democracy was to be extended throughout the society, from the management of work organizations through the composition of the political system. A basic principle was that power should be decentralized, with the political system based on the autonomous commune rather than on the state per se. In addition, the legislative bodies were meant to involve close participation of different segments of society, particularly the working class, by requiring that legislative bodies be composed of delegates from other self-managing institutions.

The long, complex constitution of 1974[7] was meant to provide the structure for the realization of a society based on the principles of self-management. One of the institutional forms of self-management was to be a new form of law, self-management law, and new courts to implement it. These will be discussed under "Law and Self-Management" in this chapter and in the whole of the next one. First, however, it is necessary to examine more closely some of the basic concepts of self-management, since they provide the ideological foundations for the CALs and for the labor relations with which they deal.

Basic Concepts of Yugoslav Self-Management

As we have seen, one of the basic ideas separating the Yugoslav theoretical approach from that of the Soviets was the Yugoslav embrace of Marx's concept of the free association of producers as the crucial element of communist society (Rusinow 1978:51ff.; Pašić and Grozdanić 1978; Pašić 1978:54–55; Supek 1978:53). This reference was made explicit in the report of the president of the SFRY Assembly on the occasion of the passage of the Associated Labor Act in 1976 (Gligorov 1977:14). *Associated labor* is the term used to describe and define the institutional structure of the Yugoslav attempt to embody this concept. Workers associate to manage social resources jointly: this is the essence of Yugoslav self-management. Thus the second basic concept is that of social resources, or *social property*.

The close connection between social resources and associated labor as the key concepts of self-management is clear in Najdan Pašić's discussion of the latter concept:

> *Associated labor* is the general concept which encompasses all of the relations and institutions which are established between working people organized in self-management who work together and together manage [*upravljaju*] with social resources for production and—in accordance with the Constitution and statute—dispose of [*raspolažu*] that social income which is the result of their joint labor. In that sense associated labor represents the *contents* and *institutional* form of the new socialist relations of production—relations which join workers as *equal*, interdependent and responsible self-managers, voluntarily and freely associated in the work process itself and in all forms of association of labor and resources and of management and decision which are connected with it.
>
> Thus understood, associated labor is identical with Marx's idea of the association of free producers. (Pašić 1978:54–55, emphasis in original)

This interrelationship is also clearly shown in Article 2 of the Law on Associated Labor (1976), which states that associated labor is to be founded on social ownership of the means of production.

Associated Labor (Udruženi Rad)

Of the two concepts, associated labor is the least problematic. Simply put, while the 1974 Yugoslav constitution gives all workers the right to work with social resources, it requires that workers join in various kinds of organizations in order to do so (Constitution, Articles 13–23). It is the organization, rather than the individual worker, that then has the legal right to create income through the exploitation of these resources, although each individual worker has the right to a personal income from the income of his or her organization (Article 20). This requirement of association avoids the problem of individual ownership of the means of production. The constitution and the Law on Associated Labor (1976) contain detailed provisions concerning the formation and management of organizations of associated labor; these provisions will be described below under "Law and Self-Management."

Social Property (Društvena Svojina)

Social property[8] is simultaneously the most important innovation of Yugoslav legal theory and one of the least clear aspects of self-management. Recognizing the potential dangers to the general welfare of control over the means of production either by private interests or by a bureaucratic state, the Yugoslavs have tried to create a form of property that avoids the negative aspects of both traditional private property and Soviet-style state property. Just as the Yugoslav geopolitical position is "somewhere in between" East and West, so this central concept of Yugoslav law is "between State property and private property, being in fact neither, but partaking in some measure of both" (Chloros 1970:163).

Since Yugoslavia under the 1974 constitution is a socialist country ruled by a communist party, it is not surprising that private ownership of the means of production is viewed with disfavor, although private ownership of homes and small businesses is permitted. More noteworthy is the Yugoslav departure from Soviet concepts and doctrine of ownership. In creating the concept of social property, the Yugoslavs explicitly rejected Soviet-style state property as undesirable and productive of "bureaucratic despotism" (see Chloros 1970:163). Where Soviet theory has seen state ownership as necessary in socialist society, because only the state represents society, the Yugoslavs have endeavored to create a form of property that is owned by the working people themselves, without the intermediation of the state. It is this concept of direct ownership of the means of production by the working people rather than the state that is the essence of social property.

As a category of political and social theory, the principle of social property is reasonably clear: social property is owned neither by the state nor by individuals, but rather directly by the whole of society. Individuals may join together in organizations of associated labor and acquire the right to work with social property, but they may not, as individuals, own social property. The 1974 constitution identifies social property as "[t]he means of production and other means of associated labour, products generated by associated labour and income realized through associated labour, resources for the satisfaction of common and general social needs, natural resources and goods in common use" (Article 12).[9] In the same article, it is stated that "[n]o one may acquire the right of ownership of social resources." Greater specificity is given to this point in the Basic Principles of the Constitution:[10]

> Since no one has the right of ownership over social means of production, nobody—not socio-political communities, nor organizations of associated labour, nor groups of citizens, nor individuals—may appropriate on any legal-property grounds the product of social labour or manage and dispose of the social means of production and labour, or arbitrarily determine conditions for distribution.

It must be stressed that social property is *not* state property. The Yugoslav state continues to own some property (e.g., the guns and tanks used by the army, to use Chloros's example [1970:162]), but this is a limited category. It is very clear that the state does not own the means of production, which are seen as belonging to the entire society. It is in this regard that the Yugoslav position is most different from that taken by Soviet and East European scholars, who see the state and collectives or cooperatives as the only possible holders of property under socialism (see Knapp 1975). This divergence has prompted sharp attacks on the Yugoslav concept by Soviet scholars (Chloros 1970:162–167).[11]

That the concept of social property is an explicit rejection of the Soviet model is hardly surprising, because it was first developed in the period following the break with Stalin in 1948, when the Yugoslav leadership was faced with the need to create a new form of socialist thought that would justify the abandonment of Stalin's system. As we have already seen, the solution was to insist on the immediate importance of the withering of the state by insisting on the importance of direct self-management by the working class. The development of the concept of social property, which removed one of the major functions of the state, was plainly an important theoretical step toward that end.

A major difficulty has developed, however, in that while it has been possible to identify social property, as in the constitutional provisions given above, it has not been possible to *define* it. Divergent views emerged in the first extensive discussions of the problem in the early 1950s, and they have never been resolved. They involve the identity of the holders of social property and the distribution of rights over it, or, more succinctly, whether the concept of *ownership* is applicable to social property, and the implications of either answer to this question.

One school holds that in fact, social property is not owned; that it is actually the negation, or withering away, of property (Coronna 1985:233–234).[12] Basic to this position is the proposition that since social property is owned by society without the intermediation of the state, it is owned by everyone and hence by no one. Instead, workers have various rights of use and of disposition of the income they produce, which are then regarded as quasi-property rights. At least one author has cited the constitutional provisions given earlier in this section for the proposition that under the present constitution the nonownership position is the only possible one (Coronna 1985:234, citing A. Finžgar).

The position that recognizes ownership in social property was most fully developed by Andrija Gams, formerly of the Law Faculty of Belgrade University. Writing in the 1950s and early 1960s, Gams proposed a theory of divided ownership of social property (see Coronna 1985:231–232; Chloros 1970:172–173). This reasoning starts from the Marxist distinction between the economic and legal aspects of property, finding in use-rights and in the right to dispose of the income received from working with social property an effective economic ownership (cf. Bajt 1968). Gams also saw ultimate title to social property residing in the state, although it was limited by the use-rights accorded other social persons.[13] However, this approach did not gain approval. As Gams noted in 1982 (p. 3), a treatise on property that he had completed just before his 1973 retirement, and which developed his approach further, was not published due to the official adoption of the non-ownership position (which Gams [1982:3] calls the "non-property concept of property").[14] Certainly it was the non-ownership position that was adopted with the 1974 constitution.

The problem of defining social property may be based in part on the limitations of the conceptual tools provided by the civil law tradition, from which all of the socialist legal systems of Europe are derived. That legal tradition takes a highly restricted view of property, seeing ownership as crucial, and viewing ownership as a unitary concept; that is, one that cannot in principle be divided into various specific rights (see Beekhuis 1975).[15] Thus the view of Gams, that the non-ownership position represents a "non-property" concept of property accords with the definitions of the civil law tradition, although Gams's own development of the separability of use-rights also seems counter to the traditional view.

The potential practical implications of this jurisprudential muddle are important, as the vagueness of rights under social property has been blamed for promoting inefficient investment and management policies by self-managed firms (see, e.g., Furubotn and Pejovich 1973; Gams 1985). The definition of social property should also be crucial in the specific context of the CALs, as one of their basic charges under the constitution (Article 226) is to "decide . . . about demands for the protection of the right to work with social resources and [for the protection of] other self-management rights and of social property" (translation by author). The protection of social property is a basic feature of the constitutional structure, which entrusts both the courts and a new kind of official, the "social attorney of self-management," with this task. Indeed, some authors see such protection as the basic function of self-management law (see Rajović 1978). Nevertheless, we will not concern ourselves further with this definitional problem, because, as will be seen below, cases calling for the protection of social property are an almost negligible part of the work of the basic, trial-level CALs.

Despite its lack of clarity, the basic concept of social property, as distinct from state and private property, is an essential element of the Yugoslav self-management concept because it avoids, at least initially, the problems inherent with the state's assumption of ownership of the means of production and the inevitable problems caused by concentrating economic power in the hands of the few who run the state. Furthermore, despite the apparently insolvable problem of defining social property, the view that workers in associated labor have a quasi-property or quasi-ownership right in the use of the social resources with which they work permits the theoretical development of *worker* rather than *state* control over the means of production. However, to avoid the specter of private property, this formulation also must specify that rights in the use and disposition of social property reside with workers in associated labor rather than with the individual workers. Thus we return again to the close connection between the two basic concepts, social property and associated labor.

Socioeconomic Organization: Organizations of Associated Labor

The concepts of social property and associated labor are united in practice in the institutional structure created by the 1974 constitution and the Law on Associated Labor of 1976.[16] The basic socioeconomic institutional form is the organization of associated labor (OAL), which comes in several varieties. The generic term, OAL, stands for "economic and non-economic organizations which carry out activities with socially-owned means of production and resources, and which are organized on a self-management basis" (Jugoslovenski Pregled 1980:127). However, OALs exist only in more specific forms, the most important being the Basic Organization of Associated Labor (BOAL).

The BOAL is defined as "each unit of a work organization which makes up a working whole (a plant, a technological unit, etc.) in which the results of joint labour can be expressed in terms of value on the market or within the work organization concerned" (Jugoslovenski Pregled 1980:123). Under the 1974 constitution the BOAL is truly the basic unit of the Yugoslav economic system, replacing the traditional enterprise, or firm (see Rusinow 1978:328–329), which is now made up of independent BOALs. The BOALs may choose to join together to form a Composite Organization of Associated Labor (COAL), in effect, the traditional firm. But under the structure of the 1974 constitution and the Associated Labor Act, the firm itself has no income of its own, as all income from production belongs to the BOAL producing it (Constitution, Article 17; Law on Associated Labor Article 45). The COAL has no income of its own, as all such income must be distributed among the BOALs that have taken part in its realization (Law on Associated Labor Article 82). Further, until 1983, only a BOAL could maintain a bank account (Law on Associated Labor Article 146). However, in November 1983, that law was "supplemented" (in effect, but not in name, amended) to permit the establishment of bank accounts for OALs other than BOALs, with contributions coming from the latter.[17] According to one eminent Yugoslav legal scholar, the effect of this change has been to reestablish the traditional enterprise.[18]

All utilization of socially owned resources must be carried out in the OAL framework. The constitution sets out the basic principles of these organizations in its first chapter, and the details on their organization are provided by the Law on Associated Labor (LAL). Article 320 of the LAL provides that workers in a work organization have "the right and duty" to form a BOAL when their part of that organization meets the requirements for a BOAL, as outlined above, and may not organize one if any of the requirements are not met (Article 325). Detailed provisions are given for the formation of a new BOAL (Articles 328–337), the separation of a BOAL from other work organizations (Articles 338–341), and the dissolution of a BOAL (Articles 342–345).

Labor relations within and between OALs are also governed by the LAL, as is the organizational structure of management (Articles 490–522). All of the workers in a BOAL form the workers' assembly, which decides major policy issues (Articles 461–471). In BOALs with more than thirty workers, a workers' council has to be elected, by secret ballot by and from the workers' assembly, as the actual management body of the organization (Articles 490–497). The LAL then devotes a chapter (Chapter 6, Articles 573–615) to the regulation of self-management relations within and between OALs through a new kind of law, "self-management enactments."

Since OALs are empowered to work with and to dispose of social property, it is necessary to have some form of oversight over their use of those resources. The constitution and the LAL between them have created a new kind of legal officer, the Social Attorney of Self-Management (*Društveni Pravobranilac Samoupravljanja*), charged with protecting social property and also with protecting the self-management rights of workers in associated labor (see Trajkovski 1978). This position is discussed in detail in the next section.

In the most basic sense, these legal provisions constitute the new socioeconomic institutions of self-management. Thus law is integral to the new society. However, legal institutions, particularly the new self-management courts, are also charged with regulating the self-managed society, and it is the regulatory function that dominates legal activity. Even when constitutive provisions of law are drawn upon (e.g., the definition of the requirements for forming a BOAL), the effect is to regulate ongoing or proposed activity. Finally, the self-management legal system is supposed to facilitate the resolution of disputes. These three tasks are also those of state law, but just as social property is supposed to differ from traditional concepts of property, so self-management law is meant to be of a different order from state law. Thus it is necessary to look more closely at the Yugoslav view of state law and its self-management counterpart.

Law and Self-Management

State Law

Before considering the specific features of Yugoslav conceptions of law, it is necessary to make a brief digression on the subject of law itself. I do not intend to attempt to define law, as that task, which is perhaps the basic question of jurisprudence, has already been attempted by a vast legion of scholars. For purposes of sociological research on legal topics it is also undesirable to attempt to define law narrowly, because of the necessary exclusion thereby of relevant "law-related" phenomena, including most anthropological investigation (see Abel 1974:221–224). Nevertheless, it is important to point out that Yugoslav views of the nature of law are significantly different from those that dominate modern Anglo-American jurisprudence and which may be more familiar to English-speaking readers.

Perhaps the classic nineteenth-century statement of law in English was that of John Austin (1832): that law is the command of the sovereign, backed by the threat of the application of physical force if the command is not obeyed. The resultant philosophy of law is generally known as "positivism," and has as basic tenets the propositions that law, as commands of the sovereign, can be objectively identified and studied and, moreover, that these laws have no necessary connection with morality: the sovereign can issue an immoral command that will nonetheless have the status of law.[19] In this school, the sovereign himself is above the law, and consequently the idea of constitutionality as a form of legal relationship is impossible: the sovereign cannot bind himself. Thus Austin proclaimed that constitutionality was positive morality rather than law. In such a system the idea that individuals might have legal rights against the state was, as Bentham put it, "nonsense on stilts."

In twentieth-century Anglo-American jurisprudence, positivism has undergone sustained attack, on several grounds. First, even those who purport to accept much of the basic positivist position that law is a special set of rules backed by coercive force have modified the Austinian view of "commands" to include rules that empower individual initiative, or, more basically, that state how commands may be given (see Hart 1961). Others have attacked the idea of the unlimited sovereign, seeing constitutionality as law and individuals as having legal rights that no sovereign can violate (see Dworkin 1978). Still others have questioned the basic division between law and morality, saying that rules that are immoral are simply not law (see Fuller 1964). Finally, the basic jurisprudential concept of law as a determinate set of rules has been questioned by social scientists, who are concerned with how such rules are used (rather than applied) in different kinds of social interactions (see Moore 1978; Comaroff and Roberts 1981). These social scientists are generally quite willing to see law as existing in non-state societies and the international community, which, because of their lack of a sovereign, are problematic cases for positivists.

Whatever the refinements of their particular arguments, no reputable modern philosopher of law in the Anglo-American tradition holds to the pure Austinian form of positivism, with its rigid separation of law and morality, disbelief in constitutionality, and disregard of individual rights. Socialist and communist lawyers, on the other hand, are perhaps the purest Austinians left, although they do not cite Austin. They follow the civil law tradition of continental Europe, which has remained more positivistic than the Anglo-American common law (see Merryman 1969:20–25), but with some further refinements.

Inga Markovits (1982) has examined the concept of legality, as embodied in the constitutions of the Soviet Union and the East European socialist countries,[20] and finds it to be a matter of commands to citizens, rather than limitations on state action. Individual rights, even when enumerated, are subject to limitations, and individuals are also subjected to duties, a category not found in Western democracies.[21] Certainly, the state is supreme; the communist concept of law links it inextricably with the state, and sees law as totally dependent on state sanctions. Constitutionality in the Western sense is missing, as the state is absolute. The only difference between this communist position and the stance of classical positivism is that communist theorists see a unity between law and morality. However, communist concepts of morality are enough at variance with those of the positivists that the similarity is more apparent than real.

In socialist law, as in the civil law, only state acts, specifically, legislation and administrative orders, are law per se, with the minor exception of certain customs. Court decisions, which are the heart of the common law, are not considered to be law. This is a further manifestation of the positivism of those legal traditions.

Yugoslav views on law are in some ways unique, but they are certainly within the communist tradition. Thus law is inextricably linked with the state. As one major introductory text puts it,

> When one says *law*, then one also says *state*, because . . . law and state are tightly bound and indivisible social phenomena. Accordingly, when we say that we teach law in the law faculty, we are really abbreviating the expression, because law really cannot be taught apart from state. . . . [T]he proper name for the law faculty would be *state-law* [*državnopravni*] faculty. (Lukić 1985:3; emphasis in original)[22]

At the same time, Yugoslav legal theory seems more willing to separate law and morality. This same author distinguishes law from morality in both the introductory legal text (Lukić 1985:27–29) and a celebrated study, *The Sociology of Morality* (Lukić 1982). Law is only that set of norms that is sanctioned by the state, and morality does not enter into the equation.

It would thus seem that the Yugoslavs may be the last of the true positivists. When Yugoslav writers think of law, they are inevitably also thinking of the state, at least until the invention of the concept of self-management law, to which we shall return. Further, they are used to seeing law only in the express acts of governmental legislation or regulation, and not in legal decisions.

On the other hand, the Yugoslavs differ from the positivists in taking seriously the idea of constitutionalism. The constitutions of 1963 and 1974 contain chapters on constitutionality and legality and provide for the existence of review by a constitutional court when the constitutionality of a law or other enactment is questioned (see Srzentić 1984). Such constitutional review is rare in the civil law world, since it seems to contradict the positivist principle of sovereignty, usually seen as residing in the legislature (Merryman 1969:20–25). Yugoslavia is the first socialist country to create a constitutional court, and this court is active: between 1964 and 1982, the Constitutional Court of Yugoslavia heard 7,644 cases (Srzantić 1984:27n.19).

The Yugoslav view of the inseparability of law from the state is not compromised by the existence of the constitutional courts, which are state institutions. However, the tight connection between state and law presents an obvious conceptual problem for a system that is meant to be based on the diminution of the role of the state, and hence of law, for barring the attainment of true communism, there is no doubt among socialist writers that some form of law is necessary (see Kelsen 1954). Yet if law must be state law, how can the role of the state diminish? The Yugoslav solution to this puzzle has been the creation of the new form of law, self-management law.

Self-Management Law

The basic principle of self-management law is clear enough. Self-management law is meant to be the embodiment of the classic Marxist position on the withering of the state and law: self-managed relations are by definition not regulated by the state, and

as law *in [the process of] formation [u nastajanju]*, self-management law regulates those social relations which state law has ceased to regulate, and in that sense

> self-management law slowly replaces state [law], and in the contemporary phase of social development and further sustains itself as a system of norms with which are protected socialist social relations, the development of society and the management of social affairs on a self-management basis. (Nikolić and Perović 1980:46; emphasis added)

Similarly, it has been suggested that

> Yugoslav law is characterized by the process of withering away of law as the exclusive creation of the state, and by the taking place of a new kind of law emanating out of new relations within the sphere of production and in the socio-economic relations in general and the ones that are being created by the working class and by the working people. (Jovanović 1981:15)

The new kind of law is, of course, self-management law.

We must note the fluidity implied in these definitions: self-management law is something that is coming into being, or developing, and not a static category. Fluid substances are hard to pin down, and self-management law, like social property, has proven hard to define. However, again like social property, it has been possible to identify some kinds of normative phenomena as forms of self-management law even in the absence of a generally accepted definition. The most important of these are self-management agreements (*samoupravni sporazumi*) and social compacts (*društveni dogovori*). The former are adopted by workers within self-management bodies (e.g., within BOALs) to "regulate and control their interests," while the latter are adopted by such organizations, between themselves or with state entities, in order to "regulate socio-economic and other relations of common concern, as well as relations of general concern to the community" (LAL [official English translation], "Glossary"). Both forms of agreement are conceived of as voluntary, not imposed, and as replacing the role of the state with self-management activity.

The legal nature of these provisions has been the subject of some debate. Some authors, who see state sanctions as the defining feature of law, are rather dubious about applying that term to normative acts that are not so sanctioned (see Lukić 1985:445–446). Others see self-management laws as being (quasi) contractual in nature (see Jovanović 1981:24–25). One sociologist of law has suggested that as self-management laws are neither civil contracts nor state-enacted norms, they are "'beyond status and contract,' or maybe somewhere in between the two" (Jambrek 1983:186).

The trial-level CALs are usually confronted with practical problems of application rather than theoretical problems of definition. As expressed by the dean of Yugoslav constitutional scholars, the essence of the self-management courts is as follows:

> To protect self-management relations and social property, these courts settle disturbed relations, and their function is not to wait for disputes, to which they then apply authority, but to avert arguments and disputes, so that relations between and within self-management subjects function in accordance with law; that is, ever more in accordance with the norms of self-management public law. From this it follows that these courts strive, understandingly [*sporazumno*] and rationally, in the spirit of self-management, to resolve disputes with a call for all to participate in the formation of self-management norms, which is the essence of negotiation and coming to an agreement in a new social relationship. (Djordjević 1982:817–818)

All of this is meant to distinguish the self-management courts from the classical forms of juridical bodies. If the details of the distinctions remain vague, it is nevertheless clear that self-management institutions, including self-management courts, are to foster discourse and voluntary agreement rather than simply implement commands or enforce laws. This is the basic conceptual innovation of self-management law; its institutionalization will be explored in the next chapter.

Chapter 4
Courts in Modern Yugoslavia

The self-management courts can only be properly understood in contrast with the other components of the Yugoslav judicial system, particularly the regular courts.[1] However, these new courts were not simply added to the regular courts and the other parts of the judicial system that existed before 1974. Rather, these other parts of the judicial system were themselves changed by the new constitution of 1974 as part of the attempt to structure a judicial function "within a unified system of power and self-management by the working class and all working people" (Constitution, Article 217). These changes provided the context for the creation of the new, self-management courts, and for the specific form of the new CAL system. For this reason, in this chapter I first describe the development of the court system before the adoption of the 1974 constitution and the way labor cases were handled until that time, and then discuss the changes brought about under the new system, including the institution of the various self-management courts. The chapter concludes with a detailed discussion of the structure and work load of the CALs.

Before the 1974 Constitution

The First Court Systems

Yugoslav legal scholars make a sharp distinction between the judicial system of prewar Yugoslavia and that of the modern, socialist state. The judicial system of the latter is seen as having its inception in the courts that were created in the territories controlled by the partisans during the war. Courts were created in these areas as early as 1942, and by 1944 a judicial system had been established throughout the liberated territories (Bastaić 1954). These courts heard not only criminal cases, but also civil matters such as those involving debts, property, and boundaries. The first courts were military courts, but regular courts were created in 1944, and judicial systems were included in the governments that were forming in what would become the republics and autonomous provinces of postwar Yugoslavia. On 3 February 1945, the provisional authorities established a Supreme Court and a prosecutorial office, thus completing the first judicial hierarchy before the end of the war.

This hierarchy was refined and embodied immediately after the war in the first constitution of the new Yugoslavia (1946).[2] Chapter 13 of that instrument, entitled "Peoples' Courts," established a hierarchy of regular courts (Article 115[1]), provided for the establishment by federal statute of military courts (Article 115[2]), and provided that special courts could also be created by statute (Article 115[3]). These three categories of courts remained the basic components of the judiciary until the enactment of the 1974 constitution, which added to them the new category of self-management courts.

To begin with the regular courts, the 1946 constitution called for a uniform hierarchy of communal (*sreski*) and circuit (*okružni*) courts plus a supreme court in each republic or province, with the Supreme Court of the Federal Peoples' Republic of Yugoslavia (FPRY)[3] as the highest court in the country. The circuit courts heard appeals from the lower, communal courts, and also heard some cases as courts of original jurisdiction. The supreme court of each republic or autonomous province assessed the legality of the final decisions of the lower courts within its own territory, hearing regular appeals from the circuit courts and extraordinary appeals from the communal courts. Finally, the Supreme Court of the FPRY was pronounced the supreme organ of justice in the country (Article 122[1]) and was empowered to assess the legality of final decisions of all courts in regard to the application of federal laws (Article 123[1]).

The federal nature of this system is clear: each of the components of the federation had a separate hierarchy of courts, with the only link provided by the oversight of the federal supreme court. At first glance, this system might seem to be more decentralized than that of the United States, in which a hierarchy of federal courts exists alongside the state courts within the federal units.[4] However, what is missing from the Yugoslav system is the autonomous *republican* courts. The 1946 constitution provided that the powers to create courts and to define their essential features, including the nature of the judicial function, kinds of courts, jurisdiction and procedures, were within the jurisdiction of the federation, and these provisions were included in succeeding constitutions until, as we shall see, 1974. From the start, the Yugoslav system was thus a unified federal system, a kind of centralized federalism. Yugoslav theorists see this kind of federal system, in which the basic elements of the entire court system are established by the federation rather than by the states, as the more modern form of federalism, with the American model representing an older concept (Djordjević 1982:798–799).[5] The 1946 system was derived from that found in the Soviet constitution of 1936,[6] and similar unified court systems are found in other federal states (e.g., India; see Galanter 1984:477–490).

The 1946 constitution also established certain other basic principles of the judicial system, including the independence of the courts (Article 116), the election of judges (Article 121), the requirement that most cases be tried by panels or benches of judges (Article 119[1]), the participation of lay "jurors" (*sudija-porotnika*) in judgment (Article 119[2]), and the right of citizens to use their own languages in the courts (Article 120). As we shall see, these principles have remained basic to the regular courts.

The regular courts, like the regular courts in other countries, had general jurisdiction for most criminal and civil matters. In terms of both numbers of courts and numbers of cases, the regular courts were the most important components of the judicial system. In these courts, most cases were to be tried by the communal courts, with an automatic right of appeal to the circuit courts. Civil matters of great economic value and more serious criminal cases were to be tried by the circuit courts, with an automatic right to appeal to the republican/provincial supreme court. Exceptionally, appeals were permitted to the federal supreme court. This delineation of original and appellate jurisdiction in the regular courts has remained, with some modifications, in succeeding constitutions.

The 1946 constitution also provided for military courts (Article 115[2]) and for the creation of other special courts for particular kinds of cases (Article 115[3]). The military courts handled cases involving military personnel and some civilians connected to the military, as well as certain kinds of cases involving military matters and state security. The provision for military courts was a reflection of the importance of the army during the war and immediately afterward; in fact, the draft constitution had listed the military courts along with the regular courts in the first clause of what was to become Article 115, as one of the basic elements of the judiciary (Narodna Skupština FNRJ 1946:830). The placement of the provision for military courts into a separate clause was accomplished during the constituent assembly debates, on the grounds that the military courts were indeed special courts rather than courts of general jurisdiction, and also that they might have to deal with state secrets (Narodna Skupština FNRJ 1946:401–420). The military courts have their own hierarchy of trial courts and a supreme military court. They have been continued as special courts in succeeding constitutions.

The other important category of courts established in the early years was that of the economic courts. In the first constitutional regime, state arbitration courts were established to handle cases between firms and other economic actors; such state arbitration courts are common in the socialist countries of Europe (see Knapp 1975). These arbitration panels were later transformed into economic courts, which remained under the later constitutional systems (Djordjević 1961:700; Kuhar and Jovanović 1971:25–27).

The Constitutional Regimes of 1953–54 and 1963

After 1946, Yugoslav constitutional history is complex and potentially confusing, particularly in regard to the judicial system. Yugoslavia's break with Stalin in 1948 and the subsequent abandonment of the Soviet model of communism made the 1946 constitution, which had been patterned on the Soviet constitution of 1936, inappropriate. Consequently, a "Constitutional Law" was promulgated on 13 January 1953, which stated in its preamble that its purpose was "to bring the Constitutional system into harmony with the changes in the foundations of the social and political organization in the country" (Union of Jurists' Federations of Yugoslavia 1960:43). This new law replaced almost the entirety of Part 2 of the first constitution, "Organization of the State." However, it was not until July 1954 that the "Law Relating to Courts of Justice" was passed. This law had constitutional effect, voiding Chapter 13 of the 1946 constitution and becoming itself the constitutional source of the Yugoslav judiciary (Djordjević 1982:792).[7]

The 1954 law did not change the essentials of the earlier system, but it did provide it with greater specificity. Thus Article 1 of the new law specified that "justice shall be administered by regular, economic and military courts,"[8] with the organization and jurisdiction of the last two kinds of courts to be determined by special law; this provision essentially served to codify the existing practice. The 1954 law also strengthened the centralized federal nature of the court system by specifying that "[c]ourts of justice may be established and abolished by Federal law alone" and that the jurisdiction of the courts was controlled by law (Article 2), and that "[t]he Federal Supreme Court shall safeguard a uniform application of the law" (Article 4). The new law restated the basic principles of the judicial system established by the 1946 constitution, except that the right of any citizen of Yugoslavia to use his own language in the courts was no longer mentioned. The 1954 law did provide for one further basic principle: that the right of appeal against the decision of a court of first instance was ensured (Article 6). This provision of the so-called right of two stages of trials (*dvostepenost sudjenja*) has remained part of the succeeding constitutional regimes.

The constitution of 1963 also did not change the essentials of the judicial system, but rather served to give them greater refinement. The first article of the chapter "The Courts and the Public Prosecution" thus provided for a "uniform judicial system" of courts of general jurisdiction and courts of special jurisdiction and restated the existing hierarchy of regular courts and the categories of economic and military courts (Article 132). It also gave constitutional specificity to the jurisdiction of the regular courts, stating that they were to judge "personal, property, labour and other rights of the citizens and their obligations as well as property and other rights and obligations of organizations and socio-political communities," in addition to criminal and administrative law cases (Article 135).[9]

The centralized federal nature of the courts was reinforced by the specification that the court system was a uniform one (Article 132[1]) and by the mandate of the federal supreme court to "[p]ass basic rulings and legal judgments in matters of significance for the uniform enforcement of federal law by the courts of general jurisdiction and courts of special jurisdiction" (Article 239).[10]

The 1963 constitution did create two new kinds of courts, however. First, it established a Constitutional Court of Yugoslavia and provided for the creation of constitutional courts at the republican/provincial levels (Chapter 13). No other socialist state had established such a court, and the Yugoslav experiment in that regard is still unusual for such states. As in the other civil-law countries that have created constitutional courts, these courts are not part of the regular court system, but rather are completely separate from it (see Merryman 1969:140–148). Thus constitutional questions cannot be decided in the ordinary course of litigation of a case before the regular courts, but must be taken by a special procedure to the constitutional courts, which can rule only on those questions. These constitutional courts have been continued under the 1974 constitution (see Srzentić 1984).

The second major innovation of the 1963 constitution was a provision for the establishment of informal, voluntary courts, such as arbitration (Article 133[1]) and conciliation councils (Article 133[2]).[11] The decisions of the former were enforceable by the courts, but those of the latter had only the effect of out-of-court settlements and were not enforceable (Kuhar and Jovanović 1971:29, 31). The conciliation councils were predecessors to certain of the self-management courts, as we shall see in the next section.

The judicial system before the promulgation of the 1974 constitution could thus be summarized as follows:

1. Regular courts (i.e., courts of general jurisdiction). These courts, the basic judicial institutions in the country, heard most cases, both civil and criminal. In late 1969 there were 385 communal courts and 61 circuit courts, plus one supreme court in each republic or province, with the federal supreme court overseeing the entire system. In that same year these courts considered 360,237 criminal cases, 736,060 civil cases of first instance, 1,062,992 judicial payment orders (i.e., collections), 621,454 civil enforcement proceedings, and 1,822,269 other voluntary civil cases. In addition, the supreme courts, both federal and republican and/or provincial, heard 67,239 cases of administrative litigation (Kuhar and Jovanović 1971:22–23).

2. Commercial courts. These specialized courts heard "commercial disputes concerning the rights and duties of work and other organizations and socio-political communities, maritime disputes and administrative-accountancy disputes" (Kuhar and Jovanović 1971:25). These courts had a separate hierarchy of thirty-two circuit, seven superior, and one supreme commercial court. In 1969 these courts handled 137,366 disputes at first instance, 893,902 judicial payment orders, and 586,016 civil enforcement proceedings (Kuhar and Jovanović 1971:26).

3. Military courts. These courts handled criminal cases involving military personnel and some civilians involved in military matters, administrative litigation against the acts of military authorities, damage claims against the military, and other cases involving military activities. There were military courts of original jurisdiction and a Supreme Military Court; in addition, some cases could be appealed to the Supreme Court of Yugoslavia (Kuhar and Jovanović 1971:27–29).

4. Courts of arbitration. These courts settled property disputes voluntarily submitted to them by the parties, with the arbitrators selected by the parties. Decisions of these courts had the effect of legal decisions. There were special arbitration courts for international trade disputes and for disputes involving the army (Kuhar and Jovanović 1971:29–30).

5. Conciliation councils. These were mediation agencies, established for specific territories or within organizations, to which people could submit disputes, unless the matter was required to go to court. The decisions of these councils had the same legal status as voluntary

agreements and could not be enforced. It is perhaps worth noting that they provide an additional example of an alternative, mediatory dispute institution that did not succeed in attracting cases: in 1969 there were 6,073 conciliation councils in Yugoslavia, which attracted 70,125 cases, or 11.5 cases per council (Kuhar and Jovanović 1971:31).

Labor cases were assigned by the 1963 constitution (Article 135) to the regular courts, where they were heard by benches that specialized in such matters. While figures on the numbers of labor cases in the courts are not available, it was a well-established branch of law, particularly in areas of importance to individual workers, such as work assignments, payments, vacation, and the discipline and responsibilities of workers (see Brajić 1974).

In essence, this judicial system was one in which courts, as implements of state power, handled the usual array of civil, criminal, and administrative law cases. It was not much different from those systems found in other continental European countries, except perhaps for the importance placed on the military courts. The unified hierarchy of courts, headed by the federal supreme court, was in keeping with the centralized nature of the polity created by the 1963 constitution and had no particularly unusual features.

This constitutional structure was greatly modified, however, by a series of forty-two amendments, passed in three acts during the period 1967–71.[12] These amendments became famous for two reasons. First, the so-called "workers' amendments" (Nos. 21–23) introduced many of the basic concepts and terminology (e.g., the BOAL) that would be developed in the constitution of 1974 (see Rusinow 1978:284). Second, and perhaps just as important, was the extent to which the amendments altered the federal structure of Yugoslavia. Particularly important was Amendment 16, passed in 1968, which made a radical change in the respective responsibilities of the federation and the federal units.

In place of Article 119 of the 1963 constitution, which had essentially given the federation exclusive power to regulate and enact legislation in a wide range of activities, Amendment 16 provided that the republics also had responsibilities for the "performance of tasks and the conduct of affairs falling within the sphere of the Federation's exclusive powers and duties." Further, the same amendment authorized the republics to pass legislation on matters that the constitution had put within the federation's purview. Thus the amendments weakened the power of the strongly centralized federation that had prevailed in Yugoslav constitutions to that point.

The amendments had special importance for the judicial system. Amendment 16, which granted so much power to the republics, stated that its provisions superseded paragraphs 3, 4, and 5 of Article 132 of the 1963 constitution, the article that had governed the basic structure of the judicial system. The effect of this amendment was to grant most of the power to create courts to the republics and, in accordance with Amendment 18, similarly to the autonomous provinces (Alagić 1970:234–236). These provisions led to a much more decentralized federal judicial system than had ever obtained in the past. This decentralization was built into the structure of the constitution of 1974, and we shall discuss it in the next section.

The Judicial System Under the 1974 Constitution

As was explained in the last chapter, the 1974 constitution represented a further development of the concept of self-management, and it was in that context that the self-management courts were created. At the same time the new constitution also codified a much less centralized federation (Rusinow 1978:330–331; Burg 1983), and this political fact was central to the structures of both the regular court system under the new regime and of the new CALs.

The Dual Court Systems

Regular and Constitutional Courts

In Chapter 2 of the 1974 constitution, entitled "The Foundations of the Socio-Political System," it is stated that "[j]udicial functions shall be performed by regular courts of law as organs of state power, and by self-management courts" (Article 92). This basic provision is elaborated in Chapter 5, "Courts and the Office of Public Prosecutor" (Articles 217–236). The basic distinction between the two kinds of courts is restated in the first article of that chapter: "Justice shall be administered within a unified system of power of and self-management by the working class and all working people by regular courts as agencies of state power, and by self-management courts"[13] (Article 217). The basic outlines of these two kinds of courts are set out in the rest of that chapter.

The present constitution actually mentions two kinds of regular courts (i.e., "instruments of state power"): military courts and regular courts (of general jurisdiction). The military courts retain roughly the same attributes as their predecessors under the earlier 1963 constitution: to decide cases involving military personnel, national defense, and state security (Article 221). Since these courts have such limited jurisdiction we will not be much concerned with their activities.

The regular courts of general jurisdiction have maintained much of the mandate they had under the earlier constitution: to decide disputes involving "basic personal relations, the rights and obligations of citizens, and the rights and obligations of the socio-political communities" as well as criminal and administrative law cases, and "disputes concerning property and labour relations, *if the settlement of such disputes has not been vested in self-management courts*" (Article 221; emphasis added). This last provision has important implications for the new category of self-management courts, as will be seen below.

Of the other courts existing under the 1963 constitution, arbitration and the conciliation councils have become self-management courts, as will be discussed below. The commercial courts have ceased to be a federal constitutional category, but instead are within the jurisdiction of the republics and provinces (Djordjević 1982:812–813). Consequently, the federal Supreme Commercial Court no longer exists, and the structures of the economic court systems within the republics and provinces are no longer uniform (see Trajković 1980). Slovenia and Vojvodina have eliminated economic courts entirely, giving jurisdiction in economic cases to the regular courts. In Montenegro and Kosovo the appellate commercial courts have been eliminated, with appeals from the trial commercial courts going to the supreme court of the republic and province, respectively. Only Bosnia-Herzegovina, Croatia, Montenegro, and Serbia proper have retained the full system of commercial courts.

At the head of the judiciary established by the federal constitution is the Federal Court (Articles 369–371). However, the Federal Court has a much more restricted jurisdiction than its predecessor, the Supreme Court of Yugoslavia. Where the Supreme Court had been charged with ensuring the uniform enforcement of federal law and was given jurisdiction over appeals from the republican supreme courts, the Federal Court has jurisdiction primarily over matters involving different federal units and federal administrative acts. As a former judge of both the former Supreme Court of Yugoslavia and the present Federal Court put it, "[T]he Federal Court is not the highest court in the land, or a supreme court, but rather—the court of the federation" (Perović 1980:102). The implications of this change for the federal nature of the Yugoslav courts will be considered below.

The constitutional courts that had been created by the 1963 constitution were maintained in much the same form and with much the same jurisdiction as before. As these courts are still considered to be separate from the judicial system, however, we will not be much concerned with them.

Self-Management Courts

If the great legal innovation of the 1963 constitution was the institution of the constitutional courts, the most interesting provisions for the judicial system in the new regime were those for the self-management courts. These new courts were empowered to decide

> specific kinds of disputes, as laid down by the constitution and statute, arising out of socio-economic and other self-management relations, and also disputes entrusted to them by working people in organizations of associated labour, self-managing communities of interest and other self-managing organizations and communities, which disputes arise out of mutual relations which they independently regulate, or which stem from rights of which they freely dispose, unless it is specified by statute that certain kinds of disputes must be decided by regular courts. (Article 224)

The general goal of creating self-management courts is to socialize the judicial function (*podruštvljavanje sudske funkcije*). As shown in chapter 2, a basic principle of Yugoslav self-management is that the role of the state in social life should be diminished, and the self-management courts are meant to further this process. In fact, they are seen as essential to the development of self-management. As expressed by Djordjević (1982:815), "The essence of these courts lies in the striving of the constitution to develop and guarantee institutions with which are expressed and realized the type of self-management socialism and its appropriate self-management political system."

A similar view is put forth by Mirko Perović:

> [S]elf-management relations . . . have as their component and integral part an accompanying development of the judicial social function. That function can no longer be established only in the classical state-political manner. It must be further socialized and carried out as a social, self-management function. . . . Finally, all this is in accordance with the general concept of the withering of alienated power and government, the socialization of politics, government and administration. (1980:145)

At the risk of redundancy, one could say that the general principle is that the self-management courts should handle cases involving the rights of self-government and other self-management rights: those rights that the state is no longer concerned with. Some cases are assigned to these courts, but others are expected to come under submission by citizens and organizations, concerning rights that are under their exclusive control. Just as self-management law should regulate those social relations that are no longer regulated by the state, so should the self-management courts, rather than state courts, handle questions concerning the application of self-management law.

The CALs were established by federal and republican/provincial statutes, which will be discussed in the final section of this chapter. The constitution (Article 223) also provides that self-management courts can be established by self-management act or by the agreement of the parties. The same article provides that the jurisdiction, organization, composition and procedure of these courts may be regulated either by the act establishing the court or by statute.

The constitution specifies that "self-management courts shall be established as courts of associated labour, arbitration tribunals, conciliation councils, chosen arbitration courts, and other kinds of self-management courts" (Article 225). As Jovan Djordjević says, all of these institutions except the CALs have parallels in other societies (1982:816), which is what makes the latter interesting. Before discussing the CALs at length, however, we should briefly describe conciliation councils, arbitration, and the other self-management courts, and how the two systems of courts, regular and self-management, relate to each other.

1. Conciliation councils (*mirovna veća*). These courts are essentially mediation centers within factories and communes. They are the only self-management courts that have received any empirical investigation. It will be recalled that they had been originally established under earlier constitutional regimes, although they did not attract many cases. Under the present constitution, the provisions for the establishment of conciliation councils have been enacted by republican/provincial legislation; there is no federal legislation regarding the establishment of these courts (Čok 1984:478). And under these provisions about 7,000 conciliation councils have been created in Yugoslavia (Čok 1984:483).[14] Although the constitution envisions conciliation councils in neighborhoods, work organizations, and other self-management bodies, in fact almost all of them have been established in neighborhoods (*mesne zajednice*) (Čok 1984:283). Very few have been created in work organizations (Miloševic 1985).

Although there are no federal statutes regarding the establishment of the conciliation councils, their jurisdiction does have a federal component. The constitution leaves procedure in the courts as a federal responsibility (Article 281[12]), and both the Law on Criminal Procedure and the Law on Civil Procedure contain provisions that affect the conciliation councils. Under Article 445 of the Law on Criminal Procedure, in certain cases involving privately initiated prosecutions for offenses against reputation, the case must be referred by the regular court to a conciliation council for an attempt at mediation. Similarly, under Article 468 of the Law on Civil Procedure, civil suits over small amounts must be referred to a conciliation council if the parties live in the same commune or work in the same organization;

similar requirements for jurisdiction are stated in the criminal procedure provision. Both the civil and criminal statutes provide that if the mediation attempt is not accepted by both parties the case returns to the court, and one study of such cases in the republic of Slovenia indicated that 76 percent of such cases were returned to court in this way (Jambrek 1983:193).

Apart from these federal provisions, the jurisdiction of the conciliation councils is in general limited to those disputes submitted to them by one or both of the parties. Most cases are concerned with interference with property rights, damage claims, and fighting (Čok 1984:481, table 2).

In terms of caseloads, the conciliation councils have still not been very successful in attracting voluntary use. Data from the republic of Slovenia show that in 1979 there were 627 conciliation councils in the republic, and that they "treated" 1,265 cases, or slightly more than two cases per council (Jambrek 1983:192–193). The only comprehensive figures for the whole country are not specific as to the time period involved, which apparently varied with the respondants to a questionnaire of local authorites (Čok 1984:478n.13).[15] If we assume that the respondants provided data on calendar years (which would likely have been the form in which it was most easily available to them), and if we take the higher of the totals that can be derived from the public report (Čok 1984:480–481, tables 1 and 2),[16] we find 76,685 cases in the councils. This figure, which probably errs on the high side, would indicate that the conciliation councils in Yugoslavia handle about eleven cases per council, just as they did in 1969 (see above). Further, as perhaps 36 percent of the total caseload was referred under the Law on Criminal Procedure or the Law on Civil Procedure (Čok 1984:478, table 1), the voluntary use of the councils would be even less, perhaps 7.2 cases per council.

2. Arbitration (*arbitraža*). In addition to the CALs and the conciliation councils, the constitution mentions arbitration as a form of self-management court. Actually, two kinds of arbitration are mentioned: arbitration tribunals, and "chosen courts" (*izbrani sudovi*) or voluntary arbitration. These courts have not received much empirical study, although there is one thorough monograph on their legal structures (Musa 1982). The arbitration tribunals are found in work organizations, which must create some kind of institution for the resolution of internal disputes (Law on Associated Labor §§ 40, 372, 578). When they exist, they must be utilized before any other formal legal institution can be invoked. Appeals from these arbitration tribunals can be made to the trial-level CALs, as shall be seen below. Voluntary arbitration can be agreed to by contract or stipulation, as in many other legal systems.

3. Other self-management courts. The constitution provides that other forms of self-management courts may be established in addition to the ones specifically mentioned. Thus far, the only other such courts are the "courts of honor" (*sudovi časti*), essentially boards of ethics, which have been established in the Board of Trade of Yugoslavia (*Privredna Komora Jugoslavije*), other such trade organizations, some voluntary and professional organizations, and the Yugoslav Peoples' Army (Musa 1982:30–31; Perović 1980:193). These courts may issue warnings and reprimands, and in some cases repeated convictions before them may lead to administrative action against the wrongdoer.

Relations Between the Two Court Systems

The relationship between the two court systems, the regular courts and the self-management courts, has remained unclear. The constitution (Article 233) states that the question of when and under what conditions a legal remedy will be allowed against the decision of a self-management court will be regulated by statute or by the act establishing the court, and that the conditions under which the decisions of a self-management court may be disputed before a regular court will be established by statute. The same article also states that the enforcement of the decisions of self-management courts will be regulated by statute. These provisions imply the subordination of the self-management courts to the regular courts. Thus Djordjević (1982:816) takes this constitutional situation to mean that "a decision of a self-management court is not final, in that there may be established a specific relationship between them [the self-management courts] (the possibility of their hierarchy) and between this court and another (constitutional or regular) court." This conclusion is too drastic for some other writers, who hold that there should be no hierarchical relationship between the two court systems, as they regulate different social relationships in different manners (Perović 1980:171–175).

This question has been most important in regard to the CALs. Article 10 of the first (1974) federal law regarding these courts had envisioned the possibility of their decisions being challenged before the regular courts. However, this was not often done in practice, and the second federal law on the CALs (1984) no longer mentions such a possibility (see chapter 9, under "The Law on the CALs, 1984"). Thus, for our purposes, the question of a possible hierarchical relationship between the dual judicial systems remains one of greater theoretical than practical moment.

The New Federalism: Poli-centric Centralism

We have already mentioned that the constitutional amendments of

1967–71 greatly altered the federal structure of Yugoslavia by weakening what had until then been a strongly centralized system (see Burg 1983). The 1974 constitution accentuated this process, creating what Yugoslav political scientists have come to refer to as "poli-centric centralism." The meaning of this oxymoron is that the political system within each of the eight constituents of the federation is centralized, but there is no longer an overriding central power to coordinate their activities. This situation seems rather more than similar to that obtaining in confederations, although it is usually denied that Yugoslavia is a confederation in the classical sense (see, e.g., Djordjević 1982:610).[17]

For our purposes, the effect of this decentralization on the judicial system is most important. We have already mentioned the drastic curtailment of the supervisory powers of the Federal Court over the other components in the court system, as compared with those of the earlier Supreme Court of Yugoslavia. The effect of this development has been to create judicial systems within the federal units that need no longer necessarily exhibit uniformity between them. To be sure, there are still mechanisms to provide some uniformity, such as the continued federal control over the regulation of criminal law and economic offenses, and over court procedures (Constitution, Article 281[12]). In addition, the constitution (Article 371) provides for joint sessions of the Federal Court and delegates of the republican and provincial supreme courts to "jointly take stands of principles on questions of concern for the application of federal statutes;" this mandate has been expanded by the federal Law on the Federal Court (Article 33),[18] which provides that these courts may agree that such joint sessions may also consider additional questions of mutual interest. Again, the decentralized nature of the system is clear, in that all of the courts, including the Federal Court, are represented by equal numbers of delegates, so that no one court can impose its views. In contrast, a similar provision for joint sessions under the previous constitution had given overwhelming representation to the Supreme Court of Yugoslavia (Perović 1980:107).

The result of this decentralization of the judicial system has been a certain amount of nonuniformity in the judicial systems of the republics and provinces. Least changed are the regular courts. Although these are now regulated by republican or provincial statutes rather than by the constitution or federal law, all of the regular court systems have maintained the structures set up in 1946: communal courts, circuit courts, and a supreme court in each republic or autonomous province. The commercial and economic courts have changed the most, ceasing to exist in Slovenia and Vojvodina, and losing their appellate levels in Kosovo and Montenegro; the federal Supreme Commercial Court was also abolished.

Since the Federal Court is now one of extremely limited jurisdiction, the effect of the new federalism has been to create an assortment of individual judicial systems without many mechanisms for unifying them. Without further constitutional changes, it may be that the Yugoslav federation goes from its earlier position of a predominantly federal judiciary without the independent republican and provincial courts, to one where the republican and provincial courts dominate and there is no federal judiciary.

The fragmentation of the federal judicial system may be most evident in the CALs. In these courts, as will be seen later, there are no federal components. There is not even the limited oversight provided to the regular courts by the Federal Court, as that court has no jurisdiction over appeals from the self-management courts. While there is a provision for joint sessions of the republican/provincial CALs, there is no federal CAL, and thus for most matters the decisions of the highest CAL in each republic or province are supreme within that territory. Nevertheless, the CALs are all derived from the same federal legislation and so exhibit some common elements. Thus we turn to a closer examination of the formal structure of the CALs in the next chapter.

Chapter 5
The Courts of Associated Labor, 1974 to 1984: Formal Structure

The legal status and structure of the CALs is complicated by the decentralized federalism of the present Yugoslav state. The CALs are mentioned specifically in the federal constitution, the republican/provincial constitutions, federal statutes, and republican and provincial statutes. We will first sort out these multiple layers of reference in general terms, and then look at the specifics of the provisions governing such important questions as the jurisdiction, composition, and procedures of the CALs. To give the discussion of these points some specificity, we will concentrate on the CALs in Serbia, as the case study was conducted in that republic. The chapter will conclude with a discussion of the work loads that have developed in the CALs, and particularly in Serbia.

Constitutional and Statutory Provisions

Constitutional Provisions

The CALs are the only courts other than the Federal Court to which an entire article of the constitution is devoted (Article 226). This article gives their basic jurisdictional charge: to decide on whether the conditions exist for the creation of BOALs and other work organizations, and to handle disputes concerning the formation, division, or fusion of such organizations; to protect self-management rights and social property; to decide on the conclusion and implementation of self-management agreements; and to decide on "other kinds of disputes arising out of socio-economic and other self-management relations, as specified by statute." Very similar language is used in the constitutions of each of the republics and autonomous provinces.[1] The constitution also specifies that "principles concerning the formation, jurisdiction and composition of the courts of associated labour and proceedings before these courts, shall be laid down by federal statute" (Article 226).

The Federal Law on the CALs (1974)

These basic constitutional provisions were given some specificity in the federal Law on Courts of Associated Labor,[2] which was one of the first acts passed after the promulgation of the 1974 constitution. The swiftness of the law's enactment was a reflection not only of the importance of the self-management courts to the conceptual scheme of the constitution, but also of the particular importance of the CALs as the premier examples of self-management courts. This law set out the basic structures of the new courts, with all subsequent legislation, at both federal and republican/provincial levels, following this initial model, at least until the passage of the new federal Law on CALs in 1984 (see chapter 9, "The Law on the CALs, 1984").

The first section of the 1974 federal law contained general provisions, such as guarantees of the independence of the CALs in exercising the judicial function (Article 2), the public nature of their work (Article 5), the requirement that cases be heard by benches (Article 8), and that the decisions of the CALs have validity throughout Yugoslavia (Article 10). These provisions simply restated basic principles that the federal constitution requires for all courts. Of greater interest are several provisions that are unique to the CALs. Perhaps the most interesting of these is the rule stating that while a proceeding in a CAL is begun by the proposal of a participant, further proceedings are carried out by the court as its official responsibility (Article 6). This provision is in theory a significant departure from the situation prevailing in regular courts, where the parties control the course of litigation and may choose to settle the case if they wish.

In contrast, the CALs statute provided that private settlements could not be made once a case was begun unless the court specifically determined that such a settlement would not violate self-management rights or be detrimental to social property (Article 33). In addition, the CAL was put under an obligation to determine for itself the truth of the facts involved in the issue, even if the parties did not dispute them and even if they did not adduce evidence on them (Article 28). These provisions were in keeping with the general view that the CAL was not simply to decide legal questions, but rather was to resolve disputed relationships in all of their complexity. They are also in accordance with the duty of the CALs to protect social property (see Rajović 1978:222–226).

Despite these substantive innovations, however, another basic provision specified that the CALs should use much of the Law on Civil Procedure, "insofar as it is appropriate to the nature of the disputes that the court decides and if it is not contrary to the provisions of this statute" (Article 13). This adoption of the procedures of the regular courts has been criticized, both because of the presumed unsuitability of that procedure for self-management disputes and because it seems that the constitutional provision calling for the regulation of the CALs procedure by statute (Article 226) implies a separate procedure (Pantović 1985:9). In fact, following the enactment of the new Law on the CALs (1984), an attempt to enact a Law on Procedures in the CALs has been initiated, but has so far not succeeded (see chapter 9, "The Law on the CALs, 1984").

The second major section of the 1974 federal law concerned the organization of the CALs. There it was established that these courts would exist at two levels, as trial courts (Article 14) and as republican or provincial CALs as appellate courts (Article 15). Further, their basic jurisdiction was defined on a territorial basis, with a provision that some special CALs could be created to hear particular kinds of cases (Article 14).

A third major section dealt with the subject-matter jurisdiction of the CALs. A long (33-clause) Article 18 gave some specificity to the general expressions of jurisdiction used in the constitution. This topic will be considered in some detail below.

In addition to the basic provision specifying the use of the Law on Civil Procedure in many CAL cases, procedures in these courts also merited a separate major section of the 1974 act. The provisions of this section specified who could initiate proceedings in the CAL, who could otherwise participate in such proceedings, time limits, and other regulations concerning appeals. This section also contained the provisions specifying the duty of the court to determine the facts and the impossibility of private settlement or withdrawal of cases once initiated. These provisions, too, are considered in detail in the next section.

The last major substantive section of the 1974 federal law was concerned with appeals to the basic CAL of the decisions of internal arbitration boards within work and other organizations. As we have seen, such cases were expected to account for much of the work of the new courts.

The 1974 law concluded with several "transitional and concluding provisions" concerning the transfer of appropriate cases already initiated in the regular courts to the CALs and a statement that the new law would go into effect on the day of its publication in the *Official Gazette of Yugoslavia*. One important substantive provision was also contained in this section, however. Article 54 stated that

[1] Decisions of the courts of associated labor that are initiated for judicial execution, are [to be] executed by regular courts according to the regulations for proceedings in execution. [2] The execution of other decisions of courts of associated labor are ensured by the assembly having jurisdiction, which towards that aim accepts the measures envisioned by the constitution and statute.

The problem of execution of the CAL decisions has remained an important one, however, even with the passage of the new law in 1984.

Other Federal Statutes

While the CALs are mentioned in a number of federal statutes (see Rajović 1979:224), the references to them in the "little constitution," the Law on Associated Labor (1976), are probably most important, due to the prominence of that act in the Yugoslav system. Not surprisingly, some of the provisions of both the constitution and the federal Law on CALs are reflected in the provisions of that law. In the first part of the act, entitled "Basic Provisions," the CALs are mentioned among other institutions for settling disputes and disagreements involving self-managed relations (Article 40) and for the protection of self-management rights and social property (Article 41). In Chapter 5, entitled "Protection of Workers' Rights," the CALs are given prominent attention. The first article of the chapter (Article 220) mentions them as among the institutions from which workers may seek protection of their rights. Further, Article 224 specifies the CAL as the court to which a worker who is dissatisfied with the handling of his complaint by his work organization may appeal the organization's actions. Later in the act, the CALs are charged with determining whether the conditions exist for the formation of a new BOAL or the separation of a BOAL from another work organization (Articles 330 and 331), just as in the Law on CALs.

In general, the various federal statutes, including the 1974 Law on the CALs, can be seen as mainly serving to provide some specificity to the very general provisions of the constitution regarding these courts. In the process they sometimes broaden the scope of the CALs' jurisdiction by, for example, including other kinds of self-management organization in addition to the BOALs and work communities mentioned in Article 226 (Rajović 1979:217). But this specificity is still not meant to be definitive of the actual structure or work of the courts, as there are no federal CALs and the constitutional mandate of federal legislation regarding these courts is only to establish *principles* for their organization and work. The federal Law on CALs (Article 4) itself empowered the republics and provinces to regulate the "formation, composition, location, jurisdiction and organization" of the CALs. Therefore we must turn to that level, of the constituents of the federation, to examine the specifics of the CALs.

Republican and Provincial Statutes

Just as the constitutions of all of the republics and autonomous provinces have articles concerning the CALs, so have all of these polities enacted statutes creating and structuring these courts in 1974 or 1975.[3] In the main, these statutes are closely parallel to the federal Law on CALs, with some exceptions. Since procedure is a matter solely within the prerogative of the federation (Constitution, Article 281[12]), none of the republican or provincial statutes contains provisions on that subject.[4] Also, none of these statutes contains provisions on the appeal of arbitration decisions. All except those of Bosnia-Herzegovina and Kosovo have special provisions concerning the selection of judges and, in addition, the Serbian statute has a section on the president and administration of the court.

All of the republics and provinces have created basic CALs, with one appellate CAL in each of these federal units. There have thus been established forty-seven basic CALs and eight appellate ones in all of Yugoslavia. Moreover, Slovenia has taken advantage of the provision of Article 14 of the federal law, permitting the establishment of special CALs to hear particular kinds of cases, in addition to the regular, basic CALs in the republic, whose jurisdiction is territorially defined (Rajović 1979:90). As of 1979, five such special CALs had been formed in the republic, one each in the fields of pension funds, sports, culture, research, and education.[5] However, as of that time only the special CAL for pension funds and sports had received any cases (Jambrek 1983:192). Since only Slovenia has created these special CALs, and they have not been very active, we will not be concerned with them further.

The most important provisions concerning the CALs are those governing jurisdiction, procedures and the composition of the courts. We will look at these provisions in the specific context of the CALs in Serbia, as the case study was carried out in that republic.

The CALs in Serbia

Jurisdiction

Article 4 of the federal Law on CALs states that "[t]he formation, location, jurisdiction and organization" of these courts are to be determined by republican or provincial statute. The Law on Courts of Associated Labor of the Republic of Serbia created nine basic CALs (Belgrade, Šabac, Zaječar, Čačak, Kragujevac, Niš, Požarevac, Titovo Užice, Vranje [Article 14]) and one appellate CAL, the CAL of Serbia, located in Belgrade (Article 11). Each of the basic CALs was given jurisdiction over specific communes (*opštine*), and the CAL of Serbia has jurisdiction throughout the entire republic except for the territories of the two autonomous provinces, Kosovo and Vojvodina.

The subject-matter jurisdiction of the CALs has reference to the federal law. Although the provisions of the federal law are stated by the constitution to be principles governing these courts, they seem often to have been absolutely determinative of the republican/provincial acts. For example, the Serbian Law on CALs (Article 19) adopts almost word for word the introduction and the following thirty-three clauses of Article 18 of the federal Law on CALs, defining the jurisdiction of the courts. The Serbian statute does add two more clauses, giving the CAL the power to decide disputes initiated by the trade unions concerning the application of certain agreements which they have not signed (Article 19[34]) and disputes about the disposition of assets after a work organization has been liquidated (Article 19[35]).

The Serbian statute (Article 20) also adopts almost word for word Article 19 of the federal Law on CALs, giving the basic CAL in the republic the duty to decide about other disputes involving the self-management rights and obligations of workers in associated labor. Article 21 of the Serbian law empowers the CALs in the republic to decide appeals from internal arbitration (cf. § 5 of the federal Law on CALs). Article 23, like Article 20 of the federal act, sets the rules for determining which CAL has jurisdiction when the parties are from different communes and, in fact, adopts most of the language of the federal statute. Finally, Article 22 of the Serbian statute states the subject-matter jurisdiction of the CAL of Serbia: to decide appeals from the basic CALs in the republic, as well as those concerning the legality of the acts of certain political bodies as they affect organizations of associated labor; to issue rules concerning the procedures in the CALs; and to assume "other jobs which are placed in its jurisdiction by the constitution or by statute."

Since the federal and Serbian statutes are so similar, it is fair to sum up both by saying that the legislators seem to have intended that the CALs be used primarily for the resolution of disputes concerning the use of social property and the structure of organizations of associated labor. These disputes, which are called "status disputes" in the literature on the CALs, are the kinds encompassed by the general clause of the long article on jurisdiction in both acts, with the remaining thirty-odd clauses in that article serving mainly to give greater specificity to the general statements. The provision giving the CALs the power to decide other kinds of cases concerning the rights of workers seems residual. However, as we will see, it is this residual category, which includes individual labor disputes, that has been most important in the caseload of the CALs, both in Serbia and in the other parts of the country.

Composition and Organization

Like the federal statute and the constitution, the Serbian statute on CALs requires that these courts sit in panels (*veća*) to exercise the judicial function. Again, the republican law provides greater specificity than the other legislation by providing (Article 6) that these panels consist of three judges, of whom only one may be a judge of a regular court. The same article provides that all three members of a panel are equally competent in the rendering of judgment; none is superior to the others in regard to that function, even though one of them is the president of the panel.

The judges of the CALs are nominated by the Socialist Alliance and elected by the republican assembly (Article 28). Their mandate is for four years, renewable for another four years (Article 29). There are no particular requirements for election as a judge of the CAL, other than that one must be "a Yugoslav citizen who is politically and morally suitable for the exercise of judicial responsibilities and who has the necessary experience and expertise [*stručnost*]" (Article 32). A judge of a regular court may also be elected judge of the CAL (Article 33). Although most CAL judges retain their regular jobs, a certain number of full-time judges in the CAL may be elected and paid as they were paid in the year before they took up that position (Article 31). CALs are to be independent in their exercise of the judicial function (Article 2), and their judges may not be called to account for their thoughts when giving judgment or be held criminally responsible for their actions without the permission of the assembly that elected them (Article 35). A judge of the CAL can be removed from office only for criminal activities that make him unsuitable for further service as a judge (Article 43).

The most noteworthy features of these provisions are that there are no specific requirements for service as a judge and, specifically, that there is no requirement that members of a panel have legal training. Coupled with the provision that all judges of a panel are equal in the exercise of the judicial function, the rules make clear that, in

Serbia, at least, the CALs are designed not to be subject to domination by legal professionals, that they are to be lay courts (cf. Čalija 1982).[6]

Procedure

Every lawyer knows that the supposedly clear distinction between substantive and procedural laws is in reality anything but, and the distinction is particularly murky in the case of the CALs. Writers on the subject find it necessary to start their analyses with repetitions of the basic principles governing the CALs, such as those of judicial independence, judgment by panels, nonprofessional elected judges, and the social character of these courts, as also being basic principles of their procedure (Rajović 1979:153–186; Pantović 1985:66–80). Furthermore, as we noted above, the federal law provides (Article 13) that the provisions of the Law on Civil Procedure should be applied by the CALs unless the court decides that they are unsuited to the nature of the dispute at hand. This provision makes the procedural rules dependent on the court's assessment of the substance of the case, and a more solid conjuncture of substance and procedure would be hard to imagine.

Apart from this provision, there are a number of specific procedural innovations in the federal law. The most important of these are based on the special charge of the court, to restore disrupted relations rather than to decide narrow legal questions, and are aimed at facilitating this task by widening the sphere of participants involved in cases before the court.

One step toward such increasing participation is the avoidance within the statute of many of the usual terms for the stages and parties in a lawsuit. Thus a CAL issues a "decision" (*rešenje*) rather than the traditional "verdict" (*presuda*). The standard adversarial terms for the parties in civil litigation, plaintiff (*tužilac*) and defendant (*tuženik*), are also avoided. Instead, the statute refers only to participants (*učesnici*), with the distinction between the two traditional parties being expressed as proposer (*predlagač*) and other participant (*drugi učesnik*). But "other participants" are not limited only to the traditional defendant, nor must the proposer or initiator be only the one who has directly suffered an injury. The federal statute provides for wider participation from both sides, to the point where "the law [on CALs] does not recognize the concept of parties [to a dispute]" (Rajović 1979:193).

This expansion of the definition of who may take part in proceedings before a CAL is, in fact, a major departure from the normal rules of the civil law tradition regarding participation in civil cases (see generally Rakić-Vodinelić 1982). In general, in civil-law countries, the ability to be a party to a lawsuit is based on the concept of legal capacity: one must be a physical or legal person with the capacity to act on one's own behalf (i.e., to be of full age and of undiminished mental facilities). However, in the CALs, unincorporated or ad hoc groups of workers, for example, may be participants in cases, even though they would not have standing to bring a case in a regular civil court, so long as the members of the group are the subjects of the self-management rights at issue in the CAL proceeding. Again we see the mixing of substance and procedure (Rakić-Vodinelić 1982:46).

We may look first at the initiators, or proposers. The first article of the procedures section of the federal Law on CALs (Article 23) provides that a proposal may be initiated by a worker or by a variety of self-management organizations and institutions, when there is a question of the protection of social property, and by individual workers in an organization if that organization has interfered with their self-management rights. This last category could include a collective or group of workers which does not otherwise have any legal identity or capacity. In addition, sociopolitical communities, the social attorney of self-management,[7] and the trade unions are empowered to initiate proceedings regarding the protection of self-management rights and social property. This enlarged circle of potential proposers is clearly aimed at encouraging wider participation in the initiation of proceedings to resolve self-management disputes than is customary in civil procedure.

In addition to the initiators, the range of other participants is also much wider than is usual in civil cases. Article 24 of the federal law defines these other participants as "everyone who is a bearer of the rights and responsibilities which are [to be] decided upon in the proceeding." Again, this category could include groups of workers or even of nonworkers who would not otherwise have legal identity or capacity. All of these people are considered to have an interest in the matter before the court and are entitled to equal participation in the CAL's proceedings. At the same time, all such people are bound by the decision of the court, even if they have not actually taken part in the proceedings (see Rakić-Vodinelić 1982:46). This situation has led some commentators to conclude that a CAL has a duty to identify all potential participants in an action initiated before it and to notify them of the case so that they may actually participate (see Rakić-Vodinelić 1982:46).

Another provision that seems aimed at increasing participation in CAL cases states that no taxes are incurred in proceedings in these courts (Law on Courts of Associated Labor, Serbia [LCAL-S], Article

9). This rule is a significant departure from those governing cases in the regular courts, where taxes are levied on the various stages of the proceedings, from complaint, cross-complaint, answer, and other filings, to decisions or the registration of settlements, through the stages of appeal. According to the law in effect in 1982, these taxes ranged from a minimum of 10 ND for disputes concerning amounts of less than 100 ND, to 825 ND plus 1 percent of the amount in dispute for cases valued at over 50,000 ND, with a maximum of 20,000 ND.[8] Some stages of court proceedings (e.g., the answer, or a request for execution of a decision) incurred taxes of only half the regular amounts. The total elimination of these taxes from CAL proceedings makes them much more accessible to all potential participants.

The social attorney of self-management and the trade unions may also participate in proceedings that they have not themselves initiated simply by announcing that they will do so (Article 24). And the CAL must inform the social attorney of self-management about cases that the latter has not initiated (Article 25). This provision is a clear indication of the expectation of the legislators that the cases handled by the CALs would be of relevance to the wider society.

This same expectation can be seen in the provisions for broadening the scope of the substantive discussions in CAL cases. By the Law on Civil Procedures (LCP),[9] the parties in civil lawsuits largely define the issues involved themselves, because while the court is obligated to decide questions properly brought before it, it may only decide within the boundaries of these questions and is not required to decide any questions not properly presented to it (LCP Articles 2 and 186). Furthermore, in an ordinary civil case in a regular court, the case may be withdrawn or settled more or less at the desire of the parties (LCP Articles 212–218). In the CALs, however, while a case can only be commenced by the proposal of a participant, further proceedings are carried on as the duty of the court ([federal] Law on Courts of Associated Labor [LCAL] Article 6). The CAL is obligated to determine for itself the facts involved in the matter at hand, regardless of the representations of the parties or whether they have even presented certain information (LCAL Article 28). In addition, a CAL is not bound by the proposals of the participants in rendering its decisions (LCAL Article 32). Thus, the intent of the legislators seems to have been that once proceedings were initiated in the CAL, the further processing of the matter would be based on the court's perception of the interests of the public rather than on the desires of the participants.

In Serbia these federal provisions regarding procedure in the CALs were supplemented by a set of rules (*pravila*) to govern the operation of the CALs in the republic (excluding those in the two autonomous provinces) (see note 4). These rules were issued in early 1978 by the CAL of Serbia, the appellate CAL in the republic. The rules do not contradict the procedural provisions of the federal Law on CALs, serving instead to provide greater specificity to them and uniformity to the work of the CAL in the republic (Rules of the CAL in Serbia, Article 1).

Conclusions: The CALs and Their Caseloads

To conclude this part, we may look again at some of the descriptions of the way the CALs were supposed to work and at the gross figures on their caseloads. Since the CALs were to be a completely new kind of legal institution,[10] discussions in the public media and in legal professional journals concerning their proper function and role arose immediately after the passage of the federal Law on the CALs. This literature provides some good descriptions of the concepts these courts were meant to embody.

All of the commentators at the time of the creation of the CALs argued that these courts, and the self-management courts in general, must be different from the regular courts. As one writer in the Zagreb law journal *Naša Zakonitost* put it, "The courts of associated labor cannot be a different name for the regular courts. . . . The authority of their [CALs'] decisions cannot be based exclusively on the possibility of their forcible execution but rather on their internal power" (Matović 1974:974). The intent was plainly to create a social, mediatory institution rather than a strictly legal one. The idea was perhaps most succinctly put by a participant in a seminar to discuss a draft of the proposed Law on the CALs in the republic of Serbia on November 1974:

> Disputes which are decided by the courts of associated labor, so-called "self-management disputes," do not have the character of lawsuits between parties, because there are not parties in dispute, but rather participants, a procedure for these disputes is different in substance from ordinary civil procedure. The accusation as a means of initiating procedures has been changed to the proposal of a participant, and the verdict has become a decision of the court by which the disputed situation is untied and relations restored. The court of associated labor, in greater measure than the other courts, applies not only self-management law but also legal morality. It must do that because it does not decide a lawsuit in which one man stands against another, but rather puts in order an internal relationship in which more people are involved and have an interest in the restoration of that relationship. (Trifunović 1975:25)

To be sure, not all legal scholars were convinced that the CALs as constituted by the new legislation would actually meet these goals. At that same conference, one professor of law from Belgrade University expressed some skepticism, suggesting that, by his understanding, the judicial function was always a state function.[11] Other participants questioned particular aspects of the jurisdiction assigned to the CALs as determined by the federal law and draft of the republican statute. Nevertheless, the bulk of scholarly opinion at the time of the creation of the CALs did accept the sharp distinction between them and the regular state courts.

This same idea also carried over into the popular press. An article in the Zagreb weekly *Start* in early 1978 on the work of the then-new CALs in Croatia said that they were "a real little revolution in the history of the judiciary, an innovation without precedent in that history, which traditionally had shrunk from innovation" (Miles-Jašarević 1978:20). After discussing the concept of the self-management court and the new practice of the CALs, the article concluded that with some exceptions, "it seems that we are a very good way towards the destatification [*na vrlo dobrom putu deetatiziramo*] of one more function which had always been a typical attribute of state power" (ibid., p. 22). This article was accompanied by a cartoon of an overalls-clad female worker, seated on a girder, wielding the sword and scales of justice (see cover), a graphic representation of the popular image of the CAL as a "workers' court" (*radnički sud*), as was the title of the article: "Justice in Worker's Overalls" (*Pravda u radničkom kombinezonu*).

As we saw in chapter 1, the forty-eight basic (trial) CALs in Yugoslavia quickly developed large caseloads, from 26,000 cases in their first full year of operation (1976) to 80,000 cases in 1980. While I do not have later figures for the entire country, such figures are available for the republic of Serbia for the period 1976–1984. In those years, the numbers of cases filed were as follows (from GSURS 16:31 [1984]):

Year	Cases
1976	11,221
1977	13,717
1978	17,584
1979	21,418
1980	24,560
1981	27,696
1982	27,436
1983	29,873
1984	30,255

With the exception of 1982, when the number of filings actually declined slightly from the previous year, we see a constant growth, although the growth rate slowed in the most recent years. And, as we have already seen in chapter 1, most of these cases were filed by individuals, at a rate per 10,000 workers that was much higher than those in the Warsaw Pact countries. These raw figures certainly seem to indicate that the CALs have been successful in attracting use by workers. Whether they have actually functioned in the way expected of self-management courts, however, is another question, which the case study that follows was designed to answer.

Part III

The Case Study of the CAL in Belgrade

Chapter 6
The Court and the Research

The Case Study: The CAL in Belgrade

Why Belgrade?

An obvious question for any case study is why the particular institution, location, or phenomenon studied was chosen. The Belgrade CAL was an attractive candidate for the study for several reasons. It was (and is) the busiest CAL in the country in terms of numbers of cases filed. This heavy work load meant that I was likely to be able to observe a wider variety of cases than might have been the case in a smaller court. Also, the heaviest concentration of lawyers in Serbia is in Belgrade (see chapter 8), which meant that I would probably be able to see more lawyers in action than in a smaller town, where the small size of the bar may have affected relations between lawyers and court personnel.

On the other hand, the Belgrade CAL was perhaps an unrepresentative court, for some of these same reasons. First, the heavy caseload of that court may mean that it handles cases differently from its less busy counterparts. Similarly, the larger concentration of lawyers may mean that matters are handled more formally or in some other way differently than in courts where the "bargaining arenas" are smaller (cf. Galanter 1984b). One of the problematic features of many ethnographic studies of courts is that their subjects are urban rather than rural institutions and may not be representative of the latter (cf. Daniels 1985). At one stage I had hoped to be able to control at least partially for these problems by studying a smaller CAL for contrast, but it was not possible to do so. However, some data from other, smaller CALs are available, which indicate that the Belgrade court is probably not atypical in its handling of cases; these data are discussed below.

Another possible objection to the choice of the Belgrade CAL as the site of the case study is that Yugoslavia is a very diverse nation, and Belgrade, which is the capital of both the federation and of the republic of Serbia, is perhaps the least representative site in the country. The merits of this objection are hard to gauge, however, because of the lack of nationwide data with which to compare Belgrade institutions. Most sociological work in Yugoslavia is done on a republican or provincial basis, and thus the present study, limited as it is to one site, is within the general pattern of social research in and on Yugoslavia.

As a practical matter, the specific subject of analysis for a case study is often determined by its accessibility. A researcher cannot force entry to a research site, for ethical reasons and for the very practical one that participant observation is dependent on acceptance by the people being observed. In the present study, the likelihood of gaining access to the CAL in Belgrade was certainly one of the reasons that that court was chosen for study. I had been able to make contact with several scholars from Belgrade before undertaking the study, and had also been able to arrange for affiliation with a research institute there for the time required for the study.[1] These scholars assured me that they could arrange for me to receive access to the Belgrade CAL, and it seemed best to accept this arrangement rather than to try to obtain different affiliations or access to a CAL outside of Belgrade. In the end, whatever limitations on data and interpretation are caused by the peculiarities of the Belgrade court, the case study is still valuable, for, as they say in Yugoslavia, *bolje išta nego ništa*—better something than nothing.

The Conduct of the Research

The core of my research on the CAL was the observational study carried out in the court in 1982–83. These observations were supplemented by interviews, the collection of statistics, and a survey of the professional legal literature and the popular press for materials on the CAL. In addition, I was able to follow up events after 1983 in the course of return visits to Belgrade in September 1984, August through December 1985, and March–April 1986. The various stages of the research need to be described so that the reader has some means with which to evaluate the data and analysis.

The Observational Study, 1982–83

The research process began when I arrived in Belgrade in August 1981. From then until April 1982 I worked on acquiring facility in Serbo-Croatian and on learning the essential features of the Yugoslav legal system and the statutes governing the CALs. This knowledge was gained through interviews with law professors and struggling through legal materials; the latter process made for tough going to a beginner in the language, but was effective in terms of learning the specialized language of Yugoslav law.[2]

My actual entry into the CAL was delayed until formal permission from the city of Belgrade could be obtained. Although my research project had been approved at the federal level in early 1981, local approval took much longer to obtain. Once it came, however, no restrictions were placed on my activities, so long as I worked under the auspices of the institution with which I had been affiliated.

In April 1982 I was notified that my project had been approved by the city of Belgrade. I was then introduced to the secretary of the Basic CAL in Belgrade, who showed me around the court administrative offices and introduced me to the personnel working there. All of these people were very gracious and offered to answer my questions and to otherwise assist me in the research. In particular, I was told that I could have access to the court's records of cases.

The administrative offices, which were quite crowded, were located on the sixth floor of a building in which the elevator went only to the fifth floor. In addition to the offices of the president of the court and the secretary, this building also held other court administrative offices, the court's library, and the offices of the court's technical and professional staff. However, there were only two courtrooms in this building. Most cases were heard in a building about a half-mile away, which contained seven courtrooms.[3] The secretary of the court took me to this second building and introduced me to one of the judges. That introduction marked the start of my observational research.

The judge to whom I was first introduced was one of the full-time members of the court. He was quite amenable to the idea of my observing the operation of his bench, of which he was, of course, the president. I began my observations that same day.

The CAL courtrooms were very small, holding only a large, long table with three chairs on one side of it for the judges, a chair at one end for the stenographer, and an additional chair, usually between those of the judges and that of the stenographer, for the secretary of the bench. In addition, there were always two chairs on the side of the table opposite the judges for the parties or their representatives. When a chair was found and brought in for me, the judge,[4] secretary, and I agreed that the best location for me would be next to the stenographer and the secretary, where I would be able to see and hear everything taking place. I assumed that position in all of the courtrooms that I visited.

For the next three months I concentrated my research on that judge and his panels. Thus I only attended the court one day per week, when his court sat, and used the remaining time to continue library research on the CAL and to talk with people in the court's administration. I did not want to be too demanding on the court's personnel and particularly the first judge, as I wanted to establish a sound relationship with him in the hope that I would thus gain a good reputation in the court. And that approach seemed to be successful, for when I did start to make broader contacts in the court I received assistance from the first judge.

Almost without exception, the personnel of the CAL were receptive of my presence and helpful in my research. They were, in fact, pleased that I was interested in their activities. Before too long I was known as "our American" (*naš Amerikanac*) and introduced as such: "Have you met our American?" The reputation seems to have lingered. On return visits to the court in 1984, 1985, and 1986, I still was introduced to new personnel as "our American, you've heard about him."

The first judge was patient and took pains to ensure that I understood what was going on. He would not only answer my questions, but also asked me if I understood certain specific points, and if my explanation did not satisfy him, he would explain the matter. He also encouraged me to read the file of each case before it was heard. There was nearly always an opportunity to do this just before the parties were called into the courtroom, as cases were generally scheduled for every half-hour but hearings usually did not last more than half that long.[5] Thus in the time between cases I could scan the file of the upcoming case and ask the secretary or the judge for clarifications, which they were always willing to provide.

Cases were scheduled from eight in the morning until early afternoon. At around eleven there would be a break of about forty-five minutes, when the members of the bench, the secretary, and I would go to a small restaurant in the basement of the court for "breakfast" (*doručak*), which could be fruit juice and snack, or coffee, or a hot dish and a beer.[6] As the members of other benches would also have breakfast at about the same time, this break in the restaurant provided a good opportunity for me to meet more of the people who worked in the court.

In the courtrooms I took notes on the activities involved in each case, recording case numbers, issues, attendance by parties and/or lawyers, who spoke to which issues, questions from the bench, and the progress made at the hearing; when decisions were made, I recorded those as well. In many instances I was able to get a copy of the record from the stenographer.[7] Only once did someone ask who I was and what I was doing there, and in that instance it was a plaintiff who was a chronic litigant and who had several cases filed in the court at the same time. The judge simply responded that I was observing, without explaining who I was, and that was the end of the matter.

The court divides its cases into six categories, which will be discussed in the next chapter. Each panel specializes in cases from one of these classifications, although sometimes they do hear other kinds. After my three months of observing only the cases heard by the panels headed by the first judge I met, I told him that I wanted to see how other kinds of cases were handled and how other judges and panels worked. He had no objection to my doing so and suggested that I observe several specific panels. I took his suggestions, but later also observed other panels whose judges I had met on my own.

The court was nearly dormant in August, as most of the judges and other personnel were on vacation. When cases began to be heard again in September I started to attend different panels. My concern was that I should observe the processing of enough cases from each of the classifications that the court makes so that I would have a clear understanding of the kinds of issues involved and how the members of the court think that these issues should be decided. As an anthropologist I was interested in the subculture of the court—the terms and concepts that court personnel used in dealing with cases, apart from or in addition to those provided by the formal law (cf. Mather 1977). At the same time, I wanted to ensure that my observations were not biased by the idiosyncracies of one judge or panel and so took care to observe the way each kind of case was handled by at least two different panels.[8]

In all, my observations extended over fifteen months, until July 1983. During that time I observed more than 400 hours of activity in the CAL, involving more than 240 cases and fourteen judges. In addition, and for contrast, I also observed for about 100 hours in a communal (lower-level) civil court in Belgrade. These observations formed the heart of my study, as they allowed me to become thoroughly familiar with the way cases are processed in both kinds of courts. However, these observational data were not of themselves sufficient to evaluate the work of the court, and so I also spoke with court personnel outside of the courtrooms and gathered statistical data on the court's work throughout the time of the observational study. These materials were later updated on revisits to Belgrade in 1984, 1985, and 1986.

Interviews

When I was not in the courtrooms I frequently visited the court's administrative offices, where I spoke informally with judges, administrators, and secretaries of the benches. These talks were very useful for clarifying my understanding of some of the actions I had seen in the courtrooms or read about in case files and also provided detailed knowledge of the out-of-court work of the court personnel.

While my meetings with the court's personnel were sufficient to give me detailed knowledge of their activities and opinions of the way the court functions, I had less opportunity to speak with lawyers and particularly with the most important users of the courts, the parties. My opportunities for such interviews were limited by the need to remain in the courtrooms after the parties were dismissed, in order to hear the discussions there; I also did not want to be seen talking with one side in a case and not the other. I did have some opportunities to speak with lawyers who practice in the CAL when I met them on other occasions, but my lack of systematically obtained data from them must be acknowledged as a weakness of the study. However, since I was not able to hire research assistants and had to depend on only my own activities, this weakness could not be avoided. Thus the study is not as complete as one could hope, but it is a pioneering effort, and, again, *bolje išta nego ništa*.

Statistics

In order to put the cases I observed into context, I needed statistical data on the court's work load. Fortunately, Yugoslav social and political institutions are usually required to report to the appropriate assembly once a year, and the CAL in Belgrade produces an annual report for that purpose. This report contains information on the numbers and kinds of cases filed and disposed of during the year, the methods of disposition, average time for disposition, the number of cases scheduled for each bench and how many of these were heard, and a wealth of other information on the year's work. In addition, the annual report contains discussions of the work of the court over the year just past and its plan for the year to come. I was able to obtain these reports for every year from 1981 through 1985.

Apart from these reports, which provide aggregate data, I was also able to obtain the raw data on the cases filed in the first nine months of 1981, including detailed information on parties, issues, outcomes, and whether the case was appealed and the outcome of the appeal, for more than 6,000 cases. These data will be reported in the next chapter.

Finally, the CAL of Serbia publishes a journal (*Glasnik Suda Udruženog Rada Srbije* [GSURS]) twice a year, which provides data on the activities of all of the CALs in the republic as well as the republican CAL. These data were also very useful.

The CAL in Belgrade: A Profile

Establishment and Growth of the Court

The Basic CAL in Belgrade, like the other CALs in Serbia, was established by republican statute in 1975. In the beginning it was a small operation with only twelve full-time employees: a president and a secretary of the court, two full-time judges, one beginning or apprentice employee (*pripravnik*), one "administrative technical person," five stenographers, and a cleaner.[9] Of course, most judges were not full-time employees of the CAL, and thus do not show up in the employment figures. Other CALs apparently also started small. In Požarevac, for example, the Basic CAL had ten employees in its first year, including the president of the court and one other full-time judge (Vukičević 1985:8–9). By the end of 1976, the Basic CAL in Belgrade had received 3,863 cases and resolved 2,021 of them, while 1,791 were carried over into the next year.

Over the next ten years the caseload of the Belgrade CAL grew fairly steadily, and so did the number of full-time employees in the court. In 1977 3,918 new cases were filed and the court staff increased to thirty-seven. In that year four new job categories for professionals were created: deputy president of the court, technical secretary to the president of the court, economist, and "secretary of a panel" (*sekretar veća*). This last category, which will be fully described in the next section, has become one of the most important positions in the court. These secretaries, almost all of whom are recent law graduates, work like American law clerks. Each is assigned to several benches and briefs the cases, drafts opinions, and otherwise provides expert legal assistance to the members of the bench.

The court's caseload continued to increase by about 20 percent a year until 1981, when 9,390 cases were filed. In that year the court's staff also hit its peak size of 102 full-time employees, including the president of the court and six other judges, thirty-six secretaries of benches, eleven beginning workers, twelve "administrative technical persons," twenty-five stenographers and a head stenographer, and three cleaners.[10] There were also two experts on particular kinds of cases ("work relations" and "work organizations"), plus the economist. This cadre was maintained through 1983, while the caseload declined slightly in 1982 but returned to its 1981 level in 1983. In late 1983 the court moved into new quarters which it shared with several other courts, and the nonprofessional staff of the CAL merged with that of these other courts. Thus by 1985 the staff of the CAL in Belgrade numbered fifty-five, including thirty-eight secretaries of panels, and 10,112 cases were filed in it.

These figures make two general features of the court's development clear. First, the court attracted a constantly growing caseload in its first six years, from 3,863 cases filed in 1975–76 to 9,390 in 1981, after which the caseload has shown only slight increases. This nearly threefold increase in the caseload of the Belgrade court is representative of the growth of caseloads in all of the CALs in Serbia over the same period, which was from 11,221 to 27,696 cases (GSURS 16:31 [1984]). Furthermore, the staff was also increasingly specialized. Of the original twelve employees of the court in 1975, only five had been professionals. By 1983 there were sixty-three professionals and in 1985, fifty-five professionals.

We have already seen in chapter 1 that more than 90 percent of the cases in the CAL have been initiated by individuals. This caseload will be discussed in detail in chapter 7. The specialized professional court staff is central to the structure of the institution and should be examined immediately, as it would be difficult to follow the description of the research without some knowledge of the institutional players.

Personnel: The Professionalization of the CAL

The President and the Secretary of the Court

The Serbian statute on CALs (Article 12) specifies that each of these courts is to have a president. His or her specific duties are to determine the composition of the benches (Article 13), to "represent the court, to judge, to direct the work of the court administration and to ensure the regular and orderly performance of work in the court" (Article 44), and to establish the work assignments in the court (Article 47). The president, like all of the judges in the court, is elected by the Belgrade city assembly (Article 28) and has a renewable term of office of four years (Article 29).

Although the president of the court is always a lawyer and is specifically charged with judging cases, most of his or her time is spent in administration. The contrast is most clear with the other full-time judges in the court (see below). In 1981, for example, while the full-time judges each heard cases forty-one days out of the year (with the rest of their time spent primarily on research and writing opinions), the president of the court heard cases on only thirteen days (*Osnovni Sud Udruženog Rada u Beogradu, Izvestaj* [OSURBI] 1982).

The other major administrator in the court is the secretary of the court. This position is not specifically mentioned in the statute, but the position is plainly an essential one and most if not all CALs employ such a person. In the Belgrade court, the secretary was a lawyer and worked full-time as an administrator; he was not a judge.[11]

The Judges

There are two major categories of judges in the CALs in Serbia, those who hold that position as a full-time job and those who instead hear cases only twice a month. In the Belgrade CAL in 1981 there were seven full-time judges, plus the president of the court, and 242 other, part-time judges (OSURBI 1981). All of the full-time judges held law degrees; the qualifications of the other judges will be discussed below.

As might be expected, the full-time judges handled a disproportionate number of cases. While the other judges were each scheduled to hear cases on approximately twenty-one days during 1981, the seven full-timers were each scheduled for forty-one days (OSURBI 1981). I do not have the actual figures on the number of cases handled by each category of judge in that year, but such figures are available for 1985 and indicate that the full-time judges accounted for approximately 25 percent of the cases completed in that year (OSURBI 1985). In addition to the time that these judges spent hearing cases, they also drafted opinions in the cases they heard, reviewed other opinions, and substituted on panels on which there was a temporary vacancy. In addition, each of the panels was assigned to a section, corresponding to the court's substantive categories for cases, which will be described in chapter 7. Each full-time judge was responsible for supervising the work of the panels in his or her section.

Despite the disproportionate work load of the full-time judges, panels headed by part-timers still account for 75 percent of the cases disposed of in the Belgrade CAL. In regard to the ideal of the deprofessionalization of justice in the CAL, these judges should be of greatest interest. During 1981 there were 242 of these judges, and during 1982, 266. The background of this last group is known: forty (15 percent) held law degrees, eighteen (6.7 percent) had finished high school, forty-five (17 percent) had finished middle school, twenty-two (8 percent) were professionals (six doctors, ten engineers, six economists), eighty-six (32 percent) were highly qualified workers, forty-four (16.5 percent) qualified workers, and the remaining eleven (4 percent) had other unspecified qualifications (OSURBI 1982). Thus only about a fourth of these part-time judges were professionals, while the rest were workers.

Each of these part-time judges was scheduled to hear cases about twice a month. The part-timers had no obligation other than to come to the court on the days that they were scheduled and to hear the cases. They did not have to take part in writing opinions or in any other aspects of the work needed to keep the cases flowing to decision. Thus while the majority of these judges were not legal professionals, they were also not concerned with the operations of the court apart from the actual process of hearing the cases. Even then, the role of the nonprofessionals was limited by the structure of the panel system and the presence of the secretaries of the panels.

The Panel System

The effective work unit in the Belgrade CAL is not the individual judge, but rather the panel (*veće*, literally "council"). The entire body of judges, full- and part-time, is divided by the president of the court into permanent panels, each consisting of a president and two other judges. During the period of the research, each panel convened on the same day of the week in every second week. The full-time judges each participated in two such panels and thus heard cases on at least one day every week. By the rules of the court, only a full panel could hear evidence or make decisions in cases. However, "full panel" in this context meant only that three judges be present at any given stage of the process, not that all three regular members of a panel be present. It was for this reason that the full-time judges were employed as substitutes when a judge did not appear as scheduled. This kind of substitution will be discussed in greater detail in chapter 8.

Three-member benches are common in the civil law systems of Europe and usually take the form of a professional judge assisted by two lay judges. Such benches are used in the regular courts in Yugoslavia, where the judge (*sudija*) is assisted by two "jurors" (*porotnici*). However, the CAL panels are a departure from normal European and Yugoslav practice in that all of the members of a CAL panel are formally equal: all three are judges and there is in theory no terminological, conceptual, or practical difference between them. This equality of CAL judges is mandated by the Serbian statute on CALs (Article 6): "Judges have equal rights in trials."

Despite this theoretical equality of the members of a CAL panel, the president does have greater power than his or her fellows in the trial process because he or she is the person charged with conducting the trials. Thus it is the president of the panel who calls witnesses, discusses matters with lawyers, and dictates the record to a stenographer, who is present in every Yugoslav courtroom.[12] The degree to which the participation of the president in trials differs from that of the other two judges will be discussed in detail in chapter 8. For the moment it must only be recognized that there is a potentially important difference in role.

In light of the special role of the president in the conduct of trials, it is interesting to note that in regard to their training, these people comprise a very skewed sample of the total population of judges in the CAL. We have already seen that lawyers make up 15 percent of all of the judges in the CAL, with professionals another 8 percent in 1982. In 1981, however, the court's figures show that of eighty-four presidents of panels, seven (8 percent) were full-time judges in that court, eighteen (21 percent) were regular judges in other courts, and twenty-seven more (32 percent) had law degrees. Thus 61 percent of all of the presidents of benches had had legal training. In addition, eight more (10 percent) were professionals in other fields, while only twenty-one (25 percent) were "workers" (OSURBI 1981). Thus the most important position on the bench of each of the "workers' courts" seems likely to be filled by a professional rather than by a worker, and most often by a legal professional.

The Secretaries of the Panels

The largest single category of employees in the Belgrade CAL was that of secretary of a panel, and the job was clearly critical to the smooth functioning of the court. These secretaries were almost all young women,[13] mainly recent law graduates. Each was assigned to at least two panels, thus ensuring that she heard cases on at least one day per week. As stated in the 1982 report of the court, the job of the secretary of the panel was that she

> takes care of the execution of the orders of the Court, obtains documents and regulations necessary for decisions, reports the assertions of the participants and other information to the bench, assists in the conduct of discussions and prepares drafts of decisions. [She] takes care that the panel fulfills the planned number of judicial days with 10 hearings per judicial day and composes 17 draft decisions [per month] which resolve disputes by the decision of the court. (OSURBI 1982:5)

The writing tasks were given even greater specificity in the "Plan for Work in 1983" attached to the 1982 report:

> The secretary of a panel . . . prepares proposals for discussion according to the rules for two panels, prepares orders [*naloge*] and decisions which the court passes and takes care that each decision is delivered to participants within the time specified by statute. Also, each secretary of a panel is required to: prepare at least 440 and at most 660 hearings for about 44 or 66 judicial days in the

course of a work year of 222 days, to write at least 245 decisions with which a dispute is ended or proportionately 22.5 decisions per month, within five days from the conclusion of the hearings and other chores besides. (OSURBI 1982)

It is clear from these descriptions that these secretaries work much like American law clerks, briefing cases, drafting opinions, and gathering materials to assist their judges. Since each panel is assigned a secretary,[14] competent legal talent is available for even the non-legally trained judges. Further, as the secretaries sit with their panels in hearings, as will be described in chapter 7, this assistance is available at all times in the court process.

Other Professional Personnel

The secretaries of the panels are all generalists; each could, at least in theory, handle any of the kinds of cases coming to the court, and each could substitute for another. In fact, the secretaries do sometimes substitute for one another when one of them cannot be in court. In addition to these generalist positions, the court in 1982 employed several legal specialists. Two "advisors for court practice" (*savetnici za sudsku praksu*) worked to ensure that the court's decisions were consistent with each other and with the formal law, answering questions about interpretations and alerting the full-time judges and the secretaries of the benches to changes in the law. They also notified other courts, political bodies, and other interested entities about the work of the court. In addition, the court employed administrators (*referenti*) to coordinate the processing of particular common kinds of cases.

These job categories and descriptions indicate that despite the CALs' reputation as workers' courts and the large number of ordinary workers who serve as part-time judges, the court in Belgrade at least has a large cadre of legal professionals to assist the lay personnel, and there is no reason to think that this court is unusual in that regard. The importance of the permanent professional staff will become clear in chapter 7, when we look at participation in the court process.

Chapter 7

Cases Brought to the CAL; or, Who Uses the Court, and for What?

Numbers of Cases

The CALs in all of Yugoslavia quickly developed both a substantial caseload and a backlog. The basic (trial-level) CALs were established in 1975 and 1976; in 1977, the CALs in all of Yugoslavia received 36,798 new cases, in 1978, 50,594 (Perović 1980:107), and in 1980, more than 70,000 new cases (Korać 1981:8). This caseload exceeded the capacity of the courts to process cases: 28,652 cases were finished in 1977 and 40,230 in 1978 (Perović 1980:107). Similar caseloads were seen in the various republics: in Slovenia, 2,152 cases were filed in 1976 and 4,091 in 1978 (Jambrek 1983:189), while those same years saw the filing of 11,221 and 17,548 cases, respectively, in Serbia (GSURS 12:19).

In 1981, the year before the fieldwork began, the CALs in Serbia[1] received 27,696 new cases. In Belgrade in 1981, the Basic CAL received 9,392 cases. Of these, 32 percent concerned the allocation of housing, 27 percent involved workers' claims for salary or other monetary benefits, 14 percent the establishment of work relations, 9 percent claims for compensation for damages, 8 percent workers' appeals from disciplinary measures, and 7 percent were challenges to job assignments (OSURBI 1981:table 3). Since these categories are not self-explanatory, they will be examined in detail in the next section.

Kinds of Cases

The CAL in Belgrade recognizes nine substantive categories of cases, which are given below. Each category is followed by its percentage of the total 1982 docket, as given in the court's *Report* for 1982. Descriptions of a few cases in each category are also provided. Although I chose the particular cases because they are good examples of the matters that I observed, these examples do not constitute any kind of representative sample, and thus must be seen as illustrative rather than exemplary. The cases presented were among the ones that I observed in 1982–83. For this reason, some of them do not report outcomes, as the cases were not concluded during the time of the fieldwork.

Salary/Remuneration (*novčana potraživanja*; 24.6 percent)

These cases involve disputes over monies that workers claimed to be owed by their work organizations,[2] but did not include damage suits (see "Compensation for Damages," below) or challenges to fines (see "Disciplinary Measures," below). Most of the cases in this category involve claims for salaries, for the reimbursement of expenses, and vacation pay. In the 1980s, many involved claims by workers who had worked overseas for Yugoslav firms, for payment in hard currency for that work, generally either as expenses or as per diem amounts.

The court recognizes the importance of these cases to workers, saying that they "touch on the basics of existence" and that the worker is therefore "prepared to wage a dispute over the most insignificant infringements" in this regard (OSURBI 1981:4). At the same time, the cases are often complicated in terms of evidence, forcing repeated adjournments to allow the gathering of documents and witnesses:

Case 1: Plaintiff claims one day's salary, which was not paid because the organization said that he was not at work. He claims he was, and that he has witnesses; the case is adjourned until those witnesses can be called.

Case 2: This case is on its fourth appearance in the court. Plaintiff claims overtime that was not paid, saying that he worked weekends for twenty months, and brings documents showing that he worked those times. But the respondent organization presents a witness who says that the plaintiff worked on weekends to make up for time off the job during the week. Plaintiff claims that is not so, and the case is adjourned to permit plaintiff to gather further evidence.

Sometimes a claim is made for equal pay for equal work, though not necessarily successfully:

Case 3: Plaintiff works as a telephone operator in a large firm. Her co-worker on the same job, who was hired later, earns one and a half times as much. Plaintiff wants equal pay with her co-worker and back pay of the difference since the time the latter was hired. However, on questioning by the court, the plaintiff admits that the co-worker's qualifications (training and previous experience) are better than her own. The court decides in favor of the organization and rejects the plaintiff's claim.

Perhaps the single most frequent class of claim, however, was one that was essentially a form of subterfuge: a claim by a pensioner that his pension had not been paid, requesting that the court order his former employer to pay him. This kind of case was not, in actuality, a matter of dispute, because the claims were never defended. Instead, the respondent would simply send a written answer stating that the pension had not been paid because there was no money in the pension fund and that the firm therefore could not legally pay the plaintiff. In fact, this defense was true, because under the accounting practices of the time, funds were allocated at the beginning of the fiscal year and could not be spent on a different purpose without a court order. That last provision, of course, was the key to the matter: when the CAL ordered that the pension be paid, the organization could legally use monies from another fund to do so.

Establishment and Termination of Work Relations (*Zasnivanje i prestanak radnog odnosa*; 15.9 percent)

Virtually all of these cases involved a claim that the plaintiff had been denied a job for which she or he was better qualified than the person hired. These latter cases are common because recruitment for employees in most Yugoslav firms must follow detailed, explicit procedures, designed to ensure impartial selection. This is not an unreasonable concern in a society in which the importance of "connections" (literally; *veza*) is acknowledged by all and well represented in folk aphorisms.[3] Not infrequently, a disappointed applicant sues to have a hiring decision reversed; also not infrequently, such a plaintiff wins. In the 1980s, unemployment was already high in Belgrade and rising rapidly, so many disappointed job-seekers had plenty of incentive to take their claims to court.[4]

Examples of work relations cases:

Case 4: Plaintiff answered an advertisement for a position but was not hired. The firm had ranked candidates by assigning points for various factors, with the position to go to the higher-ranking people. The selected candidate (who appeared personally at the hearing) had been ranked 96th, with 53 points; the claimant had been ranked 90th, with 54 points. The CAL decides in favor of the plaintiff.

Case 5: A disappointed job-seeker asks that a hiring decision be reversed. In fact, there were two competitions for the job in question: at the time of the first, the plaintiff was better qualified than the selected candidate. However, that competition was voided as a result of litigation in the CAL. In the subsequent competition, different criteria were listed, by which the selected candidate was superior to the plaintiff. While the plaintiff tries to challenge the new criteria, the court sides with the organization: decision for defendant.

The importance of the poor job market for these cases is clear from the following example:

Case 6: The plaintiff had worked for the defendant organization for ten months as a temporary worker and had passed an examination for an apprentice position (pripravnik).[5] *After she had passed this examination, a competition was held for an apprentice position, but the plaintiff was not given the job. She sued in the CAL and lost in the trial court, but gained a remand from the CAL of Serbia. The case is now said to hinge on the text of the advertisement she responded to when she took her temporary position. However, after all of this litigation, the plaintiff fails to appear on the appointed day. The defendant's attorney says that she has not come because she found a new job, and the case is considered by the court to be withdrawn.*

Sometimes a case leads to the invalidation of a recruitment process, but not to the employment of the plaintiff:

Case 7: The respondent organization is an elementary school, which had advertised for an English teacher; the plaintiff claims to be better qualified than the selected candidate. A decision against the plaintiff by the trial-level CAL was reversed by the CAL of Serbia and remanded. On remand, the school claims that plaintiff is not qualified because he does not have the qualifications listed in the school's regulations as necessary for an English teacher. But the defendant says that those requirements were not stated in the advertisement for the position. Since the advertisement and the regulations are in disagreement, the entire competition is now cancelled by the CAL—but the plaintiff does not get the job.

Despite the lack of immediate results, the plaintiff in a case such as this last one may see the cancellation of the original competition as a promising victory, hoping for better results in a new one. And even if he or she does not ultimately win the job, spite is often cited by the judges as a motive for lawsuits.

Transfers to a Different Work Assignment (*Premeštaj radnika na druge poslove i radne zadatke*; 6.5 percent)

These are cases in which a worker challenges a transfer to a different job category within a work organization, usually following a reorganization of the employment structure of the latter. The court generally does not interfere in such cases unless there is evidence of malfeasance (*zloupotreba*) or some other discrimination against the worker who is complaining; it recognizes that economic factors or new technological advances may necessitate reorganizations (OSURBI 1981:7–8). Thus plaintiffs usually lose these cases, although they may obtain some limited satisfaction (see Case 9, below):

Case 8: Four plaintiffs, employees of a restaurant organization, were transferred to another of the organization's restaurants as a result of a reclassification of jobs. They want their old jobs back; the organization says that those jobs no longer exist and introduces the new job classification scheme. The court rules for the organization.

Case 9: As a result of a reorganization of job categories, plaintiff has been given a job that pays less than the one he had held until the reorganization. He wants his old job back, but the organization claims that it no longer exists. Under questioning from the court, plaintiff admits that he really is more interested in getting his old salary than he is in working the old job. The court orders that such an arrangement be made.

A second type of transfer case refers to the problem of the employment of the handicapped or others who can not work a normal load (*invalidi*). Most of these cases arise in heavy industry, building, and transportation contexts, when a worker who can no longer do heavy work asks for a transfer to a less demanding job—a transfer to which he is entitled. This situation leads to several types of problems: an ordinary worker displaced by such a transfer brings an action requesting reinstatement, or a handicapped worker denied a lighter load on the grounds that there are no such positions available requests the court to order a position for him. The CAL, plainly feeling itself caught in the middle, has called repeatedly for better coordination between work organizations and the commissions that determine whether and which jobs a handicapped worker can work (see OSURBI 1981:8; OSURBI 1982:12) and decides the cases as they arise on the court's assessment of the particular situation.

Case 10: The plaintiff worker has been officially determined to be an invalid, but he wants to continue working. He is entitled to continue working at a job that is not physically demanding, but he says that the job to which he has been assigned is too hard, in part because it requires travelling five to six kilometers per day on public transportation. The court decides that the plaintiff's job should be evaluated by the commission that regulates affairs for the handicapped and adjourns the case until the evaluation is made.

Disciplinary Measures (*disciplinske mere*; 8.4 percent)

These cases are challenges by workers to disciplinary measures taken against them by their employers. They present perhaps the most difficult issues for the CAL in terms of its relations with the outside world, because the court takes the position that the procedures mandated by law for the protection of the rights of workers must be followed in disciplinary cases; unfortunately, many organizations do not do so. This puts the court in what it recognizes as a dilemma: What to do "when a violation [by a worker] is apparent and serious, but the disciplinary commission [of the organization] was not properly constituted?" (OSURBI 1982). In such cases, the court feels compelled to uphold the formal law regarding workers' rights and to overturn the disciplinary sanctions imposed on the worker, but this action leads to the frequent accusation that the CAL "protects slackers [*neradnike*]" (see OSURBI 1982). This common perception has induced serious political difficulties for the CAL, as will be seen in chapter 9.

Disciplinary cases center on a few common types of sanctions. The best figures are available for 1981 (OSURBI 1981): in that year, 740 new disciplinary cases were filed. The most common forms of sanctions against which appeals were taken were termination of employment (431 cases), "removal" from a specific assignment (74 cases), "warning" (73 cases), fines (57 cases), and reassignment to a different task (66 cases).[6]

Examples of disciplinary cases:

Case 11: Plaintiff had been fired from his job, on the grounds that he had not written up a sale properly and had thus lost 310,000 ND (then about $17,000) of the firm's money. He counters that others were also responsible for the loss. The court wants evidence on the question of responsibility, but the organization is not able to provide it. In closed session, the judges agree that in the absence of evidence of the plaintiff's responsibility for the loss, the disciplinary sanction cannot be imposed. Thus, the court rules in favor of plaintiff.

In fact, the labor law does tend to favor workers to such an extent that it is difficult to justify a dismissal:

Case 12: Plaintiff was dismissed for missing work, but he claims that, at the time, he was entitled to medical leave (bolovanje) *on the grounds of alcoholism. On the day that the case is first heard in the CAL, the plaintiff does not even bother to come to court, although the highest administrator of the firm that has been employing him does come, along with a lawyer. In the absence of the plaintiff, nothing can be done on the case, but the manager and lawyer talk off the record with the judges, saying that the plaintiff is indeed a drunk and thus a miserable worker. They also say that they have tried without success to reform him, but he continues to miss work and to disrupt the workplace when he comes. They want to hire a real worker, but have not been able to fire the drunk. The judge expresses some sympathy, but says that all he can do is to continue the case and notify the plaintiff of the new time. After the parties leave, the judge looks at me and says: "We only get the idiots* [mangupi]; *if a worker is good, we never see him. He'll get a slip from a doctor saying that he was ill from alcoholism, and we'll have to reinstate him. We have no choice. And then people say that we coddle loafers."*

But not all plaintiffs win:

Case 13: Plaintiff had been fired from her job with a petroleum firm because she refused several field assignments. She counters that the assignments were dangerous: some because of the physical condition of the work area (i.e., leaking oil and petrol), others because she would be forced to work alone in an isolated location at night. The LAL does, in fact, mandate that workers be provided a healthful working environment. However, there is clearly animosity between the plaintiff and her supervisor, which manifests itself in a shouting match when he is called as a witness.

The case appears in the court five times in a three-month period, but the consideration of the matter at the end of the presentation of evidence is amazingly brief. In closed session, one of the associate judges posits that "a worker has to go where he's directed," and the others agree. With no further discussion, a decision is rendered against the plaintiff.

Compensation for Damages (*naknade štete*; 10.2 percent)

This category encompasses two different kinds of cases: those brought by firms against employees who have caused a loss and those brought by employees against the firms employing them, generally because of an injury to the employee while on the job. The personal injury cases are by far predominant numerically. They arise even though all Yugoslav workers are covered by social insurance which pays disability benefits, because such insurance payments are almost always less than full salary, but a worker who was injured through the fault of the employer can get full salary from the latter. Furthermore, claims by firms for compensation for damages often involve potentially criminal acts by the employee, and the CAL defers in such cases to the criminal courts. If guilt is found there, the CAL case becomes simpler, but many defendants in such cases are not able to make restitution and the case is ultimately dropped.

Examples of compensation for personal injury damages cases:

Case 14: The plaintiff lost a finger to a machine with which she worked; she has already received a payment from social insurance of about $800 in dinars at the then-current rate. However, she wants more from the firm, saying that it was at fault. The firm contends that the worker was herself at fault, but she introduces a witness who says that another worker later lost two fingers in the machine, which has now been removed. The case settles for an undisclosed amount.

As this first example indicates, many of the personal-injury cases involve negotiations over settlements, with the court essentially providing the conditions under which settlement will occur and the considerations to be taken into account—a role certainly familiar to American legal scholars (see, e.g., Mnookin and Kornhauser 1979). Often, the CAL's role is that of supplying a neutral expert (*veštak*) to determine competing claims:

Case 15: Plaintiff suffered an injury to his right kidney at work. The employer accepts responsibility in principle, but the plaintiff has claimed compensation under a variety of headings: lost wages, pain, fear, and psychological trauma. The firm wishes to have its own specialists determine these claims, but the CAL orders that the matter be referred to specialists chosen by the court. Their report will settle the matter.

And sometimes the CAL plays the time-honored judicial role of scapegoat, accepting responsibility for a decision that the parties agree with privately but cannot, for various reasons, admit to:

Case 16: The plaintiff worker had been injured two years before this case was heard and had brought an action in the CAL for compensation, which was granted. However, the original award was overturned on appeal on procedural grounds: at the time of the injury, the employer was one undivided Work Organization (Radna organizacija), *but by the time the award was made, it had been divided into four BOALs, and the appeals court said that the award had been made against the wrong BOAL. All parties admit that the organization was at fault, but the question is which BOAL should pay the damages. After a hearing, the CAL determines which BOAL is responsible and suggests that the case settle. Two weeks later, when the case reappears, the defending attorney says that there has not been a settlement and asks the court to render its own decision so that he does not have to try to convince the workers' council to settle the case; in effect, he wants the court to take the blame for an unpopular decision. The court agrees and renders a decision for the plaintiff.*

While most of the damages cases are brought by individuals against employers, some are also brought by firms against individuals who have caused losses:

Case 17: A firm sues its employee for about eight thousand dollars' worth of dinars at the then-current rate, claiming that he took samples to a trade fair and lost them. The defendant worker does not appear in the CAL; but as the matter is now the subject of a criminal case, the CAL action is adjourned indefinitely to await the results in the criminal court.

Other cases involved claims that an employee had been overpaid. Usually, employees do not bother to defend against such claims, but attorneys for the firms said that getting execution of a judgment against a worker was not easy. Thus many of the relatively few cases against workers seem to have been brought for symbolic reasons, particularly the desire to appear to be preserving social resources. However, some cases have more at stake:

Case 18: The plaintiff in this case was a major manufacturing firm which was suing its former representative in a Western European country. The employee had been given funds in hard currency to pay for schooling for his children, but they were not in school. The employer thus wants its money back. The defending employee counters that he used the funds to match rising living costs in the country where he was stationed which were not covered by his salary and allowances and asserts that the LAL assures him an adequate salary. The CAL hears witnesses on the cost of living in that country at the time. But ultimately, the case is referred to the economic courts and adjourned in the CAL.

As these examples show, it is hard for an employer to get much in tangible awards from a CAL. That these cases are brought at all seems due primarily to the local-level political necessity of seeming to pursue those who have harmed the firm and to the symbolic politics of wanting to appear to be upholding socialist legality and maintaining social property.

Apartment Assignments (*stambeni sporovi*; 28.4 percent)

The single largest category of cases, presumably because an apartment is the single most important scarce resource in Belgrade, as it is in most Yugoslav cities. Like many other developing countries, Yugoslavia has experienced a heavy influx of people moving from the countryside into the cities (see Thomas 1982; Simic 1976). And like other socialist countries (e.g., Hungary; see Szelenyi 1976), Yugoslavia has not been able to meet this demand by providing enough affordable housing. Thus there is a very tight market for rental space in Belgrade and other large cities.

As is true in regard to so many other matters, the housing market in Belgrade is also extremely complicated. Yugoslavs may own their own housing units, and thus there are many private houses and flats. Apartments in private ownership are often available, but usually at a very high rent. On the other hand, another element of the housing market is the socially owned sector. It is the obligation of socially owned enterprises to devote some of their income to providing housing for their workers. The rents for such housing are controlled and are far below the market rate for private housing.[7] However, very few organizations have a stock of housing available that is sufficient to meet the demands of its workers. Therefore, each firm develops a set of rules for the allocation of housing, and when a unit is built, bought, or becomes available in some other way, a competition will be held for it within the firm. As is true in the case of employment, the competitions for flats rank employees by a set of criteria, such as seniority in the firm, length of time on the waiting list for housing, quality of current housing, and number of people living in current housing. What results is a list that is based on the evaluation of a large number of considerations that are officially relevant, and that is thus susceptible to challenge on many grounds. Housing competitions, then, provide fertile grounds for litigation.

Housing is within the jurisdiction of the CAL because it is allocated within the work organization as part of its self-management decision-making. Interestingly, this jurisdictional question apparently was not clear when the CALs came into existence, because in their first years, they had very few housing cases. Housing cases rose from 128 in 1976 (3 percent of the docket) to 2,419 in 1982 (28 percent). By the early 1980s, housing cases before the CAL were part of everyday business for lawyers in Belgrade; in fact, for many of them, the bulk of their income came from such cases.

Housing cases are complicated for other reasons as well. When a plaintiff challenges the outcome of a housing competition, the people who won that competition are invited to participate in the proceedings as "interested parties." They frequently choose to do so and often hire their own attorneys to represent them. Thus a housing case may involve one or more plaintiffs, a respondent work organization, one or more "interested parties"—and all of these participants are likely to be represented by attorneys. Furthermore, the legal issues involved in housing cases are most complicated, since the laws themselves are complex, as are the regulations of each firm, and the whole case may depend on how these complex formal instruments were interpreted in a given case.

With these considerations in mind, it is not surprising that housing cases had the longest average duration in the Belgrade CAL.[8] It is also not surprising that the court administration assigned its most experienced personnel to them. The senior judge in charge of such cases during the period of the fieldwork was one of the seven full-time judges on the court and had earlier been a judge in the regular courts. A "lawyer's lawyer," he was highly competent in the technical aspects of housing law. He handled the cases in that way, as legal matters, not as those of self-management decision-making.

Examples of housing cases:

Case 19: This case involves three plaintiffs, all challenging the outcome of a housing competition within their work organization. Since they are all represented by the same lawyer and the cases all involved the same competition, the cases are heard together. Attending the hearings are these plaintiffs, their lawyer, a lawyer for the organization, and three "interested parties." The essence of the matter is that each plaintiff asserts that he or she should have been given more points and thus ranked higher, for various reasons, and that the "interested parties" should have been given fewer points and thus ranked lower. One plaintiff says that she was not given points on the basis of an unsatisfactory current housing situation, even though her housing is not up to officially acceptable standards; while it is claimed that one of the "interested parties" was given points for overcrowded current housing, but one of the people he listed as living with him has emigrated. The lawyer for the organization refutes these factual arguments. The court finds that the original decision was justified by documents filed with the court by the organization and upholds the competition. The case is decided in favor of respondents (and thus in favor of the "interested parties").

As the preceding case shows, the question of who is living with whom and when can be crucial to a case. This question is likely to arise in regard to the rights of children to inherit an apartment. The Law on Housing Relations (*Zakon o stambenim odnosima*) of Serbia recognizes the right of children living with a parent who has the right to live in a flat to inherit that right, but a nonresident child should not inherit. Thus the following case:

Case 20: Plaintiff's father had the right to live in a flat belonging to the organization for which he worked. He has now died, and plaintiff is requesting that the right to live there be assigned to her. The respondent organization asks that the flat be returned to it for reassignment, on the grounds that plaintiff did not actually live there. The question becomes one of fact: if the plaintiff did live with her father until he died, she may inherit; if not, she cannot. The case is adjourned while the court calls witnesses suggested by the plaintiff. The respondent does not suggest any witnesses.

In theory, the question of residence should be easily resolved, since Yugoslav citizens are required to list their current address on their personal identity cards and to report changes of address to the police, who issue the cards. In practice, someone may continue to list a parent's address even after moving out (e.g., after marriage, assuming that the other spouse has better housing), precisely to avoid losing the right to the parent's flat. Belgrade folklore abounds with stories about such people. The court may call witnesses, but folklore also recognizes a tendency toward unreliability among people involved in disputes involving this issue. Thus the determination of a residency question by a CAL may itself be challenged, one of the reasons that housing cases tend to be more prolonged than other types of cases in the CAL.

Despite the complicated legal structures aimed at determining who is entitled to a social flat, housing situations are always subjective. Sometimes a plaintiff who already has a social flat claims that he or she deserves a better one:

Case 21: Plaintiff, who already has a three-room flat from his organization, wants to enter a competition for a newer, more desirable flat that is now available. The organization contends that those who have nothing should receive preference and that plaintiff has to stay in his assigned flat even if something better comes up. The court agrees and renders a decision for the organization.

And sometimes a plaintiff makes what are perceived as unreasonable demands:

Case 22: Plaintiff has won a competition for a flat, but has rejected the one offered to him. He claims that by the appropriate regulations, he is entitled to a flat with two rooms and a total floor area of fifty to sixty square meters. The flat offered has two rooms, but only forty-eight square meters. A rather incredulous judge explains to the plaintiff that he gets either *two rooms* or *fifty to sixty square meters, but not necessarily both. The court decides against the plaintiff, who now loses everything, because the organization's rules specify that a worker who refuses a suitable flat moves to the bottom of the ranking.*

Yet this plaintiff is not necessarily acting unreasonably, since if he takes the small flat he will probably be "locked in" to it, as the previous case shows. Thus, rejecting a small flat now may preserve one's access to a larger one later.

The kinds of cases presented thus far account for more than 95 percent of the docket of the CAL in Belgrade. Almost all of them are initiated by individual workers, and the respondent is primarily the work organization employing the plaintiff. The three remaining categories of cases differ from this alignment of parties because they represent matters between organizations, with no individual parties involved. As will be seen in chapter 9, there is a certain irony in the low numbers of such cases, because the CALs were originally envisioned as handling primarily disputes between organizations rather than between individuals and organizations. In terms of the research reported here, the paucity of the interorganizational cases made it hard to observe them. Thus the remaining categories will be described, but no examples will be given.

Benefit Groups (SIZ, or "self-management communities of interest," *samoupravne interesne zajednice*; 1.2 percent)

The (in)famous SIZ is one of the most abstruse creations of the self-management structure institutionalized in the 1974 constitution and the LAL. A SIZ is a nongovernmental agency through which social services are funded and administered and which serves employment, price-setting, and other economic functions. In essence, the SIZ is meant to link the providers of social services (e.g., health, education, culture) with the people who use those services by having representatives of both groups in the SIZ, which allocates resources for these purposes. In practice, the SIZ is something of a mystery to most Yugoslavs, including those involved in the CAL.

Cases involving the SIZ come into the CAL primarily in connection with health insurance, since the provisions of the (Republic of Serbia) Law on Health Insurance[9] establish that court's jurisdiction in questions involving the determination of rights and obligations concerning medical insurance, both of individual workers and of organizations, vis-à-vis the SIZ. Yet few cases come in under this heading. The most important cases that did come to the CAL in this regard in 1982–83 concerned the establishment of the right to SIZ-supported health care outside of Yugoslavia. This kind of case could arise when a worker traveling in a foreign country fell ill and asked for reimbursement, or, less often, when an ill worker requested that the SIZ send him or her out of the country for medical procedures not then available in Yugoslavia (e.g., kidney transplants). Both types of cases would be likely to involve fairly large sums, in hard currency, which is probably why they were more likely to be brought to the court (OSURBI 1981:3).

Self-Management Organization (*samoupravno organizovanje*; 2.7 percent)

These cases involve the establishment of BOALs, or the relations of self-management organizations such as BOALs to each other. In many ways, this type of case seems to have been the prototypical one in the thoughts of those who created the CAL system in the first place. Yet there were few of these cases, perhaps reflecting the tendency of businesses to try to avoid litigation in the course of their interactions with each other, a pattern identified by Macaulay in his classic article (1963) and also reported from Poland (Kurcewski and Frieske 1978). The CAL in Belgrade itself views the dearth of these cases as reflective of a desire on the part of the workers in associated labor either to avoid their obligations or simply to not want to have their affairs brought to the attention of the courts (OSURBI 1982). Further, the court itself found the small number of these cases that did come to it to be difficult and time-consuming. None of the people I spoke with at the court viewed the lack of these cases as a matter for concern.

Arbitration (*arbitraža*; 0.15 percent)

The CAL could hear appeals from arbitration decisions, but virtually none are brought to it. The court itself views the extremely small number of disputes in this category as evidence that "arbitration is not yet accepted by the workers as a form of self-management court" (OSURBI 1982) and goes on to say that even the few cases that are brought to it are not really arbitration disputes, in that they involve an arbitration decision on a matter taken "for purely formal reasons" in order to get the case into the CAL.

Party Characteristics and Win Rates

In all of the CALs for which data have been reported, the vast majority of the cases are brought by individual workers against the organizations employing them: more than 90 percent of the cases (see Jambrek 1983 [Slovenia], Korać 1981 [Bosnia-Herzegovina]). Overall rates of disposition can be seen from the figures for 1981: of the 7,388 cases completed in that year, the plaintiff's proposal was accepted fully in 30 percent of the cases, partially in 10 percent of the cases, and rejected in 37 percent of the cases. Nine percent were withdrawn and 13 percent were "resolved in another manner" (e.g., by agreement or through finding of lack of jurisdiction; OSURBI 1981). Unfortunately, the court does not provide a breakdown of results for each category of cases, so it is not possible to determine whether individual workers win or lose disproportionately to organizations. Nevertheless, since organizations are plaintiffs in so few cases (effectively, primarily in compensation for damages), it is likely that individual workers obtain satisfaction in a substantial number of cases.

The court itself notes that individual workers tend to take great interest in their cases:

> In order to satisfy their personal interests, plaintiffs [*predlagaći*] exhibit great persistence in proving their rights, insisting that the court work quickly, and many times and through many channels asking for information about the procedure in every phase, complain about slowness which often isn't slowness in [the court's] work, express doubts without cause and reason concerning the objectivity of individuals working in the court, write detailed petitions to all [official] organs, with which they burden unnecessarily not only the courts, but also other organs, and in this way themselves contribute to the elongation of procedures before the court. (OSURBI 1981:2)

Thus the court certainly views individuals as an important constituency. And their concerns do get prompt attention: in 1981, virtually all of the cases about the establishment of work relations, disciplinary measures, and the allocation of housing were finished within the year, while other kinds of cases took longer. Of course, the set of cases that received faster processing are brought virtually by definition by individual workers.

Workers' Courts, or Courts for Workers?

The figures and examples above indicate quite clearly that the CALs are courts for workers, in the sense that they are the courts to which individual labor disputes are brought. In this regard, they are quite dissimilar to the workers' courts in the socialist countries in Eastern Europe and in some ways more similar to the labor courts in Western Europe. They differ from the latter as well, however, in important ways, as we shall see.

Compared with the workers' courts in Eastern Europe, the CALs exhibit a very different picture of who uses the courts and why. As detailed in chapter 1, the so-called workers' courts in Eastern Europe are rarely invoked by individual workers, being instead primarily mechanisms by which the state imposes labor discipline. In terms of rate of use by individual workers, the CALs seem to resemble the labor courts of Western Europe. Yet the picture is more complicated than that. The labor courts of Western Europe seem to be used largely to structure the termination of work relations, the consequences of the dismissal of a worker. Thus they are not used to structure ongoing social relations. In contrast, the CALs are often used for the latter purpose, for determination of disputed issues involved in a continuing work relationship. This fact makes them somewhat unusual in the literature on law and society, since it is counter to the general principle that litigation will tend to be avoided by people who are engaged in continuing relationships; or, better, who expect their relationship to continue (see Wisconsin Law Review 1985).

This somewhat unexpected finding merits further exploration. Why should the CALs be unusual in this regard? One answer may lie in the specifics of the legal structure of Yugoslav labor relations, in that it is very difficult for an organization to terminate a worker's employment. Thus the aggrieved worker in Yugoslavia has a greater capacity to bring a suit than does his or her counterpart in the West, since the worker's job is much less likely to be at risk for bringing the action.

Yet to note this difference is to bring into question some of the presuppositions of the relational hypothesis. Specifically, the original idea behind this hypothesis was Gluckman's suggestion that, in societies in which people had multiple ties, there would be a tendency to avoid forms of legal processing that produced win-lose decisions and to favor instead compromise (Gluckman 1955:20–21; Nader 1969). As Starr and Yngvesson (1975) noted long ago, this model is not sufficiently complex; they stress the importance of considering the relative value to the disputants of maintaining the relationship, as opposed to winning the specific decision. Yet the basic point is still widely held, that in situations where people expect to continue in long-term relationships, they will generally avoid formal legal processes in favor of informal negotiations, and that it is the exceptions to this practice that need to be explained (see Macaulay 1963; Wisconsin Law Review symposium 1985).

Perhaps the most sophisticated analysis of the interaction of disputants' relations and their goals in regard to the forms of dispute processing they utilize is that of Comaroff and Roberts (1981:113–118). They distinguish two continua, of litigants' relationships (from determinate [Gluckman's simplex] to generalized [multiplex]) and of their goals (from concentrating on the preservation of the relationship to concentrating on the particular value at issue), and suggest that procedural flexibility will be sought the more the dispute is concerned with the relational ends of either continuum. Their model is more subtle than those of their predecessors, however, in that it also accounts for such features of individual disputes as the explicit invocation of norms, the importance of disputant's prior history, and the importance of the circumstances behind the immediately salient issue. In general, their model predicts "a movement from specificity to generality and, concomitantly, toward greater ambiguity" as the focus of a dispute shifts from a concern with specific actions or events to the management of a social relationship (Comaroff and Roberts 1981:131).

From this perspective, too, litigation in the CAL seems anomalous. The employment relationship is a fairly generalized one, but the issues in CAL cases are drawn fairly narrowly, in terms of the formal law. It is thus a kind of case that the Comaroff and Roberts model would envision as producing a certain amount of maneuvering for strategic advantage in the generalized relationship in the context of a specific claim. Yet there is not much negotiation in the majority of CAL cases, or striving for strategic advantage, as the Comaroff and Roberts model would predict. Instead, matters are handled in strictly legal terms, and decisions are brought by the court in the large majority of cases, rather than by the actions of the parties themselves through "bargaining in the shadow of the law" (cf. Mnookin and Kornhauser 1979).

This last point brings another anomalous feature of the CALs to the fore: the high rates of decisions by the court rather than by the parties themselves. In modern Western courts, it is clear that most cases that are filed do not result in a decision made by the court after some kind of contest or argument. Instead, the dominant forms of case outcomes are those effected by the parties themselves, taking the forms of settlements or withdrawals of the case (see Daniels 1985). In the CAL, however, the court makes the effective decision in 77 percent of the cases, with the parties themselves settling or dropping the matter in only, at most, 22 percent of the cases.

These anomalies can also be explained by consideration of the highly stable employment tie in Yugoslavia and the importance of the issues in most cases to the individual workers who bring them. Despite the presence of some appeals of terminations in the caseload (see above), it is extraordinarily difficult for an employer to terminate an employee's work relationship.[10] Since the issues are important, the incentive to fight over them is clearly present, and since it is unlikely that a worker will be terminated, there is little incentive to settle. This explanation is simple, even obvious in this context, but it raises a number of potentially interesting issues.

First, it is interesting that the idea that a generalized tie, such as employment, will be in itself largely beyond the realm of negotiation and maneuver does not seem to have entered into much of the anthropological thinking on disputes. The basic idea behind all of the models is that people engaged in a generalized tie will avoid litigation unless the stakes to them are important enough to outweigh the threat to the tie itself. This seems like common sense, yet it does not consider the possibility that there may be ties that are extremely resistant to complete disruption. In this context, the employment relationship in Yugoslavia seems inherently more stable than kinship relations in most societies, in that it cannot be broken. Kin ties, on the other hand, are often negotiable (see, e.g., Comaroff and Roberts 1981:175–215). Even in cultural settings in which ties of blood are viewed as unbreakable, ties of affection are less strong—and without affection, the blood tie is of dubious relevance.

Second, it is also interesting that the models of disputing behavior seem to presume that individual disputants themselves will tend to disfavor conflict with the people with whom they must interact, barring a fairly high stake in the outcome. But this assumption ignores the general presupposition of political anthropology—that conflict is inherent in social relations—and the long history of studies on pervasive conflict in settings in which, as Sally Falk Moore puts it, people are sentenced to a life term together (Moore 1988).[11] Perhaps the CAL experience shows us that the risk, or rather lack of it, to the plaintiff is as critical to the decision to pursue a dispute as are the stakes.

Chapter 8
Participation in the CAL Process; or, Who Talks, About What?

The ideals of the CAL system seem clear: that workers, rather than legal professionals, should decide workers' disputes. It is for this reason that the CALs operate under less strict procedural rules and have so many judges who are not professionals. The expectation seems to have been one of participation by workers in their own cases, as reflected in the terminology: "initiator" of a "discussion" rather than "plaintiff" in a legal case. One might envision the discussion of a case in the CAL as being ideally a matter of free and frank discussion among workers, with the initiator, the "other participant" and the worker-judges all taking part, with the latter drawing on their work experience to formulate a resolution of each case. This image would be supported by the words of the president of the CAL in Zagreb in an article in the popular magazine *Start*, shortly after that court began work:

> They [nonprofessional judges] are people who come from associated labor and who emphasize in their own surroundings the organization and establishment of self-management relations. The predominant number of these "non-permanent" judges come from direct production, where as performers of self-management obligations and organizers of production they have years of immediate experience with the interpersonal relations of workers and the real problems which accompany the birth of these new productive relations. Therefore their presence on our judicial panels ensures that we hold direct and intimate connection with the reality of self-management: in that way we guard against the greatest danger, that we become estranged from our task and turn into a professional institution which would examine only the legal formalities of decisions arrived at in associated labor. (Miles-Jašarević 1978:22)

Instead, the idea behind these courts was that they should deal informally with the substance of relations.

In an ideal workers' court, we might expect to find a constellation of features aimed at facilitating the discussion, by workers themselves, of the substance of work relations that have been disrupted. As the preceding quote indicates, the cases should be handled by workers themselves, rather than by legal professionals, and should not center on technical legal questions. Instead, we might expect to find more broad discussions of substantive issues. Both the lack of emphasis on legal questions and the preference for finding consensual solutions, drawing on work experience and knowledge, would seem to indicate that the services of lawyers should not be essential to the functioning of the CALs.

One of the purposes of observing cases in the CAL in Belgrade was to determine the extent to which these features prevailed. For each case observed, I noted whether the parties were represented and who spoke to what issues, both in open court (with the parties present) and in closed session, out of the presence of the parties and of the general public (my own presence was an exception to the general practice in this regard). This chapter reports those observations. First, however, it is necessary to set the stage by describing the physical setting of the discussions, the courtrooms and other areas of the CAL in Belgrade, and the physical circumstance of the research.

The Physical Setting: The CAL in Belgrade

The judicial power is one of both practical and symbolic import, since it represents the practical manifestation of ideology. Courtrooms themselves often reflect elements of the ideological structures that they are meant to make manifest, through the display of symbols (such as flags, or of a representation of justice) or through the arrangement of furniture and by the clothes worn by participants in the court ritual (see Hazard 1962). A judge sitting above the parties, for example, may be seen as symbolizing the law's majesty, as may an elaborate costume (see Atkinson and Drew 1979:222–227; Hazard 1962). Similarly, an ornate courtroom may also be seen as a manifestation of both the majesty of the law and the power of the state that it embodies.

In modern Yugoslavia, many of the regular courts are now housed in new buildings, designed and built expressly to be courts. In Belgrade, the regular courts are in such new structures, and the courtrooms have been designed to exhibit the rituals of socialist justice to an audience. In the regular courts, the regular judge and the lay judges sit behind an elevated bench. The parties sit at a table on the regular floor, and there are seats for the public, facing the bench. Cases are called over an intercom system, and the judges enter and leave the courtroom through a special door, behind the bench. The buildings are often well appointed; the Fifth Communal Court in Belgrade, for example, is a new building with wall-to-wall carpeting in the courtrooms.

The CAL, however, had a physical setting in 1982–83 that was quite different from that of the regular courts.[1] At that time, the Belgrade CAL was housed in two older buildings which were separated by about a half-mile. One building housed the administrative offices of the court, plus two courtrooms, the court's library, and work areas for the secretaries of the panels. The other building held seven courtrooms, arranged along a corridor. The corridor was lined with benches, which were used by parties and lawyers while they waited for their cases to be called. The day's docket was posted on the door of each courtroom, listing cases by file number and the names of the parties, along with the names of the president and secretary of the panel and the stenographer. The latter opened the door of the courtroom and called out the names of the parties as the time scheduled for each case arrived.

In the regular courts, the courtrooms are usually large enough to accommodate an audience, even if only a small one of ten or fifteen people. In the CAL, however, the courtrooms were tiny, having barely enough room for one large table (or two small ones pushed together) and seven chairs: three on the side of the table farthest from the door, for the members of the panel; a chair for the secretary of the panel next to them; one for the stenographer at one end of the table; and two chairs on the side opposite the judges. When I was present, an additional chair was brought into the room and squeezed in somewhere, usually next to the stenographer. From this position, I could usually see and hear the proceedings without difficulty.

This seating arrangement might be viewed as more egalitarian than that found in the regular courts, since it puts everyone on the same physical plane and in close proximity, dealing over a table. Thus the setting of the CAL could be seen as conducive to the kinds of informal, self-management discussions that were apparently envisioned by the designers of the CALs. The staff of the court did not perceive it in that way, however, and complained about the cramped, dark rooms in both the buildings occupied in 1982–83 and the newer building into which they moved in 1984 (OSURBI 1982:7). Indeed, the most likely explanation for the CAL's presence in these buildings was one of scarcity of resources rather than suitability for self-management resolution of labor disputes.

In any event, whatever the potential for egalitarian proceedings in the CAL courtrooms, the actual use of the space seems determined more by sociological considerations than by ideological ones. The critical positions in these cramped surroundings were those around the table. As explained more fully below, most parties in the CAL are represented by lawyers, and it was *always* the lawyers who took the chairs at the table, facing the judges. When the parties were themselves present, they were relegated to standing against the wall, behind the lawyers, effectively out of the action. The invariable nature of this seating arrangement was brought home to me most graphically in a case in which a very pregnant woman was a plaintiff. In ordinary circumstances, one of the lawyers, judges, or other court personnel (male or female) would have almost certainly offered a seat to this woman. Instead, her lawyer took the seat and she stood against the wall, like any other plaintiff. Yet this arrangement made perfect sense, since her lawyer was the one involved in the negotiations and she was really only a spectator, albeit an interested one.

This image, of the pregnant plaintiff standing against the wall while her lawyer argued her case, could stand as an exemplum for the social and physical arrangement of people in the proceedings in the Belgrade CAL; and it does not support the initial view of the CALs as being fora for the discussion of disputes by the workers involved in them. Yet the question of participation requires further analysis, both in terms of who takes part in discussions and what kinds of issues figure in those discussions. The remainder of this chapter deals with these questions by looking more closely at who says what in the CAL.

The Hearing Process

In Yugoslavia, as in other continental European countries, there is generally no trial as a single summary event toward which all efforts are oriented. Instead, a trial consists of a series of hearings, usually scheduled for one half-hour at intervals of two or several weeks, during which particular tasks are undertaken. Thus the opening hearing may consist of the presentation and discussion of the initial complaint and answer and ascertainment of what kinds of evidence will be required for further proceedings. Subsequent hearings will be devoted to the presentation of documentary or testimonial evidence and of arguments by the parties involved in the case. After all the evidence that can be obtained has been entered, and arguments made, the court will issue a formal declaration that the hearing (*rasprava*) is concluded; it then excuses the parties, makes its decision, and informs the parties by mail of the outcome. This procedure is used in both the regular civil courts and the CAL in Belgrade.

This system of sequential hearings rather than a single summary event seems odd to Americans, but has a number of advantages. It is both more certain and more flexible than a summary trial: more certain because there is greater opportunity to obtain needed evidence, since proceedings can be adjourned until that evidence is found, and more flexible, in that usually each hearing is only a half-hour long, and the schedules of the participants can usually be made to accommodate such a short period of time. Further, the system of sequential hearings seems to be highly effective in terms of the use of the court's time, since cases can be scheduled with precision.

Participants in the CAL Process

Parties and Their Lawyers

We have already seen that parties themselves play little active role in the discussion of cases in the CALs. Instead, they depend on their lawyers. In the cases I observed, more than 90 percent of the plaintiffs were represented by attorneys and virtually 100 percent of the respondents were also represented. "Interested parties" had lower levels of representation, but such people were not involved in most cases in any event.

Discussion of the role of lawyers in the CAL process requires some brief consideration of the general profile of the legal profession and its activities in Yugoslavia, particularly in Belgrade. The basic category of "lawyer" itself requires some explication in the Yugoslav context, particularly for American readers. The basic law degree in Yugoslavia is a first degree, the equivalent of a bachelor of arts in the United States, and is, in fact, one of the most popular fields of specialization in Belgrade University. In the late 1970s, between 7 and 8 percent of the undergraduate degrees granted in Yugoslavia were in law (Zvekić 1983:409), and each person granted such a degree is a "lawyer" (*pravnik*, pl. *pravnici*). However, not all of these lawyers practice law, in the sense of serving as an attorney (*advokat*, pl. *advokati*). For our purposes, it is only the latter, the members of the bar, who are of interest, as they are the ones who represent clients in the courts, including the CALs.

Not many law graduates become attorneys. While the law faculties in the republic of Serbia granted 8,973 law degrees in 1980 (Zvekić 1983:410), there were only 990 attorneys (*advokati*) in the republic that year (Statistički Godišnjak Jugoslavije 1981:579), most of whom must have received their law degrees in earlier years. Interestingly, the bar is the only one of the traditional professions that was never socialized in postwar Yugoslavia, and an *advokat* is free to engage clients at his or her own discretion—within the code of ethics and at fees regulated by statute. Most attorneys are solo practitioners or members of small firms and over half of the total number of attorneys in the republic of Serbia live in Belgrade.

It is the *advokati* who represent the individual workers who are plaintiffs in the vast majority of the cases in the CALs. On the other side, the work organizations that are the other participants in CAL proceedings are usually represented by members of the larger class of law graduates, the *pravnici*. While few figures on the employment of such people are available, many law graduates are employed within work organizations or in government, often on legal matters (see Jambrek and Taylor 1987). In effect, many of the *pravnici* function as in-house counsel, including representing their organizations in cases before the CAL. As we shall see, these lawyers also play major roles in the staffing of the CALs.

The configuration of parties and lawyers in CAL discussions, then, was as follows: the parties themselves would stand behind their representatives, who were seated at a table facing the bench of judges. The great majority of plaintiffs were represented by attorneys (*advokati*), while nearly all respondents were represented by lawyers (*pravnici*) who were not members of the bar. Thus the court staff was consistently confronted with people who were trained in law, rather than with workers themselves. In addition, the representatives of the parties often tried to control the discussion, discouraging participation on the part of plaintiffs. I observed attorneys who interrupted clients, sometimes very bluntly ("When I'm talking, you shut up"), and others who responded themselves to questions posed by the court that were either directed at plaintiffs or that could have been addressed by the latter. On the other hand, I never saw a representative ask a party to participate in discussion. Thus the parties seem pre-empted by the legal professionals who represent them.

Judges

The dominance of legally trained people on the parties' side of the table is largely matched, however, on the judges' side. As mentioned in chapter 6, the effective unit in the CAL is the panel (*veće*, "council"), headed by a president who is chosen by the administration of the court itself. While legal education was not a formal prerequisite for selection as a president, 61 percent of the presidents of benches in the CAL in Belgrade in 1981 were legally trained, even though only 15 percent of all of the judges in that year had law degrees.[2] Further, there were no panels in which there was a legally trained member who was *not* the president.

Judges were assigned to panels by the court's administration. Once constituted, a panel would remain as a stable body for at least one year. Most panels were specialized, hearing a particular kind of case on the same day of the week, at two-week intervals. Normally, the same secretary of the panel and stenographer worked with a panel at its biweekly meetings, and the unit of panel, secretary, and stenographer constituted a small, stable work group.

The legal training of the presidents is important because they were truly the controlling factors in discussions in the CAL, particularly in the presence of parties and their lawyers. While the formal law provides that judges are equals in deciding cases,[3] the presidents were clearly superior, "first among equals." Their dominance showed itself in several ways. First, as in other European courts, the record of the case is not taken verbatim by a court reporter, but rather is dictated to a stenographer *by the president of the panel*. Thus it is his or her phrasing that constitutes the official record of the case. Moreover, as in other European courts, questioning of witnesses is generally conducted by the court rather than by the parties or their lawyers, and the questions were almost invariably put by the president of the panel.

The presidents of the panels also dominated discussions in the courts, in both open sessions (in the presence of the parties) and closed ones. In all of my observations in the courts, I almost never heard the other judges raise questions that had not been already mentioned by the president of the panel. There was little if any free flow of discussion; virtually always, the president of the panel, when legally trained, controlled the substance of deliberations.

In fact, the courts' administrators themselves recognized the possibility of professional dominance over the lay judges and attempted to guard against it by instituting a rule that the latter would vote first in deciding cases. In practice, this means that the side judges sign the "record of deliberation and voting" (*zapisnik o većanju i glasanju*) before the president of the panel;[4] and as one of the latter commented to me, "If they vote in favor of something, I can't overrule them." Yet the usual method of filling in the form is that the decision is reached and the reasons for it stated, primarily by the judge, often through the expedient of leading questions (e.g., "What do you think, shall we do X?"; or, more bluntly, "I propose that we do X; what do you think?").

Even without such conclusionary comments, the president of the panel may steer deliberation of a case through comments made informally, either before a case starts (e.g., "I remember this case. If they produce their bylaws, it looks pretty clear") or after the presentation of evidence is concluded (e.g., "It's a clear case," followed by an opinion). These were not phrases that I ever heard voiced by other members of panels.

The domination of the president of the panel is not surprising if viewed in the context of similar panel systems in other European countries and, indeed, in Yugoslavia. In regard to the latter, I observed cases in the regular courts in Belgrade, and found that the "juror-judges" (*sudije-porotnici*) rarely said anything in court unless they were asked to comment by the professional judge, whom they then addressed as "judge" (*sudija*). In other European countries, the dominance of regular judges over the lay assessors in their courts has been documented in empirical studies of the regular courts in Hungary (Kulcsar 1982) and of West German labor courts (Blankenburg et al. 1978) and regular courts (Richert 1983). From this perspective, then, the CALs exhibit the same pattern of judicial dominance of court deliberation that is found in other parts of Europe, and the only surprising aspect of the matter is that anyone would expect anything different.

Secretaries of the Panels

The dominance of the presidents described above needs one major qualification, however: it was most pronounced when the president had been legally trained. In other cases, and even in some of those in which the president was a lawyer, the secretary of the panel became a major figure.

The secretaries were almost all women, recent graduates of the law faculty at Belgrade University. They performed duties similar to those of law clerks in America: briefing cases, drafting opinions for judges, and, in general, assuring that the court ran in accordance with legal requirements. A secretary was assigned to each panel except those of the seven full-time, professional judges in the CAL. Each secretary spent two days per week in the courtrooms assisting in the trial procedures and then devoted the rest of her time to doing research and drafting opinions for the judges on her panels.

The position of secretary of the panel seems to have been an innovation in the Yugoslav legal system. When the CALs were created in Serbia in 1975, the position of secretary of the panel did not exist and they are not found in the regular courts. The first three secretaries were hired in the court's second year of operation, in 1976; in 1977 and 1978 there were nineteen of them, twenty-one in 1979, and thirty-seven to thirty-nine in the years 1980–82 (OSURBI 1982:table 4).

That the seven full-time judges in the Belgrade CAL do not have them is indicative of the need that they are perceived to fill: the full-time judges, who are otherwise regular judges, do not need their assistance, but the part-timers do.

In fact, the various CAL judges do seem quite dependent on the secretaries of their panels. Before a case is called, the secretary informs the panel of the issues involved, the status of the case, and what the day's proceedings will be expected to cover (e.g., the examination of one or more witnesses, or the presentation of documents). When the hearing is in progress, the secretary is generally not openly involved, but she will monitor the proceedings closely and may inform the judge if he makes an error of procedure or law. On several occasions I observed secretaries who signaled to the judge that there was a problem, without seeming to do so, so that he would dismiss the parties temporarily; and in their absence, she would point out a procedural problem that required immediate correction.

In briefing the cases, the secretary isolates and thus defines the salient issues that the proceedings should address. In doing so, however, the secretary does not draw on any wealth of experience as a worker or self-manager. Instead, she will base her comments on the formal law, on statutes and judicial decisions. This is not any kind of conscious slighting of the supposed ideals of self-management, but is rather a reflection of the general opinion held by those who serve in the CAL, that it is a *court*. As one judge put it, "The workers' courts judge according to law" (*radnički sud sudi po zakonu*), rather than according to more informal norms.

This orientation toward the formal law is also reflected in the opinions that the secretaries draft. These are practically identical in form and style to the opinions filed by judges in the regular courts, citing statutes and occasionally the decisions of CALs in other cases. The latter, as mentioned earlier, are readily available in the bulletin of the CAL of Serbia (GSURS), which reports the decisions of the republican CAL in every issue. Other legal publications also report on the decisions of the CALs, along with those of the regular and constitutional courts.

Summary of Participants: Who Speaks?

From the foregoing descriptions, it is clear that the discussions in the CALs are dominated by legal professionals. An attorney (*advokat*) for a plaintiff is likely to be arguing against a lawyer (*pravnik*) for a defending firm before a panel that is likely to be headed by a person with legal training, all under the supervision of a secretary of the bench, herself a *pravnik*, whose primary concern is to ensure that legal forms are followed and legal norms met. The plaintiff, if present, stands against the wall behind the lawyers, effectively out of the discussion. Yet this dominance of legal professionals in what should be a workers' court should not surprise us, if we recall that self-management law must be in accordance with constitutional and statutory provisions.

The general lack of participation of the side judges was brought home most graphically by the occasional practice of what I termed "panel jumping," in which a side judge from one panel would sit temporarily with a different panel in order to provide the latter with a full bench. Article 6 of the Law on the CALs of Serbia provided that there must be three judges present for a panel to issue any decisions. However, it sometimes happened that one member of a panel would not show up, rendering it powerless. In such cases, the secretary of the short-handed panel would visit the other courtrooms, trying to find someone to fill in temporarily.[5] The visitor would not make any comment or ask any questions, but would sign the necessary forms at the end of the case. The decision was effectively made in such cases by the president in consultation with the secretary of the panel.

The Substance of Discussion in the CAL

The staff of the Belgrade CAL tend to view their task in fairly narrow terms, as finding the legally proper solution for a case, rather than solving underlying problems, or as restoring disrupted relations. This attitude is made manifest in the court's pronounced policy of holding the discussion of cases to matters raised in the original plaint:

Case 23: The plaintiff in a case concerning an allocation of housing has lost the decision in the trial court and also on appeal to the CAL-Serbia. He now requests that the case be reopened, citing changes in his circumstances that would entitle him to more points in the ranking system. The secretary of the panel examines the original complaint and says that the new request raises new issues. She then says that since there are new issues, it is a new case, and the original one cannot be reopened. Thus the court refuses plaintiff's request, saying that the matter cannot be heard unless a new case is filed.

The court also tries to take a relatively narrow view of its own tasks, refusing to look too closely at the wisdom of many kinds of decisions taken by work organizations. Essentially, the position is that if an organization makes a decision in an area in which it is empowered to act, the court will respect that decision:

Case 24: Plaintiff says that he has been on the waiting list for an apartment for eight years, with no success, and that he cannot expect to ever get an apartment from his firm because the firm has no intention of ever purchasing flats. Instead, the organization gives loans to people to buy their own flats—but the loans must be paid back. Plaintiff wants the CAL to order the firm to buy and allocate flats for workers who cannot afford to pay back loans. The court refuses, however, saying that "that's a self-management decision," and dismisses the case.

On the other hand, the court will overturn a self-management decision that is patently unreasonable:

Case 25: Plaintiff works as a deputy chef at a large hotel. When the chief chef was injured in an automobile accident, plaintiff took over his duties. The organization's bylaws (pravilnik) *provide that there is no change in formal status when a worker works temporarily at a different job, for up to thirty days. Plaintiff in the present case waited thirty days and then asked for her salary to be paid at the rate of head chef, since she was acting in that capacity. The organization refused, saying that no matter what she was doing, the plaintiff was officially only an assistant chef and therefore could not be paid as a head chef. She asks the CAL to order the hotel to pay her in accordance with the work she is doing, rather than her formal rank.*

Under questioning from the court, the plaintiff asserts that she now works sixteen-hour days, seven days a week, and that the hotel has not hired an assistant chef to help her, even temporarily. The lawyer for the hotel admits these facts, but stands by his earlier answer: she is still classified as an assistant chef. Once the parties are dismissed, the judges voice incredulity at the actions of the employer, and unanimously vote to grant the plaintiff's request.

Further, some judges, at least, try to help potential plaintiffs:

Case 26: Apartment case; the plaintiff is not represented by a lawyer and has filed a handwritten claim that is nearly incomprehensible. When the case is called, the plaintiff comes, but the respondent firm does not send a representative. The judge lectures the plaintiff, informing him about the proper form of a complaint: "You can't complain until the flat is actually awarded, and then your complaint has to say: One, when the decision awarding the flat was made, and by whom; two, the address of the flat; three, the name of the person to whom it was given; four, why you have a better legal claim to the flat than that person." The case is then rescheduled for four weeks later, to give the plaintiff time to revise his plaint: "You have to say exactly what you want, and why."

This action was unusual, however, perhaps because very few plaintiffs appear without legal representation.

Like any other court, the CAL is confronted at times with questions of fact, which necessitate the taking of evidence. The procedures used in examining witnesses are virtually identical to those used in the regular courts. The witness is identified by name, name of parents, address, whether employed, marital status, and relationship to the parties; he or she is warned to speak only the truth, and is then asked questions by the judge, sometimes with supplementary questions asked by the parties' lawyers:

Case 27: Plaintiff, a butcher, was injured in an accident at the meat-packing plant where he works. The matter is unclear: plaintiff says that a side of meat fell from a hook, knocking him over, and that he cut his wrist when he fell on a knife. The firm contends that the plaintiff was drunk and that he cut himself and then knocked the meat off of the hook. Three witnesses are called: the first responds to the judge's question as to whether he actually saw the accident by saying that he did not, but had only heard about it. The defending attorney asks whether the witness had heard that the plaintiff was an alcoholic, and receives an affirmative reply.

The second witness describes the accident: plaintiff cut a vein in his wrist while he was cutting meat, which was hanging on a hook.

Question from the judge: "Are you sure he cut a vein?"

Answer (by second witness): "Yes, here" [pointing to his own wrist].

Question (judge): "Did the meat fall?"

Answer: "I don't know. I was too concerned with the spurting blood."

Question (plaintiff's attorney): "Did he perhaps fall on the knife?"

Answer: "No, the knife was thrown far away, and he was holding his wrist from the start."

After this sequence of questions, the parties were excused and the judges discussed the case. The quick consensus was expressed by the judge: the injury was due to the plaintiff's own actions, not those of the organization. Thus: decision for defendant.

This case was certainly not one in which any great attention was paid to the principles of socialist self-management. Instead, it was a rather ordinary legal case, one that could have come up in any other court and which would have been handled in much the same way in courts other than the CAL. Yet it was not exceptional in this regard. Quite to the contrary, the overwhelming business of the CAL was recognizably legal, not far removed from the ordinary business of other courts.

The lack of any specific self-management character in the CAL was exhibited most graphically when one panel of judges tried to follow that model rather than the legal one:

*Case 28: Plaintiff appears without a lawyer and claims that he is being paid at a rate that is too low for someone with his qualifications and experience. The lawyer (*pravnik*) representing his work organization says that the plaintiff is* *being paid at the rate established by the firm's workers' council for the job that he holds. Under questioning of both parties, it becomes clear that the real problem is that the firm has been reorganized. The job that the plaintiff held earlier has been eliminated, and he has been assigned to a lower-paying job instead.*[6] *Plaintiff says that he would like a job that is more appropriate for someone with his qualifications and experience. The judge asks whether there are any such jobs available, but the lawyer for the respondent firm evades the question. One of the side judges pursues the matter further:*

Side judge: Are you a lawyer with that organization?

Respondent attorney: Yes.

Side judge: Then help us out!

Respondent's attorney: I don't know about jobs. I'm a lawyer; they gave me the file and told me to come argue the case.

At this stage, the court suggested that the plaintiff should petition the workers' council for a different job, and if that petition is refused, that he should then return to the court and file a new case against that decision. In the meantime, the present petition is rejected.

The judge then asks the lawyer if he could help the plaintiff draw up a petition to the workers' council. The lawyer says that he can, that it is only a matter of four or five sentences. The judge tells the lawyer to do so and then dismisses the parties.

This case was perhaps the best self-management proceeding that I observed in the court in that the members of the panel were involved along with the president and the aim of their discussion was to reach an agreement satisfactory to both parties. Yet the effort was stymied by the inability of the respondent's representative to engage in any substantive, nonlegal negotiations.

In fact, it is hard to see how this problem, of the inability of an organization's representatives to discuss substantive issues, could be avoided. It would, of course, be possible to bar representation by lawyers in the CALs, but this seems like an unlikely step, for several reasons. First, who would be a better representative of the organization? If it were mandated that senior managers personally appear in cases before the CALs, there might be disruptions of work back in the factory and probably a public outcry about the perceived waste of managerial time. Yet anyone other than a high manager would probably not be able to negotiate for the organization. But this last point raises a further question: If self-management decisions should be made by the workers' council, is it acceptable to delegate authority to negotiate particular cases to the management?

Finally, even if lawyers were to be prohibited from representing organizations, the substance of arguments in the CAL would be likely to remain centered on formal law. It should be remembered that self-management law is ultimately largely subordinated to regular law, which means that lawyers must consider decisions said to be based on self-management law, if only to see that they are not incongruent with the formal law.

Summary: Legalization of the Self-Management Courts

Observation of the CAL in Belgrade thus leads to the conclusion that, despite the ideology of self-management law and self-management courts, the court is very similar in its operations to the regular courts. In the CAL, arguments are made by legally trained representatives to legally trained judges, and decisions are based on the same kinds of sources (statutes and court practice) that are used in deciding cases in the regular courts. Further, the parties to disputes are not themselves generally involved in arguing or even discussing their own cases in the CAL. If they even come to the hearings, they are almost always relegated to the position of spectator, apart from the main action physically and in terms of social interaction.

These findings provide an explanation for one of the questions raised in chapter 1: the apparently anomalous status of the CALs, as the only informal court to attract substantial voluntary use by individuals. The appearance of an anomaly vanishes when it is recognized that the CALs are very much like regular courts. That a regular court should be used by individuals is not surprising; quite to the contrary, one of the arguments most frequently made in favor of creating alternative courts is that the regular courts are *over*used. But why should that be a problem? In the case of the CALs, why would it not be desirable that the workers' courts be used by workers?

In fact, however, a political discourse had developed in 1984–85 on this question, with the dominant position being that the CALs were failures because they were attracting so many individual labor cases and thus were acting much like the regular courts. The next chapter considers this discourse, which is important not only for understanding the career of the CALs, but also because of the questions that it raises concerning the inherent instability of social courts. This last topic, in turn, will be pursued in the concluding chapter.

Part IV

Court Use as a Political Issue

Chapter 9
Political Debates Over the CAL, 1981 to 1985

The Opening Rounds

In the 1970s and early 1980s, the Yugoslavs saw their efforts at building self-management as something of a large-scale experiment (see Rusinow 1978) and made strong efforts to monitor its progress. Less than four years after the establishment of the CALs, the Federal Executive Council (FEC), the highest executive organ of the Yugoslav federation, discussed the workings of these courts and decided to undertake a study of them. The study was done by the Federal Secretariat on the Administration of Justice and the Organization of the Federal Administration, which issued its *Analysis of the Condition and Actual Problems of the Self-Management Judiciary* (hereafter, *Analysis*) on 30 April 1980. The aim of the Analysis was stated (p. 2) to be

> to examine the position and evaluate the functioning to date of the self-management judiciary, and the degree of their organization and preparation to execute the functions entrusted to them effectively, economically, expertly and responsibly, so that the practice of the self-management courts develops in accordance with the determinations and intentions established by the Constitution and statutes and in accordance with social needs.

The *Analysis*, in ninety-seven typed pages plus ten appended tables, considered nearly all aspects of the self-management judiciary: theoretical and practical legal problems, statistics on their work in 1977 and 1978, and various questions concerning the organizations, jurisdiction, and procedures of all of the self-management courts.

The data from 1977 and 1978 on the caseloads of the CALs indicated that 93.6 percent of the cases in the CALs in those years were initiated by individual workers (p. 60). The conclusion drawn from this fact was that

[s]uch a structure of disputes forces a particular kind of work of the court, approximating specialized courts for the resolution of disputes involving particular violations of the rights of individual workers in which the decisions of the courts must be based on the regular application of legal norms, because it is only in a very small number of disputes that the court has the opportunity to act creatively on the development of self-management relations or the resolution of economic-political relations in an organization.

This fact was seen to create certain problems. First, the materials issued and the discussions in the legislature at the time of the creation of these courts did not envision this development, and the selection of judges had been made with an eye toward people who could discuss self-management relations between group economic actors (e.g., BOALs) rather than the problems of individuals (p. 61). The latter type of problem requires legal training on the part of the judges or the participation of technical assistants, "most often with legal training" (p. 61). In that context, the *Analysis* noted the presence of the secretaries of the bench with some misgivings, saying that the position had not been envisioned at the time the courts were created and, hence, that their responsibilities were not regulated by law. While their services were doubtless needed in many cases, concern was expressed that they were not really properly "selected officials" (*izabrani funkcioner[i]*), yet the courts might depend on their analyses (pp. 61–62).

The overwhelming preponderance of individual workers' disputes in the CALs was given a rather evenhanded interpretation in the *Analysis*, as having both positive and negative implications (pp. 68–69). On the positive side, the *Analysis* noted that the large and rapidly increasing number of individual labor disputes indicated that workers were growing increasingly aware of their self-management rights. On the other hand, the existence of these disputes was interpreted as indicating the degree to which self-management had not yet developed properly. Neither implication, however, was seen as casting the CALs themselves in an unfavorable light. Instead, the position of the *Analysis* was that they were responding to an environment different from the one originally envisioned.

In fact, if anything, the *Analysis* saw room for improvement in processing the individual labor disputes. It noted that in 1978, the processing time in the trial-level CALs was greater than six months in 24 percent of the cases (a figure that might make an American court administrator green with envy!) and said that this was unsatisfactory. The *Analysis* suggested that the CALs should coordinate efforts with the unions and the social attorneys of self-management to forestall labor disputes; it also castigated the latter two bodies for failing to be more involved in the work of the CALs (pp. 60–61).

The *Analysis* ended with conclusions and recommendations. The basic conclusion was that the transformation of the judiciary was taking place more slowly than had been expected, but the reasons for this were seen to lie with the unsatisfactory development of self-management relations rather than with the CALs themselves. Mention was made of the fact that, since lawyers frequently appear for both sides in cases before the CALs and the cases generally are concerned with the rights of individuals, the CALs had become much like the regular courts. The solution to this problem was seen in increasing other means of resolving workers' disputes, through the involvement of the trade unions and the creation of active informal self-management courts (e.g., arbitration) within the work place. The decisions of such courts would then be appealable to the CALs. Finally, the *Analysis* suggested the creation of special CALs to handle specific kinds of disputes, particularly those involving housing.[1]

In its concluding section, the *Analysis* considered the question of whether individual workers' disputes should be considered to be self-management disputes at all (pp. 92–93). It noted that one opinion on this question was that such cases should not be thought of as self-management matters, since they required a form of processing like that of the regular courts and thus were driving the CALs toward increasing similarity with classical judicial institutions. Yet it also noted that there was another school of thought that held that the individual labor disputes could not be separated from the consideration of other self-management questions. The *Analysis* did not essay any conclusions on this question, however.

The *Analysis*, then, offered a dispassionate review of the statistics on the work of the self-management courts, including the CALs, and of some of the issues surrounding them. While the *Analysis* itself was not published, it was discussed by the FEC on 3 February 1981.[2] The FEC's conclusions, however, were much more critical of the CALs than the *Analysis* had been, stating bluntly that the self-management courts had not developed in accordance with the intentions behind, and opportunities afforded by, the constitution and the LAL, or with the needs of associated labor. Furthermore, where the *Analysis* had seen some positive aspects to the rapidly increasing caseload of the CALs, the FEC viewed it in solely negative terms, as reflecting a flaw in the design of the courts. The "key problem" was determined to be that the CALs were not housed within work organizations. This was viewed as a flawed design because self-management disputes should be resolved only by the workers involved in them.

Following this assessment of the unsatisfactory nature of the self-management courts, the FEC called for a new Federal Law on the

CALs, and assigned the task of drafting it to the Committee on the Judiciary of the FEC. The Committee prepared the Proposal for the Passage of a Law on Courts of Associated Labor[3] which outlined a complete revision of the CALs. While the proposal had many provisions, the most important one was aimed at the "key problem" identified by the FEC, and it proposed that the CALs be placed within BOALs, rather than remain as independent agencies: "Courts of associated labor are formed . . . in organizations of associated labor and other self-management organizations and collectives" (Proposal, Article 16).

The proposal was discussed by the full Committee on the Judiciary on 5 February 1982. The president of the committee argued that it was of utmost importance that the proposal be placed on the schedule of the FEC meeting to be held five days later, with a recommendation "without qualification" that it be enacted as law immediately. However, in what the newspaper accounts indicate was a lively session (*Borba*, 6 February 1982, pp. 2, 4; *Politika*, 6 February 1982, p. 5), this suggestion was not accepted. Representatives of the Federal Trade Union objected to such haste, saying that they had not been given an opportunity to hold discussions on the proposed new law. Other representatives objected specifically to the proposal to create CALs within BOALs, saying that courts in such a position would fall under the influence of the "technobureaucratic forces and leadership structures" of the work organizations and thus not be independent in their judgment. The Committee on Sociopolitical Relations of the FEC weighed in with similar arguments and proposed that the FEC require that the Committee on the Judiciary prepare a new draft of the proposed law, taking these objections into account.[4] Faced with these objections, the president of the committee backed off on the proposal for an accelerated parliamentary procedure and agreed that the proposal could serve only as a discussion draft, not as a proposal for a statute.

An analysis in the official paper of the Socialist Alliance, *Borba* (6 February 1982, p. 2) raised an issue that would haunt the proposal to change the CALs. It argued that the CALs had until that time functioned to protect the rights of workers, as shown by the willingness of workers to bring cases to them. It then asked why there should be a radical change in this system and, particularly, why the CALs should be put into work organizations. The article pointed out that since most complaints by workers are directed against the leadership of their work organizations, putting the CALs into BOALs would leave the worker in the untenable position of having to complain to representatives of that leadership. The analysis emphasized this point by citing a saying from Serbia's five hundred years under Turkish rule, comparing the proposed new CALs to Muslim *kadi* justice: *kadija te tuži, kadija ti sudi* (the *kadi* accuses you and the *kadi* judges you).[5]

Over the next several days, the proposal was discussed by the Committee on the Judiciary, the Committee on Work, Health, and Social Politics and the Legislative-Legal Commission of the FEC. All three bodies recommended that the proposal be treated as a discussion draft rather than a proposed text for a statute, and the latter two bodies raised questions concerning the desirability of putting the CALs into BOALs.[6] At the next session of the FEC, on 10 February 1989, the president of the Committee on the Judiciary, the original proponent of the new law, spoke in its favor and urged the need to reform the CALs in such a way as to make them true self-management courts instead of institutions that resembled the regular judiciary. In the end, however, he acknowledged the discussion of the draft law in other working bodies of the FEC and said that "with the enriched knowledge" gained from these discussions, the Committee on the Judiciary would prepare a new text of a draft law on the CALs, for the later consideration of the FEC. Following his speech, the FEC accepted the proposal that there be a new law on the CALs, and charged the Committee on the Judiciary with preparing a new draft "on the basis of the thoughts, comments and proposals which were given in the discussions about the Proposal for passage of this law."[7]

The Public Debate

The debates and political activity concerning the proposal for a new law on the CALs continued for more than two years. The proponents of the new law kept insisting that the CALs as then constituted were "outside of associated labor" and had to be within BOALs to be true self-management courts. They prepared a new draft law that kept that provision, and it was circulated in mimeograph form in March and printed for public discussion in September 1982 (*Borba*, 14 September 1982, special section). This provision, however, was criticized, not to say ridiculed, by most commentators. Thus an article in *NIN* said that even though the proponents of the new law said that it was "revolutionary," the real question should be whether it would protect workers better than the existing law—and used the saying about *kadi* justice to suggest that the answer to that question was no (*NIN*, 4 April 1982, p. 23). This article provoked a letter to the editor in response from the president of the Committee on the Judiciary, who called the article "disinformation" and defended the proposed law against the *kadi* justice charge by pointing out that the new law provided for appeals of the decisions of the trial courts (*NIN*, 11 April 1982, pp. 2, 3, 6). Other letters published in the same issue and the following one, however, also criticized the proposed new law—and also the president of the Committee on the Judiciary (*NIN*, 11 April and 18 April 1982).

Reporters were not the only ones to criticize the draft law. The members of the Federal Legal Council, meeting in May 1982, "could not find even a single good word to say about the draft law on courts of associated labor." While serious criticisms were aimed at virtually every article of the draft law, the proposal that the CALs be established in work organizations drew the most criticism (*Politika*, 15 May 1982, p. 6). After the draft law was published, the criticisms continued. In January 1983, a satirical piece in the official party organ, *Komunist* (7 January 1983, p. 5), repeated the *kadi* justice crack in the course of criticizing the whole idea of reforming the CAL. The Belgrade nightly newscast on 23 January 1983 carried a report on the proposed new law, including interviews with workers, all of whom were against it.[8] The news report also noted that the unions were solidly against the new law. Later in the year, another piece in *NIN* suggested that the country could not afford all of the new CALs that would have to be created if they were to be established in work organizations and also pointed out that jurisdiction would be confusing in organizations that contained more than one BOAL (*NIN*, 12 June 1983, p. 16). In a similar vein, a joint session of the appellate CALs of all of the republics and provinces sent a communication to the FEC criticizing various aspects of the draft law, but particularly the provision to put the CAL into work organizations (GSURS 13:20–25).

The alignment of forces against the proposed changes in the law was of some interest. The opposition of the lawyers was perhaps predictable, since practice before the CALs was (and is) an important and profitable part of their work. Similarly, the appellate CALs might have feared a dramatic decrease in their work load if the proposal to put the CALs into organizations were to be enacted, since the number of cases in the "reformed" courts would have declined. The trade unions' opposition to the law seems less easily explicable, in view of their infrequent use of the existing CALs. However, even if the unions have not been going to court very often, they have still been active in resolving individual labor disputes within work organizations (Zukin 1981). From 1977 to 1981, the unions aided 77,000 workers in defending their individual rights (*Borba*, 13 October 1982, p. 2). Since the power to obtain concessions in negotiations may depend heavily on the existence of an outside forum to which recourse could be taken (see, e.g., Mnookin and Kornhauser 1979), the unions may have been concerned with preserving one of the resources then available to them.

The arguments raised by both sides in the debate ranged from the polemical to, particularly on the side of the opponents of the new law, the practical and sociological. The proponents of putting the CALs into BOALs used ideological, almost definitional, arguments: the CALs were not within associated labor and thus could not be self-management courts. This argument was encapsulated in the justification given for putting the courts into work organizations that was provided with the published version of the draft law on CALs, as follows:

> The consistent establishment of the leading position of workers and working people in associated labor and in society demands, along with the fact that they regulate socio-economic relations in organizations of associated labor and other forms of associated labor and means, that they be directly responsible for the elimination of contradictions and disputes which, because of the pluralism of self-management interests, remain in those relationships. Therefore, the socio-economic position of workers in associated labor requires that they be the bearers of the judicial function, above all in associations of associated labor and other self-management organizations and collectives in which are reflected in embryonic form the entirety of the relations of social reproduction. . . . In connection with this it is envisioned that courts of associated labor be established: 1). in organizations of associated labor and other self-management organizations and collectives. . . . (*Borba*, 14 September 1982, special section, p. 13)

This hermetic logic did not sway the opponents of the new law, who in general sought to insert new elements apart from the definitional assertions that institutions not physically within self-management organizations did not possess sufficient self-management character and were therefore illegitimate. The oft-repeated saying about *kadi* justice, in particular, was used to ridicule the proposal. But the point made by that simile was a serious one: who would protect workers from the potential oppression of the managers of their organizations if the CALs were also located within those organizations, and subject to pressure from those managers?

One argument that could be seen as a possible counter to this question was that the action of the courts was in itself undesirable. If this were so, then the high caseload of the CALs could more easily be seen as a social problem that needed correction. In this context, the charge that the CALs protected bad workers (*štiti neradnike*) was potentially a telling one. This accusation was made frequently, as the CAL in Belgrade acknowledged in its annual report in 1981, and "horror stories" of loafers and drunks being reinstated by the CALs appeared in the newspapers in 1982 (see, e.g., *Politika*, 6 July 1982, p. 9) and even more recently (see *NIN*, 18 May 1986, p. 26). However, on investigation, this charge is not supported by evidence on what the CALs do: in 1982, the CALs in Serbia heard 1,112 cases concerning the termination of employment, and they reinstated the workers in only 21.5 percent of those cases (*Borba*, 6 April 1983, p. 4). Furthermore, when a CAL does reinstate workers, it does so because the legal conditions that would justify termination have not been met (*Borba*, 6 April 1983, p. 4)—exactly the position taken by the judges on the court (see above, chapter 7).

The arguments over the CALs can thus be seen as breaking down into two basic camps. The position for reform of these courts was based on the premise that they were not really self-management courts because they heard so many individual labor cases. Why this caseload was undesirable was explained in terms of either an "original intent" theory (the legislators who created the courts had not intended that they handle such cases) or an economic efficiency theory (the courts improperly meddled in self-management decisions, thus undercutting work discipline and the quality of the work force). From both positions there was explicit recognition that putting the CALs into work places would discourage individual complaints to the courts, but this was seen as being a desirable outcome. The opponents of that "reform" also saw it as likely to discourage individual complaints, but questioned the premise that the large number of individual cases was undesirable per se. Essentially, their position was that individual labor complaints were symptoms of problems in the work place, rather than themselves a form of social pathology. Both positions were expressed in 1983 as part of the public and professional discourse on the proposed new Law on the CALs.

The Law on the CALs, 1984

In the end, it was the opponents of the "reform" who largely carried the day. A new federal Law on Courts of Associated Labor was enacted in July 1984,[9] but without the controversial provision to put the CALs into work places. Instead, the organizational basis of the trial-level CALs remains territorial: "[t]he court of associated labor at the primary level (first instance) is established by statute for the territory of one or more communes" (LCAL 1984, Article 12). Thus the independence of the CALs from the pressures of local-level self-management politics was protected by the new law.

In other ways, the new LCAL actually may be seen as strengthening the CALs. It had long been known that one of the difficulties with the original CAL structure was that it was difficult to have CAL decisions enforced against a recalcitrant defending party (Šarkić 1986). Newspaper articles described cases in which decisions of a CAL either were not followed or else compliance was so slow as to work a severe hardship on the worker who should have benefitted from it (*Politika*, 7 February 1983, p. 5; *Politika*, 1 July 1983, p. 7). A two-day seminar on the problem of assuring compliance with the decisions of the CALs was held in June 1983 and was attended by seventy participants (*Politika*, 25 June 1983, p. 10). One of the reasons for this problem was that although the original LCAL provided that "[d]ecisions of a court of associated labor have validity and are executed throughout the entire territory of the Socialist Federal Republic of Yugoslavia" (LCAL 1974, Article 10[2]), it also stated that "[d]ecisions of a court of associated labor may be challenged by legal means [i.e., in the regular courts] in cases and under conditions established by statute" (LCAL 1974, Article 10[1]). In practice, the regular courts did often refuse to execute the decisions of the CALs (see, e.g., *NIN*, 30 May 1982, p. 20), and the sheer fact that a challenge could be mounted may have affected adversely the bargaining power of plaintiffs who won in the trial courts.

The 1984 LCAL met this problem by replacing Article 10 of the old law with one providing the following: (1) that the decisions of the CALs are "valid and are executed" in all of Yugoslavia; (2) that participants in a self-management relation that is affected by the decision of a CAL are bound to execute the decision of that court; (3) if such a participant does not execute the decision, the regular courts will do so under the provisions of the law on executory procedure; (4) if it is not possible for the decision to be executed by the regular courts under the law on executory procedure, that decision will be executed by local political bodies (LCAL 1984, Article 6). Thus the new law not only removed the possibility of challenging decisions of the CALs in the regular courts, but it also provided for an expedited method of gaining enforcement of CAL decisions in them.

Later legislation also seems to be aimed at strengthening the CALs. A draft of a proposed Law on Procedures before the CALs, presented to the FEC in October 1985, called for a composition of these courts that must include at least one lawyer (*pravnik*): "A court [of associated labor] decides cases in panels in which at least one member is a graduate lawyer [*diplomirani pravnik*],"[10] perhaps signaling a further retreat from the ideal of self-management law. While this statute, to my knowledge, has not yet been passed, the trend seems clear: the CALs will have more legally knowledgeable judges on their panels. Indeed, a joint session of delegates of the highest courts of associated labor of the republics and provinces in 1985 concluded that, notwithstanding the desire to deprofessionalize the CALs,

> it must be kept in view that the judicial function consists of the resolution of individual dispute relations by the application of legal norms, both state and

self-management. This means that it is essential that someone with legal knowledge participate in judging. . . . With this in mind, the joint session concludes that the president of a panel, in both the first instance and second instance court of associated labor, should be a qualified lawyer [*diplomirani pravnik*] who has passed the judicial examination—this is the ideal, and failing that, a qualified lawyer—as the minimal acceptable solution. (GSURS 17:33–34[1985])

Thus the trend in thinking about the CALs seems to be running against the view that they should be truly nonprofessional courts.

Interpreting the Legislative Process

The most interesting aspect of the legislative and public debates surrounding the CALs is that they did produce a retreat from the original conception of the CALs. At the time these courts were created, it seems clear that the intent behind them was indeed to develop a new form of social court, as described in chapter 3. That this conception of the CALs was apparently abandoned in the late 1980s requires some comment.

First, the debate over the CALs must be placed into the context of larger trends of Yugoslav politics in the 1980s. Beginning in 1980, the Yugoslav economy went into a protracted period of stagnation, marked by high unemployment, high inflation, and a falling standard of living. As the economy grew steadily worse, the political situation entered its own period of crisis, which prompted the beginning of serious questioning of the entire self-management paradigm.[11] In fact, the massive set of constitutional amendments promulgated in November 1988 may be seen as the beginning of a formal retreat from much of the self-management paradigm. While the debates over the CALs took place several years before the full blossoming of the political crisis, they probably partook of some elements of the challenge to the self-management paradigm that were then beginning.

The growing turmoil in Yugoslav political life probably served to facilitate the efforts of the opponents of the original "reforms" of the CALs in another way, by making the parliamentary process more combative. As the certainties of the older style of politics weakened, politicians of various stripes, including those within the parliament, became more bold. By the early 1980s, Yugoslav legislatures had developed to the point that they played a real role in policymaking, instead of simply rubber-stamping decisions made by political actors elsewhere (see Seroka 1984). Thus the defeat of the original proposal to "reform" the CALs in a way that would have served effectively to end their independent existence, and hence their utility to most workers, became possible.

The specifics of the arguments become interesting in this context. The proponents of the "reform" offered arguments that were based almost entirely on the officially dominant theory of self-management. From within the confines of that theory, the reform would appear to be necessary, because the CALs had obviously deviated from the theoretical ideal of an informal workers' court. The arguments in favor of the continued independence of the court were, in fact, implicitly arguments against the theory of self-management, particularly in their recognition that the various forms of self-managed work organizations were liable to capture by a "technobureaucratic elite." This implication of the arguments in opposition to the reform was in fact pointed out by the chairman of the Committee on the Judiciary in his polemical exchange with a critical newspaper writer in the letters column of *NIN* (11 April 1982, p. 3). By the mid-1980s, however, Yugoslav political opinion was turning away from the dictates of theory to consideration of actual social practices and conditions. The "reform" of the CALs thus foundered on the rocks of a more or less empirically based critique. This was something of an innovation in a political world in which theory had been commonly used to define "objective reality."

Finally, it should be noted that the proponents of the "reform" of the CALs were actually defending a conservative political position, in the sense that they were trying to erect an apparatus that would bring an uncomfortable social reality under control. Their position was not designed to react to workers' expressions of grievances in ways that would meet the workers' own sense of needs, but rather to eliminate the opportunity for the expression of those grievances. This tactic of conservative political action is one that appears in other settings in debates surrounding social courts, as discussed in the final chapter.

Chapter 10
Conclusions: The Courts of Associated Labor in Comparative Perspective

A Summary Analysis of the CALs: The Contradictions of Socialist Legal Theory and Practice

The Divergence of Practice and Theory

There is a certain irony to the political debate recounted in the previous chapter, in that the proponents of the "reform" of the CALs were actually correct in terms of the theoretical paradigm of self-management. The CALs had clearly diverged from the ideals of workers' courts as institutions in which workers discussed labor issues informally and in terms of workers' norms: they were controlled by legal professionals rather than workers and dealt with cases largely in terms of the formal law rather than through any self-management norms. Yet the critics were also correct in their arguments about *kadi* justice. Few workers would be likely to go voluntarily to the CALs if the courts were to be reformed, since complaining about working conditions to the management of the work organization within the confines of the work place would not likely be a profitable exercise.

Thus the debate over the CALs actually revealed an inconsistency between the theory of self-management law and the likely behavior of workers themselves. Put most succinctly, the contradiction is as follows: to be true self-management courts, the CALs would have to be staffed by workers and meet in the work place. Yet if they were structured in this way, they would not be able to attract the voluntary submission of cases by individual workers. A form of Catch-22: to be true workers' courts, the CALs would have to be structured in such a way that few workers would want to use them.

The Internal Contradiction of Socialist Legal Theory

The question could then be raised: Why was the theory inadequate to account for the practice of workers? The answer would seem to lie in an underestimation of the potential for conflict and disputes in any work setting. Where the theory seems to have been premised on the assumption that self-management would not produce serious conflicts between workers, the realists opposing the "reform" of the CALs recognized the actual likelihood of conflict between workers and any form of management. Of course, this contradiction is not limited to Yugoslav self-management; in general, the position of "a worker in a worker's state" does not seem to be particularly enviable (see Haraszti 1978). The problem may thus be more general than simply a question of Yugoslav self-management; it may lie more deeply in the theory underlying the self-management institutions and self-management legality.

As seen in chapter 3, the origin of the idea of self-management law can be found in the classical Marxist ideal of the withering of the state as socialism develops toward communism, whereupon the state disappears. This particular prognosis was also drawn upon by Lenin in his few considerations of law (see Beirne and Hunt 1988). Yet as Beirne and Hunt (1988) show, Lenin (and by extension, others drawing on the concept of "withering") simply ignored the problem of the representation of divergent interests under socialism. This might be justifiable under some theoretical formulations, but seems intensely unrealistic in practice. The only way that the theoretical paradigm can be seen as likely would be if all people in a society viewed the precepts of the theory as correct. The problem is, however, that a complex theoretical paradigm must remain counterintuitive to most people (see Hayden 1989a:803–804; cf. Ackerman 1977:10–11) and thus of dubious merit. This problem will hold true especially for hermetic theories, such as those of doctrinal Marxism, in an inverse relationship that will be nearly invariant: the more self-contained (hence hermetic) the theory, the less likely it is to be comprehensible to most people—and, therefore, the less likely it is to gain general social acceptance.

It might be possible to duck this issue through the development of a theoretical refinement, such as the Marxist doctrine of false consciousness, that justifies the imposition of the measures dictated by theory in spite of popular opposition, on the grounds that this action will ultimately lead to the betterment of society even if many or most people do not recognize this fact. Alternatively, all members of society might be taught the benefits of the theory. We might be permitted skepticism on this point, however, particularly in light of the experience of other attempts in the twentieth century to impose totalizing visions on complex societies, a process which one analyst of Eastern Europe has called a "search . . . for the despotism of the enlightened" rather than a dictatorship of the proletariat (Bauman 1987:174).

In the case of the CALs and of self-management, it seems unlikely that a theory that defines labor complaints as unjustified will gain acceptance by many workers. That the original formulations of self-management law did not consider this possibility is perhaps indicative of a bias in perspective that seems endemic to writings on socialist law, which tend to view law as a matter of command, imposing its dictates on society (see Markovits 1982). As discussed in chapter 3, socialist lawyers adhere to what may be the most pure forms of positivism left in legal philosophy. A leading Yugoslav sociologist of law, for example, has defined law as "*the body of social norms sanctioned by the force of the state apparatus* and which serves to support the form of production which is in the interest of the ruling class" (Lukić 1985:57; emphasis added). This is clearly a "top-down" perspective on law, one that envisions law as forced upon litigants, rather than invoked by them to further their own ends.

It is not only writers in socialist countries who take this top-down perspective on law, however. It is somewhat curious that an analyst such as Stuart Henry (1983, 1985), for example, who set out to investigate "private" (i.e., non-state) systems of social control in socialist, communally oriented, cooperative work organizations in Britain, should concentrate so completely on discipline in the workplace, rather than on the protection of workers' rights. Why is this the key problem?

In Henry's case, this focus may be a reflection of his rejection, apparently as an article of faith, of the idea that "mechanisms of social control might be universal irrespective of whether they occur under capitalism or socialism" (1983:180), a position he spurns because it seems to rule out the possibility of "liberation" through the attainment of socialism. By concentrating on socialist discipline, Henry may have intended to show that socialist legality is a real possibility. Yet the question remains: Why should socialist legality be primarily concerned with discipline rather than rights?

The answer to this question may be found to lie more generally in the teleological nature of socialist writings, which are aimed at achieving the transformation of society. If socialism is the ultimate goal, than the imposition of the dictates of socialist theory is justifiable. In the case of cooperatives or other communally oriented work organizations, discipline is key, because without it the organization cannot survive in a hostile capitalistic environment (see Henry 1983, 1985). Or, to paraphrase Lenin, it is not possible to have socialism in one cooperative, and extreme vigilance is required until the total revolution. The point holds more generally, however: socialist legal discourse functions on the level of command because the purpose of the exercise is to foster the discipline needed to transform society.

This basic point is not itself new and has been pursued by others at various levels of polemic (see, e.g., Djilas 1957 [high polemic]; Beirne and Hunt 1988 [low polemic]). I raise it now, however, for several reasons. First, it accounts for the persistent avoidance of concern with rights that is common to legal analyses aimed at fostering the development of socialism. The traditional argument from this corner is that individual rights hinder the advance of socialism because they impede governmental efforts to bring it about. This is an old problem for the left (see Chase 1984; Sparer 1984), but one that has been given new life by recent writers in the Critical Legal Studies school in the United States (see, e.g., Tushnet 1984; Klare 1981). The difficulties with the position are reasonably obvious; however, they are exemplified nicely by the political discourse on the CALs. A reform of labor law that is aimed at excluding individual workers from redress from legal institutions is noteworthy, perhaps remarkable.

The implications of the teleological nature of the socialist literature on law are relevant for another reason as well: they point out the importance of looking at the larger purposes of those making the arguments concerning social courts. The view that one or another use of formal courts is undesirable is frequently associated with established relations of power: those who are in power tend to disfavor use of the regular courts by those *not* in power. This point can be seen by looking more closely at the discourses on social courts mentioned in chapter 1.

Comparing the Discourses of Social Justice

Paradigms of Argument for Social Courts

The arguments made in favor of the creation of social courts in capitalist societies are of two basic sorts. One views the regular courts as alienating and as disempowering for disputants. In this version courts either are inaccessible to people out of power or, if accessible, they take control of a dispute away from the people directly involved in it by transforming the matter into the terms and logic of the law (see, e.g., Christie 1976; Mather and Yngvesson 1980). This kind of argument, which we may call "transformational," is generally made by those who either are essentially in opposition to the government or favor social and legal changes that would benefit the less powerful in society. They advocate the creation of alternative judicial institutions as a means to increase access to justice for those otherwise deprived of it, or else as a way to limit the supposedly imperialistic influence of the capitalist state.

The second type of argument in favor of the creation of social courts has implications that are very different from the transformational ones of the first camp. This second variety, which we may call "conservative," sees the need for social courts as lying in the inappropriateness or unsuitability of regular judicial institutions for certain kinds of disputes. Unsuitability may be seen as lying in the overly adversarial nature of formal courts for some kinds of disputes; inappropriateness in the expense or intrusiveness or waste of scarce resources or economic dislocations allegedly caused by permitting certain kinds of disputes to be aired in formal courts. From this perspective, alternative judicial institutions are needed in order to prevent the inappropriate use of state power in such circumstances. The effect of the creation of social courts would thus be to limit their use, particularly by the "wrong people": those otherwise disadvantaged (Galanter 1985a:550n.32).

The two schools are at base profoundly at odds, even diametrically opposed: the first calling for the empowerment of those otherwise disadvantaged, the second for their continued disenfranchisement. However, the arguments of the first group can be co-opted by the adherents of the second, particularly in regard to the supposed inappropriateness of regular courts for some kinds of disputes. Such a process of subversive assimilation can be seen in the use of the arguments about the need for a "better way" of handling particular kinds of disputes, which ignore the questions of who should be made to use these courts (see Merry 1987).

Examples of the rhetorical use of these paradigms can be seen in the arguments for social courts in the United States and India, the countries mentioned in chapter 1. Since the American discourse has already been described in some detail and is, in any event, likely to be better known to most readers of this book, it will be given only brief consideration here. However, the development of the political and scholarly debates on social courts and other forms of "alternative dispute resolution" in the United States seems to have passed from an initial period, in which the transformational paradigm was dominant, into one in which the conservative paradigm now governs. Recognition of this shift may be found in the position of many scholars who are themselves of a transformational disposition, who now see proposals for ADR as a mask for increasing state social control (see, e.g., Abel 1982). Certainly, it is doubtful that a conservative public figure such as former chief justice Warren Burger would adopt a transformational perspective.

In India, the transformational and conservative paradigms both have long histories, which stem from the beginning of the colonial period. As mentioned in chapter 1, the British sought, from almost the beginning of their rule, to maintain what they perceived as indigenous forms of legal institutions, in a quite conscious effort to administer the country efficiently and cheaply by co-opting "traditional" practices. However, if the original rationale behind attempting to preserve institutions such as *panchayats* was to preserve Indian "custom," it was a failure: *panchayats* declined very quickly as Indian litigants themselves overwhelmingly chose to try to get their suits heard by the British courts, ignoring the "traditional" options available to them. Thus by early on in the nineteenth century, the British were already complaining about the overwhelming presence of Indian suits in their courts in terms that Chief Justice Burger would recognize: that the courts were not suitable for the cases, or, conversely, that the cases were inappropriate for the courts. An early governor of Madras wrote that recourse to the courts was "too expensive" for villagers, and that the courts were both "inefficient" and unsuitable: "I have never seen any European whom I thought competent, from his knowledge of the language and the people, to ascertain the value of the evidence before him" (Glieg 1830:518–519, quoted in Rudolph and Rudolph 1967:260). At the same time, the view that Indians were "litigious" became common sense, an element of established wisdom. The British response was to initiate a series of attempts to promote informal alternatives to courts which would supposedly be better suited to Indian cases (Meschievitz 1986 and 1987).

These British efforts to provide alternatives to courts apparently served different purposes at different times (see Washbrook 1981), but the overriding effect was to limit access to courts for many kinds of cases. Indeed, as Washbrook notes (1981:657–660), the ways that the colonial state in India ran the regular courts do not indicate that the administrations were really interested in extending the supposed benefits of British law to the Indian population. In the first half of the nineteenth century, the courts charged high fees, were not able to enforce their own decrees, and were staffed by a judiciary that was not of the highest caliber. Later, the quality of the judges improved, but execution of judgments has remained problematical, and high fees still serve as a deterrent to litigants.

The British approach seems in fact to have been one that was essentially conservative in orientation: to preserve established relations of power in the Indian countryside, in the interest of a more efficient colonial administration (Washbrook 1981). At the same time, a transformational school of argument was also developing in favor of *panchayats* and other "indigenous" legal institutions, with the aim of decreasing British control over peoples' lives and, thus, British political influence. Although this transformational approach was developed before Gandhi gained prominence, he provided it with clear shape, and it became part of the ideological structure of independent India (see Meschievitz and Galanter 1982:50–57). Yet this, too, could be seen as playing into conservative interests. Dr. B. R. Ambedkar, the primary drafter of the Indian constitution, argued that the Gandhian emphasis on the supposed morality of the village community was a myth; that the social structure of village life was itself repressive. Himself a member of one of the lowest castes, Ambedkar sought transformation of the traditional social structure of village India, and he strove to create a constitutional structure that would protect the rights of individuals. Part of the framework that Ambedkar created was a system of independent government courts, which were given the power to enforce fundamental rights (see Galanter 1984a). Insofar as *panchayats* or other informal courts divert cases from the formal court system, they serve to weaken the protections offered by the formal law and thus insulate existing relations of power in local settings from challenge.

The Yugoslav Contrast

The debate over the CALs is particularly interesting because of the variation it presents on the paradigms of argument discussed above. On the one hand, arguments of the second kind are clearly present: the basic position of those who would "reform" the CALs was one aimed at limiting access by "the wrong people"—individual workers. However, the first kind of argument, in favor of the socialization of justice as a way of increasing access to justice, is absent. Quite to the contrary: those who argue in favor of increasing access to justice take the position that the attainment of this goal requires the maintanence of *regular* courts.

Why does Yugoslavia exhibit this discrepancy? The most likely explanation is that Yugoslavia is the only one of the countries discussed that already has an avowedly socialist system in place. This condition inverts the correlations of political argument and power associated with the two paradigms in countries not so structured: those in power recite the rhetoric of socialist justice while defining it in ways that limit access, while those who are essentially in opposition to the government or who favor social or legal change point out that social courts may well further oppress individuals not already endowed with local political power.

The openness of the Yugoslav oppositional position, as well as its success, may be due to the specifics of the historical moment in which it was raised. By the early 1980s, Yugoslavia was entering a protracted period of economic stagnation that led to a crisis of faith in the political system of self-management socialism. This political disturbance has led to massive constitutional reforms in 1988 with more reforms promised for the next few years, to overt questioning of the legitimacy of the guiding ideology, and even of the legitimacy of rule by a hegemonic communist party.[1] While these events took place after the ones recounted in this book, the latter were enacted in the course of the social and political processes that stemmed from the accelerating crisis after 1980 and thus were influenced by the tenor of those times. The general ferment of the period included the loosening of restrictions on public discourse (see Hayden 1989c) and a consequent rise in the publication of works critical of the system. In the sphere of law, the idea that a socialist state was one which by definition supported the rights of working people was strongly challenged in 1983 in a work that analyzed the immediate postwar period to call into question the theoretical legitimacy of the one-party state and the restrictions on political and social rights that such a state requires (Koštunica and Čavoški 1983 [English translation 1985]; see particularly 1985:146–161). In this context, the practical argument against *kadi* justice is a restrained and limited one. Yet it is also a far-reaching one, because it brings to the fore a contradiction in the very concept of social courts.

The Contradiction of Social Courts

What the *kadi* justice arguments make clear is this: if a court is embedded in a social field, it will be of little practical value to most people who operate within that field. The political logic behind this assertion is simple, but very practical. An embedded (or social) dispute institution is unlikely to offer support or assistance to those who would challenge established power relations within its own social field. Those who directly exercise power are also likely to control the institutions, such as courts, that exercise the symbols of power, linguistic, ideological, and physical (see Bourdieu 1977:164–165; cf. Yngvesson 1984). For those with little local political clout, this situation creates enormous strategic difficulties in regard to invoking a social court. Perhaps the sine qua non for claim credibility is that the agent to whom the complaint is made is not biased against the claimant. This is not a requirement of objectivity; the claimant would presumably prefer that the intervener be biased, but in the claimant's favor. However, a claim brought to a third party who is biased against the claimant will have very little value. Since those who hold power in the social field will also generally control the courts embedded in that field, the latter are likely to be biased against those who are not powerful. Consequently, it seems that there will be little incentive for most individuals to invoke social courts, as those who already hold power can exercise that power directly, while those who are not already in power will find that the powerful already control the courts.

The traditional socialist counter to this argument is to define it in such a way as to be unproblematical. The basic position is that under socialism, the working class controls the instruments of the state, including the courts, and that the working class is always in the right. Thus if a social court acts primarily to reinforce decisions made by a local political leadership it is thereby following its proper course: the actions of the party are by definition in the interest of the working class, and those who would challenge such actions are thus by definition opposed to those interests. We see here a dynamic by which litigation by individuals is undesirable because they are, by definiton, by the wrong people.

While the explicitness of the definitional exercises in socialist systems may be due to the explicitness of Leninist political theory, the dynamic of labeling those opposed to established power relations as "the wrong people" may be generalizable. The argument is not aimed at a posited authoritarianism in Marxist-Leninist ideology, but rather is meant to point out a contradiction in the ideology of any communally oriented rhetoric that is particularly manifested in the incentives for mobilizing social courts. In a small social field, the problem faced by a would-be plaintiff or claimant is that the social court is likely to be biased against him or her, and there is thus little incentive to use it. This is one facet of the contradiction of social courts.

One might argue that the problems of using social courts to challenge established power relations are most intractable in a small social field, and that lay or informal courts may afford access to justice in less narrowly defined settings. In a larger setting, the pressures of the local political scene may be more attenuated. However, it seems unlikely that an informal or lay court in such a setting will have much to offer to a potential user. If a dispute institution does offer access to coercive power, surely that power will be controlled by other, more regular, organs of social control; no state will offer unchecked access to coercive power to ordinary people. For this reason, a social court cannot really be informal or nonprofessional if it offers access to coercive force. On the other hand, if it does not afford such access, what does it offer to prospective plaintiffs? A major function of formal courts is to induce and structure negotiation (see Mnookin and Kornhauser 1979), and if there is no coercion threatened, what will make a stronger party negotiate?

The contradiction of social courts may thus be stated as follows: If a court is embedded in a small social field, it may have the power to make and enforce decisions, but that power will be available mainly to those who are already powerful and thus not to most individuals. There will therefore be little incentive for most people to invoke such a social court. In larger social settings, if an alternative or social court affords access to coercive power, its exercise of that power is likely to be subject to control by larger political forces. In such cases, the putatively social court will in actuality be part of the regular judicial system.

This conclusion is not exactly an overly optimistic one, since there is a general tendency for regular courts to favor established power relations (Galanter 1974). Still, a choice between easy access to an institution that has little to offer and more difficult access to one that does afford some means of effecting one's wishes is likely to be decided in favor of pursuing the latter. The creation of "alternatives," however, may remove the option. Thus alternatives become favored by those in power as a means for decreasing access to the ideological and physical resources of the state.

This conclusion is somewhat at variance with those of other recent writers on informal justice, who tend to see "alternatives" to regular judicial institutions as primarily an extension of state control into areas of life that were previously independent of it (see, e.g., Abel 1982; Harrington 1985). While it is certainly true that those who use informal courts thereby fall into the hegemonic grasp of the state, it is also clear that people will not use any judicial institutions unless there is a benefit to be derived from doing so. And this puts the state into something of a bind: it can structure some forms of social interaction to some extent, but not completely, since if the services offered by the state do not suit the needs of potential litigants, they will not use them.

The Necessity of Comparison

The examination of the CALs in this book has been made in terms of the Yugoslav discourse on these courts, and the success of one specific paradigm of argument has been seen as grounded in the particulars of the historical context in which it was put forth. The details of this Yugoslav context are necessary for understanding the process of these particular courts. Thus much of the analysis of the history of the CALs can be seen as comparative only in the limited sense of not being American.

Yet there is more to both the analysis and the explanation of these courts than can be found in the specifics of their Yugoslav setting. The Yugoslav discourse on the CALs can be seen as an example of a kind of political debate that seems common to discussions of social courts in other settings, as varied as modern America and colonial India. By comparing these debates, we can see an underlying pattern: that "alternatives" to state courts are frequently advocated by those who are the primary beneficiaries of the existing court structure, as a means for limiting access to existing judicial resources. Furthermore, the political discourses on these points, at their various times and in their different languages, share a commonality of substance: those who posit the need for alternatives frequently ground their arguments in the supposition that many of the disputes coming to the courts are unsuited for adjudication by formal institutions.

This is, on the face of it, a rather odd argument: if the courts are unsuitable fora, why do so many people try to go to them? If this question is asked at all, it is answered by some variant of an argument that while the courts do indeed offer some benefit to potential users, either that benefit is itself illegitimate, or it is not appropriate for the particular kinds of people requesting it. One can see the first argument in the 1980s American polemics over liability suits (see Hayden 1989b), the second in the Indian *panchayat* discourses. The arguments for the "reform" of the CALs, of course, share elements of both positions: the CALs offer improper benefits (e.g., reinstatement to loafers and drunks), and their services were in any event meant primarily for organizations rather than individuals.

Arguments like these, which are based on the supposed impropriety of a particular type of court use, are most likely to succeed when their supposition is not examined. To return to the example of the CALs, it is hard to explain why it should be so undesirable for a workers' court to be used by workers. In America, it is hard in the abstract to explain why people who have been injured through the act or failure to act of another should not be compensated. Yet arguments such as these may avoid challenge if they draw on a body of shared beliefs, local knowledge or "common sense": the way things simply are (cf. Geertz 1983). Common sense is not a neutral body of knowledge, however. What is commonsensical is most likely to be the accepted, unreflexive knowledge of the dominant classes of a society and has been linked to the concept of hegemony (Laitin 1986:19, 180–183; cf. Messick 1988). These views go largely unchallenged because they appear to be "natural," reflections of the way the world works. "Every established order tends to produce . . . the naturalness of its own arbitrariness" (Bourdieu 1977:164).

The importance of comparison is that it makes the arbitrariness of the common sense of particular cultures apparent, thus opening up to questioning arguments that may, in their own context, go unchallenged. By doing so, comparisons serve the greater purpose of making more clear the structural elements that underlie the specifics of arguments in different cultural settings. The principle is, of course, that of Occam's razor; but before that weapon can be wielded, the roots of the various whiskers must be exposed. Or, to change metaphors, comparison necessitates a step back from concentration on the specific features of any one tree in order to contemplate the forest.

On Theory Versus Realities

Perhaps an idea is exceptionally good, but if we wish to implement it, failure to consider reality will most frequently lead, in actuality, to that idea giving birth to its own total contradiction, to absurdity.
—Commentator in Komunist *(Yugoslav Party newspaper), 7 January 1983, in regard to reforming the CALs*

REALITY CHECKPOINT
—Sign on the wall at the top of a blind staircase in the University of Wisconsin Law Library

The most basic distinction between the "reformers" of the CALs and those who wished to keep the courts open to individual workers was that the former viewed the matter strictly through the lens of theory, while the latter raised practical questions. The opponents thus posed a classic argument against the theory: that it did not fit reality.[2] This is a project that should seem congenial to most people active in social science research on law, because much of the original impetus of the law and society movement was to investigate the actual operations of legal institutions and compare the results uncovered by the research with the theories, both legal and political, said to underlie the institutions studied. Yet this kind of research has come under fire in the late 1980s by people highly placed in the law and social science enterprise (see, e.g., Silbey and Sarat 1987; Sarat and Silbey 1988; Trubek and Esser 1989). The criticisms assail social scientific research on law as "scientism," deny the possibility of empirical or objective knowledge, and advocate instead research that "displaces the aspiration for truth . . . with an aspiration for participation"; that "sees things in their singularity rather than assimilating them to general categories" (Sarat and Silbey 1988:141). The aim of the research becomes the facilitation of "transformative politics": "not to uncover some objective, external, determined reality but simply to help us cope with what confronts us today . . . our theories should be as much concerned about how the world ought to be and how we can work to transform it in the directions indicated by our utopian visions," thus making the study of law in society not the "objective yet empty enterprise that Weber envisioned, but rather . . . a process of real social transformation" (Trubek 1986:596–597).

This approach to law and society research is explicitly connected with the postmodernist and deconstructionist theories of philosophy and literature that have been influential in other fields of academia (see, e.g., Sarat and Silbey 1988:129–131), from law (Critical Legal Studies) through anthropology (see Marcus and Fischer 1986). The type of intellectual project that is thereby envisioned is at first glance an attractive one. It is also an extremely naive one, despite the apparent sophistication of the deconstructionist theory that underlies it. If the point of theory is simply to propound utopia, who need pay attention to it? Even if created initially, small utopian communities disappear with time or, if they persist, it is through their own transformation away from their ideals. At the level of attempts to transform societies, the worst excesses of the present century may be seen as resting in attempts to achieve utopia through the creation of societies that are totally respondent to a particular social theory.

Much of the criticism is tied to a political agenda, however, in which what needs to be transformed is the culture and society of advanced capitalism. In this context the situation reported in this book is loaded with irony, since the society searching for transformation is expressly a *socialist* one, the critics who confront theory with reality are confronting socialist theory, and the confrontation is not made by a possibly hostile outsider but rather by the Yugoslavs themselves. Of course, it would be possible to try to defuse the irony in this situation by arguing that neither Yugoslavia nor any other self-described socialist society has yet attained socialism, that they are all versions of state capitalism.[3] This argument need not detain us here, because the basic tenor of it is that theory can never be confronted by reality, a position that may be acceptable in terms of philosophical analysis but is irresponsible in regard to political action.

The utopian project, in fact, is nothing more than the teleological one that is the fallacy of socialist law. If the ends can be defined only by theory, without considering actual social or economic practices, then one quickly attains the inherently inefficient and internally inconsistent structures of political economy that the Hungarian social theorists Feher, Heller and Markus (1983) have identified as "dictatorship over needs." If such is not the case, however, then the utopian project vanishes into the realities of practice; the theories themselves must dissipate.

One way of avoiding this contradiction of theory by practice would be to design a theory of politics that avoids normative implications. This is the enterprise of Habermas's discourse ethics (see Habermas 1979) and, in the American context, of the developing literature on "republicanism" (see Sunstein 1985; Michelman 1986). The basic premise here is that the most moral project is to foster the maintenance of discourse, while refusing to make privileged any specific moral or ethical vision other than the commitment to communication.[4] This approach explicitly recognizes the need for the recognition of varying interests (Sunstein 1985). In so doing, it avoids the teleology of utopian projects, which become too restrictive.

The point here is not necessarily to endorse the republicanist view, but simply to identify it as one attempt to deal with the problems posed by the existence of varying interests in complex societies. Any social theory that discounts the need for consideration of arguments promulgated by competing interests is doomed to stagnation. It is for this reason that the Leninist state, which recognizes only the possibility of administration for the benefits of the working class rather than politics as the expression of competing interests, has been viewed as a "machine for the suppression of time"—Lévi-Strauss's definition of myth (Polan 1984).

The commitment to discourse presupposes that colloquy be reasonable, in the sense that positions taken must be supported by reason if they are to convince; or, conversely, that positions may be countered by reference to evidence. Otherwise, the argument must revert to teleology. While social theories remain immune to ultimate disproof, the repeated failure of the world to conform to their tenets must be recognized as instructive in realms in which political actions are made. It is this necessity of confronting theoretical postulates with evidence from social life that makes empirical research invaluable.

And perhaps also transformational. Although part of the essence of common sense is its resistance to evidence contrary to its tenets (see Hayden 1989b), the history of knowledge has been one of the ultimate refutation of accepted wisdom by the weight of evidence contrary to the precepts of what was hitherto common sense (see Kuhn 1962). If much empirical research in the social sciences is "normal science," it must be remembered that it is the results of precisely this kind of research that ultimately lead to the discrediting of theoretical paradigms in science (Kuhn 1962).

In the present case, this book has analyzed an attempt to implement a theoretical paradigm that is close to the essence of a theory of social courts. The findings of this research, and of studies of other such attempts, indicate that the ideal of social courts contains a contradiction that makes them an unattainable social form. Further, efforts to promote social courts may serve as a cover for the actions of dominant social actors to counter the uncomfortable possibility that the judicial institutions could be turned against them. This may be an uncomfortable conclusion for those who would favor the creation of communally oriented social forms. But if the evidence of social research is ignored in favor of the elaboration of theory, transformative politics must remain a form of social alchemy, dependent on the purity of social actors rather than the properties of the materials with which they must work.

Epilogue, March 1990: The Demise of the CALs?

Since the conceptual basis of the CALs was originally so closely connected with the self-management system created by the 1974 constitution and the LAL, it is not surprising that, with the decline of self-management as an ideology, the future of these courts is less than bright. They were not mentioned in the 1988 amendments to the federal constitution, perhaps because those changes dealt with topics that were more immediately pressing than the nature of the courts. This dispensation seems unlikely to last, however, as at least one concrete proposal for changes in the federal constitution, made by the FEC in February 1990, provided for the abolition of the CAL.[1] This proposal was endorsed by the Committee on the Judiciary of the federal assembly on 14 March 1990 (*Borba*, 15 March 1990, p. 3). Assuming that changes will indeed be made in the federal constitutional structure, it seems likely that the CALs will be eliminated.

Unfortunately, the reasons given for abolishing the CALs are not completely clear as this book goes to press. However, a brief newspaper account of the decision by the committee on the judiciary to eliminate them states that this step was recommended in recognition of the "general agreement on [the need for] strengthening the legal state [*pravna država*]" which makes it "necessary to ensure the greater independence of the judiciary and the selection of the most highly qualified people for these positions." The CALs are seen as unsatisfactory because of "the fact that [they] have not achieved a satisfactory level of specialization, or, more precisely, that there is too much participation by laymen in the process of judgment" (*Borba*, 15 March 1990, p. 3).

For readers of this book this rationale is rich in irony, for it seems clear that the CALs were never the lay courts that either their founders envisioned or the public imagined. It is, furthermore, an inversion of the criticisms made by those who wished to "reform" the CALs in the 1980s. But the irony compounds, in that the 1990 criticism is less accurate empirically than was that of the earlier reform campaign.

Thus the restructuring of the constitutional order in Yugoslavia may lead to the elimination of the CALs, not because they worked badly, or were not really courts, but rather because the public perception of them never encompassed the reality of their operation. For those interested in research on law and society, the elimination of the CALs, if it does occur, may thus serve as something of a cautionary tale: the fate of legal institutions may depend more on folklore than on fact. But that is one of the conditions that our work is meant to counter.

Notes

Chapter 1: Introduction

1. The problem may be even more complex, in that those who concentrate on one part of one of the larger world areas are frequently not conversant with the work of others in that same area. Thus North Indianists often ignore South India, while both neglect China; and the ignorance of Soviet specialists about Eastern Europe is often profound. This situation is itself sometimes deplored by those at the center of the wider area-studies enterprises (see, e.g., Murphy 1988). Ironically, there may be something of a the-grass-is-greener tendency in such comments: Murphy's suggestion (1988:753) that East Europeanists and Slavicists, among others, engage in more intraregional comparisons than do Asianists may come as news to the former (see, e.g., Motyl 1989).

2. Note that I say *should* change; often it seems that "common sense" on any topic can be changed only slowly, perhaps because of its resonance with political (and hence social) hegemony (see Hayden 1987).

3. In regard to socialist legal institutions, this problem is compounded by the potential political biases of supposedly empirical work on the institutions of regimes widely perceived as hostile to human rights. Works on this topic often exhibit either a blind acceptance and glorification of socialist legality or an equally blind hostility to it. While accepting the basic premise that no scientific work is ever completely apolitical, the present study aims to belong to what Christopher Osakwe (1987:1259) has identified in the Introduction to a symposium on socialist law as the "school of analytical detachment," which "carefully searches for the comparable merits and demerits of socialist law." Readers in both Yugoslavia and "the West" may judge for themselves the extent to which this goal is obtained.

4. Of course, this approach is not uncontroversial: in anthropology (and in other fields), it is currently denigrated by some writers as "orientalism" (see, e.g., Inden 1986), borrowing the term from Edward Said's brilliant polemic (1978) on the implicit politics of Western studies of Eastern cultures, which often presume European superiority over those others. Yet this problem may be inherent in any effort at cross-cultural, comparative study (see Minear 1980), and the alternative to comparison is apparently to construct increasingly detailed analyses of incomparable others. This exercise may avoid the misrepresentation of The Other, but leads to a hermetic scholarship of each "other" in splendid isolation. This would seem to doom scholarly work that is truly comparative in the broader sense, which seems pointless. Is the intellectual community likely to benefit more from a scholarship of incomparable

others or from one that endeavors to use the insights provided through consideration of a different culture to reconsider the assumptions underlying that of the writer?

5. I say impressionistic because the reports of success in the socialist courts were often based on little empirical evidence, and do not stand up to rigorous investigation. The classic example may be that of the Cuban Popular Tribunals (see Salas 1983).

6. The studies by Johnson, Kantor, and Schwartz and by Aaronson et al. were published after the Pound Conference, but were cited in earlier forms by Sander (1976).

7. This argument is not, of course, unique to socialism; cf. Barber (1984:280–281), who recommends increasing lay participation in legal cases as a means of strengthening "strong democracy" in Western societies.

8. As will be seen later, this argument has been particularly stressed in Yugoslavia, which has always taken the ideal of the withering of the state more seriously than socialist systems derived from the Soviet model (Lapenna 1964).

9. I say "supposedly" traditional since there is very great doubt that village, as opposed to caste, *panchayats* ever had great currency in most of India. Although caste *panchayats* have probably always existed in India (see Hayden 1981 and 1983), permanent village *panchayats* seem a nineteenth-century romantic notion with no empirical support (Dumont 1980:158–160, 170–172).

10. *Nyaya* is Sanskrit for truth or justice; the *nyaya panchayats*, government-created local dispute institutions, should be distinguished from both the traditional caste *panchayats* and the modern administrative *panchayats* (see Baxi and Galanter 1979; Meschievitz and Galanter 1982). It should also be noted that even though the *nyaya panchayats* are located out in the countryside they may still be several hours' walk or bicycle ride from many villages (Moore 1985:81), and thus are not really "local" for such people.

11. Such a seminar was offered to the public by Professional Education Seminars International, Ltd., in 1985 (brochure on file with the author).

12. It may seem that the idea of voluntary participation in criminal processes is inconsistent; criminal law is, by definition, a matter of the imposition of state power. Nevertheless, NJCs and other alternatives were meant to attract potential complainants away from the regular criminal courts (see, e.g., Felstiner and Williams 1978).

13. One exception to this pattern could be seen in the Community Boards program in San Francisco, which accepts only volunteered cases and does not accept referrals from other agencies or from the courts. However, this program has not in fact attracted very many cases: in the period 1977 to 1982, only 1,576 cases were initiated, and of these almost half (709) were not actually processed. By comparison, over four *months* in 1983, the police in one of the five districts served by the Community Boards handled 930 comparable cases. The Community Boards have actually been more successful in attracting volunteer mediators than disputants (Fred Dubow, presentation to the staff of the American Bar Foundation, Chicago, January 1985).

14. Merry and Silbey are certainly correct in stating that court use is generally disfavored in American culture. The late 1970s and early 1980s have seen the development of a huge polemical literature about a supposed "litigation explosion" in recent years, a literature developed largely without reference to systematic data and generally contradicted by the data that do exist (see Galanter 1983 and 1986). This literature has been produced by elite

members of the legal, business, and political communities and could be seen as itself an artifact of a cultural aversion to litigation among elites. But dislike of litigation is not limited to elites, as the data of Merry and Silbey, and those of other scholars who have studied non-elites, show (Engel 1984; Greenhouse 1985a; Yngvesson 1985).

15. Dr. Kalman Kulcsar, presentation to the staff of the American Bar Foundation, 22 April 1986.

16. References to the constitution that do not contain a date are to the constitution of 1974. References to earlier constitutions will specify the date. Translations from the 1974 constitution and from the Associated Labor Act (1976) are from the official English editions issued by the Secretariat of the Federal Assembly Information Service; other translations are my own. I do not cite the American translation of the Constitution of 1974 (Poulton 1976). Even though this translation was prepared for the Yugoslav Press and Culture Center in New York, its translation is not dependable. The translation of Article 217, for example, is wildly inaccurate in that fully half of the text was omitted.

17. The Socialist Federal Republic of Yugoslavia is composed of six socialist republics (Bosnia and Herzegovina, Croatia, Macedonia, Montenegro, Serbia, and Slovenia) and two socialist autonomous provinces (Kosovo and Vojvodina) within the largest republic, Serbia. Yugoslavia takes the principle of federation seriously, and each of the eight constituent units of the federation has substantial authority over its own affairs and a judiciary that is largely independent of federal control, as will be explained further in chapter 3. There are no federal CALs.

18. As will be seen in chapter 5, one of the largest categories of cases in the CALs involves matters concerning employer-owned housing, which is not within the jurisdiction of most labor courts. Accordingly, I have excluded housing cases in calculating per capita use rates for the CALs.

19. Inga Markovits, personal communication, 18 February 1985. This figure is a more accurate one than that found in Markovits 1982:553–554.

20. The Serbian figure is calculated from the case figures at GSURS 11:20 (1982) and the population figures in Republički zavod za statistiku S. R. Srbije, *Mesečni statistički pregled*, decembar, 1982:40. The West German figure is from Inga Markovits, personal communication, 18 February 1985 (see note 14).

Chapter 2: The Question of Method

1. Those familiar with the battles in American legal scholarship in the 1980s over the Critical Legal Studies attack on conventional legal scholarship may see the call for the departure (or removal?) of CLS adherents from law faculties as a dramatic example of this tendency (see Martin 1985). Resistance need not be so drastic or open, however. It is commonplace among members of the Law & Society Association that despite a quarter of a century of outstanding empirical and theoretical research on law in social contexts, the association and its journal, the *Law & Society Review*, are decidedly out of the mainstream of American academic law.

It is worth noting that the same phenomenon is found elsewhere, including Yugoslavia. In 1974, several members of the Belgrade University law faculty lost their positions because of their sharp criticism of the then-dominant theory of self-management and self-management law. Rather ironically, the ideas that these scholars did not accept were in many ways similar to those of the dominant theorist of CLS, Roberto Unger (compare Unger 1986 with the Introductory Part of the Constitution of Yugoslavia [1974]).

2. Lest this seem a harsh judgment, the author of one such piece called it "a kind of legal journalism" rather than a scientific survey (Alschuler 1968:52).

3. The more sophisticated view has been resisted in some academic law circles, however, by people not trained in ethnographic methods, apparently because it is incongruent with the formal ideology of American law (see, e.g., Schulhofer 1984). This rejection of social science data in favor of legal ideology is a good example of the problems involved in challenging that ideology from within.

4. I am ignoring the questions concerning the epistemological status of "empirical" data that are currently in vogue in anthropology (see, e.g., Marcus and Fischer 1986) and law (see Trubek 1984) as too far afield here, although I will return to them in the last chapter. In fact, similar questions have been raised before in anthropology, if not as tendentiously (see Naroll 1962; Epstein 1967). The solution seems to be to continue to work, recognizing the inherent incompleteness of any project in social science.

5. See chapter 6. The details of the research can be best understood after the presentation of Yugoslav self-management ideology and a description of the legal system.

6. Again, it is necessary to point out that the Yugoslav constitutional system was massively amended in 1988 in ways that may signal a retreat from self-management.

7. The substantiation of these remarks would require a small essay, which is beyond what is needed for the present study. Interested readers may consider the differences in structure between the American Association for the Advancement of Slavic Studies (thoroughly dominated by Soviet and specifically Russian studies) and the Association for Asian Studies (maintaining a balance between the different regions of Asia); it is clear enough where the resources in regard to the former are concentrated. Further consideration could be given to the long-standing support of U.S. governmental agencies for Soviet and East European Studies (e.g., the National Council for Soviet and East European Research, IREX, etc.). Of course, the phenomenon is not one-sided; it is not by accident, for example, that none of the Warsaw Pact countries has a bilateral Fulbright Commission (Yugoslavia, not part of the Warsaw Pact, does have such a commission).

The ties between the Washington policy audience and funding for American research in Eastern Europe, particularly in regard to anthropology, are explored in Halpern (1983).

8. The problems of the politics of anthropological research in Eastern Europe are discussed at length in various issues of the *East European Anthropology Group Newsletter*, published in America since 1982 and an essential element of the scholarly project of anthropology in Eastern Europe. Unfortunately, the circulation of the newsletter is extremely limited. A more generally available discussion of the topic can be found in Hann (1987).

Chapter 3: Yugoslav Self-Management and Law

1. It is necessary to reiterate that this chapter describes the political conditions and geopolitical position of Yugoslavia at the time that the research was undertaken, in the 1980s. At the time of the final revisions of the manuscript for this book (March 1990) both the internal politics and the foreign policy

positions of Yugoslavia were in flux, as was also true in the other countries of Eastern Europe. This chapter has not been revised to reflect those changes, both because they are irrelevant to the study itself, and because the author's crystal ball is murky: anything that one might hazard to write in March 1990 would likely be out of date within a few months.

2. In pointing out this historical division, however, I do not wish to be seen as implying any cultural superiority to "the West" over "the East," as is now asserted by certain scholars from the western parts of Yugoslavia, as well as by American and Western European news media and political figures. This too-easy characterization is in fact more of a caricature, and is best seen as a variant of Orientalism (cf. Said 1978).

3. Including, to a very minor extent, in Yugoslav civil law (see Chloros 1970: chapter 2).

4. Officially the League of Communists of Yugoslavia, rather than the Communist Party. By early 1990, the national League of Communists had more or less disintegrated, although multi-party elections had not yet been held.

5. These were generally short trips to neighboring countries, particularly to Trieste, Italy. Of course, some restrictions on travel are occasionally imposed on individuals, and human rights organizations use these isolated examples to criticize Yugoslavia (see, e.g., Helsinki Watch 1985:303). Further, in 1982 the Yugoslav government attempted to discourage shopping trips outside of the country by requiring a deposit from most citizens leaving on non-business trips. While Helsinki Watch (1985:304) viewed the deposit requirement as a form of repression of the right to travel, the requirement was an economic measure and not an attempt to isolate Yugoslav citizens, and it was, in any event, removed in 1985. The effects of the requirement were interesting in themselves: while in the first year the deposit requirement did cause the number of exits by Yugoslavs to fall by about half, it also led to a great increase in the number of "business" trips abroad.

6. By the late 1980s, the entire paradigm of self-management was under review and likely to be changed. This book will not consider these changes, however, but will instead concentrate on the structure of self-management as it was institutionalized during the time of the research, in the early 1980s.

In the paragraphs that follow, I cite heavily an article by the sociologist Rudi Supek, written before the 1974 constitution (Supek 1973). This is done because of that article's clear delineations of the basic concepts of self-management. For the uninitiated reader, the best introduction to the development of the concept of self-management is Dennison Rusinow's *The Yugoslav Experiment* (1978).

7. Developments in Yugoslav social and political theory induced frequent changes in the constitutional structure of the nation. The first constitution (1946), which had been closely patterned on the Soviet constitution of 1936, was clearly no longer appropriate after the break with Stalin and the Soviet system in 1948. Thus in 1953, this constitution was massively amended, in effect replaced, by a "Constitutional Law," which was itself ultimately replaced by a completely new constitution in 1963. The latter instrument was, in its turn, extensively amended, particularly over the period 1969–1971, paving the way for the "self-management constitution" of 1974. This last instrument has also been massively altered by amendments promulgated in November 1988. However, analysis of the development of Yugoslav constitutional structures is beyond the scope of this book.

8. Readers interested in this subject may wish to consult the few other discussions of it available in English: Chloros (1970: chs. 12 and 13), Van Doren (1972), and Coronna (1985:228–240). Chloros and Coronna cite the original Yugoslav literature as well as Yugoslav publications in English, while Van Doren limits his citations to those available in English. A pessimistic economic analysis of the implications of some aspects of Yugoslav social property is given by Furubotn and Pejovich (1973), but Bajt (1968) should also be consulted. Unless otherwise specified, my discussion of the basic elements of social property follows those of Chloros and Coronna, which are in substantial agreement.

9. A similar definition can be found in Article 10 of the Associated Labor Act (1976), with the exception that that act does not include the phrase "income realized through associated labor." This specification of social property represents a refinement over that used in the 1963 Constitution, which identified only "[t]he means of production and the other means of socially organized work, as well as mineral and other natural resources" as belonging to that category (Article 8).

10. The legal status of the Basic Principles is somewhat obscure. The leading Yugoslav scholar on the subject states that the Basic Principles are part of the constitution, but that their content is more theoretical than normative. He then says that the constitution is a legal and conceptual unity, without an internal hierarchy of norms, and that it must finally develop in accordance with the Basic Principles. Accordingly, this scholar calls for legal science and particularly for the decisions of the constitutional court to serve as the means for reconciling the normative provisions of the constitution with the Basic Principles (Djordjević 1982:129–130).

While the United States Constitution does not contain such a section, basic principles are often found in other constitutions, where their relevance may become a matter of sharp debate. The most noticeable case may be that of India, the constitution of which contains "Directive Principles of State Policy" as its Part IV. Article 37 states that the directive principles are not enforceable by the courts, although they are to be fundamental in governing the country. During the Emergency of 1975–77, the government of Mrs. Indira Gandhi amended the constitution to provide for supremacy of the directive principles over some of the "fundamental rights" guaranteed by Part III of the constitution, a change that provoked much political controversy (see Dhavan 1978:69–70), and was partially reversed by the Janata government that was elected in 1977.

11. These attacks continued to be made through the 1980s. At the annual Belgrade University international conference on Socialism in Yugoslav Theory and Practice in September 1985, Bulgarian and Soviet participants mounted a sustained attack on the idea of social property through pointed questions addressed to one of the founders of Yugoslav self-management theory, Najdan Pašić, aimed at discrediting social property as a Marxist concept.

12. This paragraph relies heavily on Coronna's analysis, as I do not have access to the original writings. Coronna cites R. Legradić, R. Lukić, and A. Finžgar for the essentials of this position. Though the basic writings he cites are from the 1950s and early 1960s, Coronna indicates that they are still valid, and cites some later articles as well.

13. Lapenna (1964) criticized the concept of social property as misleading, on the grounds that the state could at any time reassert direct control over it. As Chloros points out, however (1970:174–177), the fact that the state holds ultimate power is true in such countries as England (under the doctrine of parliamentary supremacy), and that the possibility that the state will withdraw rights does not effect their present validity. For an interesting analysis of the similarities of state regulation over Yugoslav social property and United States industrial property, see Van Doren (1972).

14. But, as the saying goes, living well is the best revenge. In 1986, Gams's treatise was published (Gams 1986) and in fact awarded a prestigious annual prize by the newsweekly *NIN* for the best work in social criticism of the year! (*NIN*, 24 January 1988).

15. By way of contrast, the common law tradition of England has always regarded property as including a variety of separable rights concerning use, possession and disposal (see Lawson 1975, particularly pp. 36–40). As Chloros points out (1970:178–180), the common law concepts may prove useful in discussions of Yugoslav social property, since both involve situations where a sovereign wishes to create extensive rights in possession and use of property while retaining ultimate title unto itself.

16. The following outline of the structure of self-management under the 1974 constitution and the LAL is accurate for the period during which the research for the present study was undertaken. However, it is essential to note that these structures were substantially revised by the massive set of constitutional amendments promulgated on 29 November 1988 (*Službeni List SFRJ* 26/11/88).

17. *Zakon o dopuni zakona o udruženom radu* [Law on a supplement to the Law on Associated Labor], *Službeni List SFRJ* 57/83 (4 November 1983). It is interesting that the law was not officially "amended," but rather "supplemented"; this terminological oddity seems a reflection of the unofficial constitutional status of the Law on Associated Labor.

18. Professor Vladimir Jovanović, in a talk to participants in the annual Belgrade University Seminar on Yugoslav Self-Management in Theory and Practice, September 1985.

19. All of these points are subject to endless debate and refinement. The interested reader may wish to start with H. L. A. Hart (1983[1958]), who provides a clear statement of positivist positions as well as discussions of the important debates surrounding them.

20. Markovits makes one or two passing references to the 1974 Yugoslav constitution, but she clearly does not put this document into the same class as those of the Warsaw Pact countries (see, e.g., Markovits 1982:539–540, n. 118).

21. The amendments to the constitution of India during the Emergency of 1975–77 may illustrate this difference between socialist and Western democratic views of rights. When that instrument was written, it was based on Western models, and contained a separate Part III entitled "Fundamental Rights." In 1976 the Indira Gandhi government enacted an amendment that changed much of the constitution, including adding "socialist" to the statement in the preamble that specifies the nature of the Indian state and adding a new Part IVA on "Fundamental Duties" of the citizen (see Dhavan 1978).

22. The author of this text, Professor Radomir Lukić, is one of the best-known and respected academics of postwar Yugoslavia. Lukić, until his retirement professor of law at Belgrade University, is also regarded as one of the leading figures of Yugoslav sociology.

Chapter 4: Courts in Modern Yugoslavia

1. Yugoslav legal theory views the judiciary and the judicial system in the widest sense, as including such institutions as the prosecutorial service and the public defenders (Djordjević 1982:794). In this book, however, we will be concerned only with courts, and not with these other elements of the judicial system.

2. The official text was published in *Službeni list FNRJ* 10/1946. The text of this instrument is otherwise fairly hard to find, probably because it was soon viewed as unsuitable following the break with Stalin in 1948. An English translation was prepared by the U.S. Department of State, Office of Research and Development (1946). Also of interest are the debates of the constituent assembly, published, along with the discussion draft of the constitution, by Narodna Skupština FNRJ (1946).

3. *Federativna Narodna Republika Jugoslavije*, as the country was then called. The change of name to Socialist Federal Republic of Yugoslavia (1963) was meant to be a further indication of the political distance between Yugoslavia and the Warsaw Pact countries.

4. In fact, the idea of creating federal courts below the Supreme Court was controversial at the American constitutional convention of 1787, and was resisted as an unwarranted intrusion on state sovereignty (see Madison 1984:71–73). Accordingly, the U.S. Constitution directly establishes only the Supreme Court (Article 3 § 1). The establishment of the lower federal courts was left to the discretion of Congress, which created them by the Judiciary Act of 1792.

5. This assessment, too, is in need of correction following the debates in Yugoslavia in 1988–90 over the nature of a federal state. In brief, some Yugoslav theorists now envision the Yugoslav federation as in fact a confederation, with correspondingly less power for the central government (see, e.g., Ribičič and Tomac 1989; Hayden 1990).

6. It is interesting to note that the original Soviet approach to this problem was, like the American one, to create inferior federal courts within the federal units, alongside the court systems already established in those units, although most of these inferior federal courts were removed by the 1936 constitution (Hazard 1984:1191).

7. The Constitutional Law of 1953 and the Law Relating to Courts of Justice of 1954 are available in English translation, with an informative introduction by Professor Jovan Djordjević, in Union of Jurists' Associations of Yugoslavia (1960).

8. Translations from the 1954 Law Relating to Courts of Justice are from the English version published by Union of Jurists' Federations of Yugoslavia (1960).

9. Translations from the 1963 constitution are from what appears to be an official translation, but the copy that I have used was bound (by the University of Chicago Libraries) without proper bibliographical identification.

10. The 1963 constitution was the first to separate the provisions for the courts and public prosecutor (Chapter 6) from those governing the federal supreme court (Chapter 12). This separation has been continued in the 1974 instrument.

11. Actually, earlier constitutions had provided for the possible creation of such courts, but they were not established to any great extent. The only exception seems to have been a form of conciliation council established for the resolution of disputes regarding housing relations (Čok 1985:475). I have not found data on their operation, however.

12. The 1963 constitution and all of the amendments are available in English in Secretariat of the Federal Assembly Information Service (1969; Constitution and Amendments 1–19) and Secretariat of Information of the Federal Executive Council (1971; Amendments 20–42). Discussions of the politics behind the amendments and the restructuring of the Yugoslav federation that they were meant to accomplish can be found in Rusinow (1978: chs. 6 and 7, passim) and Burg (1983).

13. The official translation of the constitution refers to the regular courts as "organs" of state power in Article 92 and as "agencies" of state power in Article 217. The original document, however, uses "organs" (*organi*) in both articles.

14. Čok does not provide data on the numbers of conciliation councils in the republic of Macedonia, although she does indicate that cases are diverted to such councils from the regular courts in that republic (1984:480, table 1).

15. The data were generated by the Institute for Comparative Law in Belgrade, which was commissioned by the Federal Secretariat for the Judiciary and the Organization of the Federal Administration to do a study on the conciliation councils. The institute sent questionnaires to local authorities, asking for information on the work of the conciliation councils from 1 January 1979 to 30 June 1981. The responses, however, varied, some citing data up to February 1982 (Čok 1984:478n.13).

16. Table 1, which reports on the sources of the cases before the conciliation councils, gives a total of 56,925 cases in the entire country. Table 2, which reports on the kinds of cases in the councils, yields a total of 79,685 cases in the entire country.

17. Nevertheless, several Yugoslav constitutional lawyers have told me privately that the closest equivalent to the 1974 constitution would be the American Articles of Confederation, which preceded the present American Constitution. In that context, it may not be accidental that the Federalist Papers were published in Serbo-Croatian translation in 1981. Again, it should be noted that the weaknesses of the Yugoslav (con)federal structure have become apparent in 1988–90 (see Hayden 1990; Rusinow 1988).

18. Zakon o Saveznom Sudu, *Službeni List SFRJ* no. 21/74 and 4/77.

Chapter 5: The Courts of Associated Labor, 1974 to 1984

1. Ustav S.R. Bosne i Hercegovine član 237; Ustav S.R. Crne Gore član 250; Ustav S.R. Hrvatske član 312; Ustav na S.R. Makedonija člen 277; Ustava S.R. Slovenije člen 281; Ustav S.R. Srbije član 249; Ustav S.A.P. Kosova član 245; Ustav S.A.P. Vojvodine član 249. These constitutions are collected in Sofronić (ed.) 1974.

2. *Službeni list SFRJ* no. 24/74, 10 May 1974.

3. Zakon o osnivanju, nadležnosti i sastavu sudova udruženog rada, *Službeni list SR Bosne i Hercegovine* 31/74; Zakon o sudovima udruženog rada, *Službeni*

list SR Crne Gore 27/75; Zakon za sudovite na združeniot trud, *Služben vesnik na SR Makedonije* 41/75; Zakon o sudovima udruženog rada, *Narodne Novine* 26/76 [SR Hrvatska]; Zakon o sodišč združenega dela, *Uradni list SR Slovenije* 38/74; Zakon o sudovima udruženog rada, *Službeni Glasnik SR Srbije* 32/75; Zakon o sudovima udruženog rada, *Službeni list SAP Kosova* 32/76; Zakon o sudovima udruženog rada, *Službeni list SAP Vojvodine* 15/75. These statutes are collected in Rajović 1979: 289–374.

4. However, the appellate CAL in at least one of the republics, Serbia, issued rules (*pravila*) concerning procedures in the CAL in that republic: "Pravila o poslovanju sudova udruženog rada u Srbiji (sudski poslovnik)," *Službeni Glasnik SR Srbije* 30/78 (reprinted in Rajović 1979:377–412). At least one authority has suggested that this act exceeded the authority of the republic, since the regulation of court procedure is a federal responsibility (Pantović 1985:11).

5. More specifically, the special CALs have been created within "self-management communities of interest" (*samoupravne interesne zajednice*, better known as SIZ). These bodies came into existence with the 1974 constitution (Articles 51–59; see Jugoslovenski Pregled 1980:26–30). These have been described succinctly by Jambrek (1983:191) as "umbrella-like permanent structure[s] providing for inter- and trans-organizational decision-making whose aim is to secure and control the flow of financial means into the field [of public service, e.g., life and health insurance, sports, research, culture, education], and of its distribution among the individual service organizations . . . according to the needs and interests of those utilizing their products." The SIZ is controlled by an assembly containing two chambers, one of "producers" and the other of "consumers" of the particular service. In theory, these two chambers should be able to decide jointly on the best course of action in the particular service field without external governmental control. Each of the special CALs is meant to handle the cases arising within the area of interest of the appropriate SIZ.

6. In some republics, however, one member of a bench must be a law graduate (*diplomirani pravnik*). See, e.g., Zakon o sudovima udruženog rada SR Hrvatske, član 13 (Law on Courts of Associated Labor of SR Croatia, Article 13).

7. The social attorney of self-management (*društveni pravobranilac samoupravljanja*) is a kind of civil district attorney charged with protecting social property and the rights of self-managers (see Trajkovski 1978).

8. Zakon o republičkim sudskim taksama, *Službeni glasnik SR Srbije* br. 53/72. These amounts seem very little by the standards of the late 1980s, since the exchange value of the dinar dropped to approximately 100,000 per U.S. dollar by December 1989, and the currency was revalued in January 1990. However, in 1972 the exchange rate was about eighteen dinars per dollar, and in 1981 it was about thirty-five dinars per dollar. The tax tables for civil cases have been revised to keep pace with inflation, but I use the older figures because they were in use at the time the research was conducted.

9. Zakon o parničnom postupku, *Službeni list SFRJ* 4/77 (14 January 1977).

10. Indeed, the entire concept of self-management courts was so much of an innovation that one of the drafters of the relevant articles of the constitution told Dennison Rusinow in 1974 that their ultimate jurisdiction was unclear even to him (Rusinow 1978:328).

11. The discussion at the conference was published in *Arhiv za pravne i*

društvene nauke 41(n.s.):40–59 (1975). The specific comment was by Nikola Stjepanović, at p. 43.

Chapter 6: The Court and the Research

1. Under the federal regulations governing research by foreigners in Yugoslavia (*Službeni list SFRJ* 22/74), almost all such research must be undertaken in collaboration with a Yugoslav partner. Most projects must also receive approval from federal, republican/provincial, and local authorities. In a social and political milieu in which one of the most important principles is that of *veza*, or "connection," the would-be researcher who attempted to work without the support and assistance of Yugoslav colleagues would be unlikely to succeed in gaining access to subjects, even in those few kinds of cases in which formal affiliation may not be required by law.

2. Competence in the local language is essential for ethnographic research, and readers are entitled to an assessment of a researcher's language skills. Although I went to Yugoslavia with very little knowledge of Serbo-Croatian, I immediately took formal instruction in the language, and I lived in an entirely Yugoslav environment with little contact with other foreigners. By the time I began to go to the Belgrade CAL, in April 1982, I understood much of the spoken language and could read legal materials fairly well. My language skills improved as I stayed longer in the country, and by the end of the observational research in 1983 I was reasonably fluent in the Belgrade dialect and quite at home with most written material in modern Serbo-Croatian.

3. In late 1983 the Basic CAL in Belgrade moved to new quarters, where the administrative offices and the courtrooms were united. However, in this study I will refer to the old setting, where the court was located at the time the study was conducted.

4. Unless otherwise specified, any references made to "the judge" refer to the president of the particular panel. This usage reflects that of the personnel of the Belgrade CAL; even though all of the members of a bench are supposed to be equal judges, only the president is called "judge" (*sudija*) in courtroom interaction.

5. In Yugoslav courts, the cases are scheduled for specific times of the day and are not, as is common in some American courts, all simply set for one day with the time not specified or with more than one case scheduled for the same time. The Yugoslav method means that the court personnel may have time between cases, but it also means that the parties and lawyers do not have to wait for their cases to be called.

6. In general, the Yugoslav workday begins at seven in the morning, and lasts until three o'clock in the afternoon. The big meal of the day (*ručak*) is eaten after work. Most people do not eat much before work begins, but rather are entitled to time for breakfast (and usually a subsidized hot meal) at ten or eleven o'clock.

7. In the CAL, the only way to obtain a copy of the record was to ask the stenographer to make an additional carbon, and usually the person making that request had to provide the stenographer with paper and sometimes with carbon paper. I was not required to do so, however.

8. The problem of sampling error is always difficult to control in a case study such as this one. The traditional way of doing so in anthropology is for the researcher to spend at least a year in the field and to gain fluency in the

language of his or her subjects (Naroll 1970), which I did. In addition to these general safeguards, a researcher should also try to combat specific sources of bias when they can be predicted, as I did by varying the benches I observed.

9. The data on employment and caseloads in the first ten years of the Basic CAL in Belgrade are taken from OSURBI 1985. This particular annual report contained more data than usual, in part because of the celebration of the tenth anniversary of the court's founding.

10. In 1978 and 1979 the court also employed a driver, and in 1979 and 1980 a courier. These positions were terminated when the Yugoslav economy entered a state of long-term crisis after 1979.

11. In 1986, however, the person who had served as secretary of the Belgrade CAL at the time the research was conducted was made a full-time judge of that court, and a new secretary was appointed.

12. In Yugoslavia, as indeed in almost the entire world except for the United States, there is no verbatim transcript of trials. Instead, the record is dictated by the presiding judge, and it is this record that is used on appeals.

13. The fact that nearly all of the secretaries of the panels were women caused some inconvenience to the court. The annual reports for both 1984 and 1985 note that productivity was less than desirable or planned for because of the number of these secretaries who took maternity leave. In general, women in Yugoslavia enjoy the right to lengthy, paid maternity leave, although the actual length of time allowed varies with each republic and province. In 1982, a woman in Serbia could combine her vacation time and maternity leave and be away from work for nearly a year.

14. The full-time judges, however, do not use secretaries to draft their opinions, but instead do their own writing.

Chapter 7: Cases Brought to the CAL

1. The figures given in this chapter for the Republic of Serbia do not include figures from the Autonomous Provinces of Vojvodina and Kosovo.

2. There is a certain terminological problem in dealing with Yugoslav labor relations, because at the time of the fieldwork, the traditional firm had been supplanted by the self-management organizational forms (BOALs, COALs, etc.) described in chapter 3, one of which is a Work Organization (*radna organizacija*). In this chapter, I will use "work organization" to refer to any of these self-management forms which were the respondents in cases in the CAL; capitalized, as Work Organization, the term will refer to a *radna organizacija*.

3. For example, "Everything [happens] by connection" (*sve po vezu*); or simply, "He's got a connection" (*Ima on vezu*) as an explanation when an unlikely personnel decision is made in someone's favor. The more unlikely the decision, the more it is seen to depend on connections, and the better the connection is seen to be: thus, "He's got a good [literally, fat] connection" (*Ima on debelu vezu*). Of course, similar phrases are common enough in other systems (e.g., Chicago's), but are perhaps more prevalent in the Yugoslav setting. It is probably not coincidental that Serbo-Croatian–English dictionaries gloss *veza* as both "connection" and "relationship."

4. The fact of employment itself is in many ways more important in Yugoslavia than it is in America because of the greater fringe benefits to Yugoslav jobs. Thus a Yugoslav worker will often be provided with a heavily subsidized hot meal in the morning, given a free pass on municipal transportation facilities, and have opportunities for subsidized vacations. Of course, only em-

ployees earn credits toward pension and retirement funds, and social and medical insurance is more easily available to the employed than to the unemployed. Finally, of course, a paycheck is virtually always better than unemployment compensation, and the latter is in any event given only temporarily.

5. The apprentice (*pripravnik*) position is a common form of probationary employment, while the temporary job cannot be made permanent.

6. It is not clear to me why the court classified reassignments as a category separate from "removal" from an assignment; the latter clearly does not constitute termination of employment, however.

7. Housing is a topic that is immensely complicated in modern Yugoslavia, as it is governed by a number of laws, both federal and republican or provincial. The complications are compounded as the system matures, for after a period of some years (ten years in Serbia), the residents of a social flat obtain effective ownership of the right to reside in it, even if the person employed in the organization that owns the flat leaves that job. Further, once vested in this manner, this right of residence can be inherited by the children of the family. Thus once this right vests in a residence, the original owners (e.g., the firm that bought the place and allocated it to its worker) loses control of it, collecting only a nonmarket rent, and unable to reassign the flat unless the residents abandon it. This situation distorts the market in any number of ways. Thus many flats stand empty for years because the people who have a vested right of residence will not abandon it, even if they emigrate, until the law requires that they do so, which may be up to five years later. Or, many people refuse employment in smaller cities because it would mean abandoning residency in Belgrade, and hence the right to their social flat there. In addition, some firms more or less abandon flats that are not remunerative for them, leaving building maintenance to the city of Belgrade. All of these considerations indicate the highly desirable nature of a social flat, and thus the incentive to litigate for it in the CAL.

8. The longer than usual duration of housing cases meant that I was not able to learn the conclusions of most of the cases that I observed. Thus many of the examples of housing cases given below report issues raised and parties involved, but not outcomes.

9. *Zakon o zdravstvenoj zaštit, Službeni Glasnik SR Srbije br*. 30/79.

10. Indeed, a revision of the legal structure of employment relations in 1989, aimed at introducing greater discipline into the work force, in part by mandating termination for certain kinds of employee misconduct, was challenged by the trade union as "unconstitutional."

11. Or, as M. N. Srinivas is reported to have said, the interaction in small-scale communities is not face to face so much as back to back.

Chapter 8: Participation in the CAL Process

1. In 1984, the CAL in Belgrade moved to a somewhat better location, but it is still housed in an older building that was not built for that purpose. The comments that follow regarding the size of the courtrooms and the arrangement of furniture and people in them hold for the new location as well.

2. Unfortunately, I was not able to elicit explicit criteria for election as president of a bench from the court administration. Clearly, legal training was a plus in this regard. Among nonlawyers, one criterion was dedication to the

work. Thus in 1982, one side judge was noteworthy because he came to the court an hour early to read the day's files, a kind of dedication not exhibited by many, and he was elected president of a panel the following year.

3. Law on Courts of Associated Labor, S.R. Serbia, Art. 6, *Sl. glasnik SR Srbije br.* 32, 26.VIII.75.

4. The form represents the differences between the president of the panel and the members of it graphically, by having two lines for the latter at the bottom left of the page and one for the former at the bottom right. The lines are labeled "Members of the panel" and "President of the panel," respectively.

5. It became something of a standing joke around the court after a while to suggest that I sit on a short-handed bench, an invitation I always declined.

6. Yugoslav labor law provides that the employment of a worker cannot be terminated if his or her position is eliminated by a reorganization; such a worker must be offered a different job. However, a worker who refuses such a new assignment is held as having voluntarily terminated his or her employment (see Baltić 1975). It is generally acknowledged that some organizations may try to use an unfavorable job reassignment as a means to induce a less-favored employee to resign. Yet given the high unemployment in the 1980s in much of Yugoslavia, and particularly in Belgrade, many employees are extremely reluctant to resign a job even when they are dissatisfied with their positions.

Chapter 9: Political Debates Over the CAL, 1981 to 1985

1. In view of the fact that the CALs themselves divide their work among panels that specialize in particular kinds of cases, this particular suggestion could be seen as missing the mark: in effect, the CALs already contain special housing courts. That this point was not raised in the *Analysis* is probably due to the dependence of that report on published figures rather than on observational studies of the actual work of the CAL.

2. See *Službeni list SFRJ* 32/81, item 334.

3. *Predlog za donošenje zakona o sudovima udruženog rada*, Skupština SFRJ, AS br. 509/1. Beograd, December 1981.

4. See Skupština SFRJ, Savezno Veće, Odbor za društveno-političke odnose, "Izveštaj o razmatranju Predloga za donošenje zakona o sudovima udruženog rada," 5 February 1982.

5. A *kadi* is a lower-level Muslim judge, who bases his opinion on religious and moral grounds. The Serbian folk saying derives much of its rhetorical effect from a presupposition that *kadi* justice is arbitrary or, in Weber's assessment, irrational; but this widely held opinion is a misrepresentation of *kadi* justice, which concentrates on local concepts of equity (see Rosen 1980–81).

6. See Skupština SFRJ, Savezno Veće, Odbor za pravosudje, "Izveštaj" (8 February 1982); Odbor za rad, zdravlje i socialnu politiku, "Izveštaj"(10 February 1982); Zakonodavno-pravna komisija, communication to the president of the FEC, 9 February 1982.

7. Stenographic report of the discussion in the FEC, 10 February 1982. See also *Borba*, 11 February 1982, p. 5.

8. Dnevnik 2, Belgrade Television, 23 January 1983.

9. *Zakon o sudovima udruženog rada, Sl. list SFRJ br. 38, 13 jula 1984* (Law on the Courts of Associated Labor, *Official Gazette of the SFR Yugoslavia*, no. 38, 13 July 1984).

10. *Predlog za donošenje zakona o postupku pred sudovima udruženog rada*, 22

October 1985. Federal secretariat for the judiciary and the organization of the federal administration.

11. Tracing the development of the internal Yugoslav discourse on the economic-political-social crisis of the 1980s would require a complete study of its own. Interested readers may see Rusinow (1988).

Chapter 10: Conclusions

1. At the time of final revisions of the manuscript of this book (March 1990) these political events in Yugoslavia were current affairs, not yet subject to scholarly analysis. Nonetheless, readers interested in the progress of the Yugoslav crisis through circa 1987 may consult Rusinow (1988), and later constitutional developments are chronicled by Hayden (1990).

2. The classical nature of this situation is illustrated by an old, old joke, attributed at various times to each of the socialist countries of Eastern Europe. In its briefest form, the joke concerns a man who walks into a clinic and demands to see an eye-ear specialist. He is told that there is no such specialty; that there are eye specialists and ear-nose-throat specialists, but no eye-ear specialists. Nonetheless, the man insists that he needs an eye-ear specialist. When the exasperated staff members ask why he needs such a doctor, the response is "because the things I hear and the things I see aren't the same."

3. It should be noted, however, that this criticism is implicit in a joke current throughout Eastern Europe in the late 1980s: "Marx was right. The advanced capitalist societies *will* be the first to attain socialism." Certainly, after 1989, the Eastern European countries will abandon the attempt.

4. Of course, this position itself can be seen as privileging a liberal conception of social order, eschewing force for "rational" discourse (Moore 1988).

Epilogue, March 1990: The Demise of the CALs?

1. Savezno Izvršeno Veće, "Prijedlog da se Pristupi Promjeni Ustava SFRJ," *Delegatski Vjesnik* no. 496, 8 February 1990, p. 4.

Abbreviations

BOAL	Basic Organization of Associated Labor
CAL	Court of Associated Labor
CAL-S	Court of Associated Labor SR Serbia
COAL	Combined Organization of Associated Labor
GSURS	*Glasnik Suda Udruženog Rada Srbije* (Journal of the Court of Associated Labor, SR Serbia)
LAL	Law on Associated Labor
LCAL	Law on Courts of Associated Labor (federal)
LCAL-S	Law on Courts of Associated Labor SR Serbia
LCP	Law on Civil Procedure
OAL	Organization of Associated Labor
OSURBI	*Osnovni Sud Udruženog Rada u Beogradu, Izveštaj* (Basic CAL in Belgrade, [annual] Report)
SFRJ	Socialistička Federativna Republika Jugoslavije (Socialist Federal Republic of Yugoslavia)

Bibliography

NOTE: The works in this list are ordered according to the principles of English alphabetization, ignoring the diacritics on Serbo-Croatian words.

Aaronson, David, Bert Hoff, Peter Jaszi, Nicholas Kittrie, and David Saari. (1977) The New Justice: Alternatives to Conventional Criminal Adjudication. Washington, DC: U.S. Department of Justice.

Abel, Richard. (1974) "A Comparative Theory of Dispute Institutions in Society." Law & Society Review 8:217–347.

______. (1979) "Western Courts in Non-Western Settings: Patterns of Court Use in Colonial and Neo-Colonial Africa." In Sandra Burman and Barbara Harrell-Bond, eds., The Imposition of Law, pp. 167–200. New York: Academic Press.

______. (1982a) The Politics of Informal Justice (2 vols.). New York: Academic Press.

______. (1982b) "A Socialist Approach to Risk." Maryland Law Review 41:695–754.

Aberle, David. (1987) "Distinguished Lecture: What Kind of Science Is Anthropology?" American Anthropologist 89:551–566.

Ackerman, Bruce. (1977) Private Property and the Constitution. An Essay in Philosophy, Economics, and the Field of Just Compensation. New Haven: Yale University Press.

Alagić, Nedžmudin. (1970) "Podjela Normativne Funkcije izmedju Federacije i Republika u Oblasti Pravosudnog Sistema." In B. Blagojević, ed., Aktuelna Pitanja Podele Normativne Funkcije Izmedju Federacije i Republika. Beograd: Institut za Uporedno Pravo.

Alfini, James. (1986) "Alternative Dispute Resolution and the Courts: An Introduction." Judicature 69:252–254.

Alschuler, Albert. (1968) "The Prosecutor's Role in Plea Bargaining." University of Chicago Law Review 36:50–112.

______. (1983) "Implementing the Criminal Defendant's Right to Trial: Alternatives to the Plea Bargaining System." University of Chicago Law Review 50:931–1050.

American Bar Association. (1977) Report on the National Conference on Minor Disputes Resolution. Chicago: ABA Press.

Appadurai, Arjun. (1986a) "Theory in Anthropology: Center and Periphery." Comparative Studies in Society and History 28:356–361.

______. (1986b) "Is Homo Hierarchicus?" American Ethnologist 13:745–761.

Atkinson, J. Maxwell, and Paul Drew. (1979) Order in Court. Atlantic Highlands, NJ: Academic Press.

Bailey, Frederick G. (1969) Strategems and Spoils: A Social Anthropology of Politics. New York: Schocken.

Bajt, Aleksander. (1968) "Property in Capital and in the Means of Production in Socialist Economies." Journal of Law and Economics 11:1–4.

Ballhatchet, Kenneth. (1957) Social Policy and Social Change in Western India, 1817–1830. London: Oxford University Press.

Baltić, A. (1975) "Termination of Work—Of the Status of Worker in the Organization." Yugoslav Law 1975, #2:23.

Barber, Benjamin. (1984) Strong Democracy: Participatory Politics for a New Age. Berkeley: University of California Press.

Bastaić, Konstantin. (1954) "Razvitak Organa Pravosudja u Novoj Jugoslaviji." In Ferdo Čulinović, ed., Nova Jugoslavija: Pregled Državnopravnog Razvitka. Zagreb: Institut za Historiju Države i Prava Pravnog Fakulteta u Zagrebu.

Bauman, Zygmunt. (1987) "Intellectuals in East-Central Europe: Continuity and Change." East European Politics and Societies 1:162–186.

Baxi, Upendra, and Marc Galanter. (1979) "Panchayat Justice: An Indian Experiment in Legal Access." In M. Cappelletti, ed., Access to Justice, vol. 3, pp. 341–386. Milan: Giuffre.

Beekhuis, Jacob. (1975) "Civil Law." In Property and Trust: International Encyclopedia of Comparative Law, vol. 6, ch. 2, pp. 3–21. The Hague: Mouton.

Beirne, Piers, and Alan Hunt. (1988) "Law and the Constitution of Soviet Society: The Case of Comrade Lenin." Law & Society Review 22:575–614.

Benoit, John. (1984) "What Makes a Successful Mediation Service? An Examination of North American Mediation Services." Paper presented at the annual meeting of the Law & Society Association, Boston, MA, June 7–10.

Berg, Ger van den. (1983) "Judicial Settlement of Individual Labour Disputes in the Soviet Union." Review of Socialist Law 9:125.

Berman, Harold, and James Spindler. (1963) "Soviet Comrades' Courts." Washington Law Review 38:842–910.

Berman, Jesse. (1969) "The Cuban Popular Tribunals." Columbia Law Review 69:1317–1354.

Blankenburg, R., R. Rogowski, and S. Schonholz. (1978) "Phenomena of Legalization: Observations in a German Labour Court." European Yearbook of Law and Sociology 1978:33.

Blumberg, Abraham. (1967) "The Practice of Law as Confidence Game." Law & Society Review 1:15.

Bohannan, Paul. (1957) Justice and Judgment among the Tiv. London: Oxford University Press.

Bok, Derek. (1983) "Law and Its Discontents: A Critical Look at Our Legal System." The Record 38:12–13.

Boorkman, David, Ernest Fazio, Noel Day, and David Weinstein. (1976) An Exemplary Project: Community-Based Corrections in Des Moines. Washington, DC: U.S. Department of Justice.

Bourdieu, Pierre. (1977) Outline of a Theory of Practice. Cambridge: Cambridge University Press.

______. (1987) "The Force of Law: Toward a Sociology of the Juridical Field." Hastings Law Journal 38:805–853.

Brajić, Vlajko. (1974) Radno Pravo u Praksi. Beograd: Službeni List SFRJ.

Brazil, Wayne, Michael Kahn, Jeffrey Newman, and Judith Gold. (1986) "Early Neutral Evaluation: An Experimental Effort to Expidite Dispute Resolution." Judicature 69:279–286.

Brow, James. (1988) "In Pursuit of Hegemony: Representations of Authority and Justice in a Sri Lankan Village." American Ethnologist 15:311–327.

Burg, Steven. (1983) Conflict and Cohesion in Socialist Yugoslavia. Princeton: Princeton University Press.

______. (1986) "Elite Conflict in Post-Tito Yugoslavia." Soviet Studies 38:170–193.

Burger, Warren. (1976) "Agenda for 2000 A.D.—Need for Systematic Anticipation" (Keynote Address for the Pound Conference). Federal Rules Decisions 70:83–95.

______. (1984) "The State of Justice." American Bar Association Journal 70:61–66.

Bush, Robert. (1979) "A Pluralistic Understanding of Access to Justice: Developments in Systems of Justice in African Nations." In M. Cappelletti, ed., Access to Justice, vol. 3, pt. 2, pp. 259–310. Milan: Giuffre.

Buss, Andreas. (1985) Max Weber in Asian Studies. Leiden: Brill.

Butler, William. (1972) "Comradely Justice in Eastern Europe." Current Legal Problems 25:200–218.

______. (1977) "Comradely Justice Revised." Review of Socialist Law 3:325–344.

Čalija, Branko. (1982) "Proces daljeg Podruštvlavanja Vršenje Sudske Funkcije u Svjetlu Novog Nacrta Zakona o Sudovima Udruženog Rada." Privreda i Pravo 21(11/12):16–22.

Cappelletti, Mauro, gen. ed. (1978–79) Access to Justice (four vols.). Milan: Giuffre/Alphen aan den Rijn: Sijthoff and Noordhoff.

______, and Bryant Garth. (1978) Access to Justice. Vol. 1: A World Survey. Milan: Giuffre/Alphen aan den Rijn: Sijthoff and Noordhoff.

Carter, April. (1981) Democratic Reform in Yugoslavia: The Changing Role of the Party. London: Frances Pinter.

Chase, Anthony. (1984) "The Left on Rights: An Introduction." Texas Law Review 62:1541–1562.

Chloros, A. G. (1970) Yugoslav Civil Law: History, Family, Property. Oxford: Oxford University Press.

Christie, Nils. (1976) "Conflicts as Property." British Journal of Criminology 17:1.

Cohen, Lenard. (1985) "Judicial Elites in Yugoslavia: The Professionalization of Political Justice." Review of Socialist Law 11:277–308.

Čok, Vida. (1984) "Mirovna Veća." Annali Pravnog Fakulteta u Beogradu 32:474–492.

Comaroff, John, and Simon Roberts. (1977) "The Invocation of Norms in Dispute Settlement: The Tswana Case." In Ian Hamnett, ed., Social Anthropology and Law. London: Academic Press.

______. (1981) Rules and Processes: The Cultural Logic of Dispute in an African Context. Chicago: University of Chicago Press.

Comisso, Ellen. (1979) Workers' Control under Plan and Market: Implications of Yugoslav Self-Management. New Haven: Yale University Press.

Cook, Royer, Janice Roehl, and David Sheppard. (1980) Neighborhood Justice Centers Field Test: Final Evaluation Report. Washington, DC: U.S. Department of Justice.

Coronna, M. E. (1985) "The Concept of Social Property and the Rights of the Foreign Investor in Yugoslavia." Review of Socialist Law 11:227–248.

Daniels, Stephen. (1985) "Continuity and Change in Patterns of Case Handling: A Case Study of Two Rural Counties." Law & Society Review 19:381–420.

Danzig, Richard. (1973) "Towards the Creation of a Complementary Decentralized System of Criminal Justice." Stanford Law Review 26:1–54.

______, and Michael Lowy. (1975) "Everyday Disputes and Mediation in the United States: A Reply to Professor Felstiner." Law & Society Review 9:675–694.

Dhavan, Rajeev. (1978) The Amendment: Conspiracy or Revolution. Allahabad: Wheeler.

Djilas, Milovan. (1957) The New Class: An Analysis of the Communist System. New York: Harcourt, Brace, Jovanovich.

Djordjević, Jovan. (1961) Ustavno Pravo i Politički Sistem Jugoslavije. Beograd: Savremena Administracija.

______. (1982) Ustavno Pravo. Beograd: Savremena Administracija.

Dumont, Louis. (1975) From Mandeville to Marx. Chicago: University of Chicago Press.

______. (1980) Homo Hierarchicus: An Essay on the Caste System (2d ed.). Chicago: University of Chicago Press.

______. (1985) Essays on Individualism. Chicago: University of Chicago Press.

Dworkin, Ronald. (1978) Taking Rights Seriously. Cambridge: Harvard University Press.

Elphinstone, Mountstuart. (1973[1821]) Report on the Territories Conquered from the Paishwa. (Reprint) Delhi: Oriental Publishers.

Engel, David. (1978) Code and Custom in a Thai Provincial Court. Tucson: University of Arizona Press.

______. (1980) "Legal Pluralism in an American Community: Perspectives on a Civil Trial Court." American Bar Foundation Research Journal 1980:425–454.

______. (1984) "The Ovenbird's Song: Insiders, Outsiders and Personal Injuries in an American Community." Law & Society Review 18:551–582.

Epstein, A. L. (1967) The Craft of Social Anthropology. London: Tavistock.

Feher, Ferenc, Agnes Heller, and Gyorgy Markus. (1983) Dictatorship Over Needs. New York: St. Martin's Press.

Felstiner, William. (1974) "Influences of Social Organization on Dispute Processing." Law & Society Review 9:63–94.

______, and Ann Drew. (1978) European Alternatives to Criminal Trials and Their Applicability in the United States. Washington, DC: U.S. Department of Justice.

______, and Lynne Williams. (1978) "Mediation as an Alternative to Criminal Prosecution: Ideology and Limitations." Law & Human Behavior 2:223–244.

Fenno, Richard. (1986) "Observation, Context and Sequence in the Study of Politics." American Political Science Review 80:3–15.

Fisher, Eric. (1975) "Comment: Community Courts: An Alternative to Conventional Criminal Adjudication." American University Law Review 24:1253–1291.

Freedman, Lawrence. (1984) Legislation on Dispute Resolution. Washington, DC: American Bar Association, Special Committee on Dispute Resolution.

Fuller, Lon. (1964) The Morality of Law. New Haven: Yale University Press.

Furubotn, Erik, and Svetozar Pejovich. (1973) "Property Rights, Economic Decentralization, and the Evolution of the Yugoslav Firm, 1965–1972." Journal of Law and Economics 16:275–302.

Galanter, Marc. (1966) "The Modernization of Law." In M. Weiner, ed., Modernization, pp. 153–165. New York: Basic Books.

______. (1968) "The Displacement of Traditional Law in Modern India." Journal of Social Issues 24:65–91.

______. (1972) "The Aborted Restitution of 'Indigenous Law' in Modern India." Comparative Studies in Society and History 14:53–70.

______. (1974) "Why the 'Haves' Come Out Ahead: Speculations on the Limits of Legal Change." Law & Society Review 9:95–160.

______. (1983) "Reading the Landscape of Disputes: What We Know and Don't Know (and Think We Know) about Our Allegedly Contentious and Litigious Society." UCLA Law Review 31:4–71.

______. (1984a) Competing Equalities: Law and the Backward Classes in India. Berkeley: University of California Press.

______. (1984b) "Worlds of Deals: Using Negotiation to Teach About the Legal Process." Journal of Legal Education 34:268–276.

______. (1985a) "Presidential Address: The Legal Malaise, or, Justice Observed." Law & Society Review 19:537–556.

______. (1985b) "Vision and Revision: A Comment on Yngvesson." Wisconsin Law Review 1985:647–654.

______. (1986) "The Day After the Litigation Explosion." Maryland Law Review 46:3–39.

Gams, Andrija. (1982) O Svojini. Beograd: privately published by Andrija Gams.

______. (1985) "U zamci 'odumiranja'" [interview with A. Gams]. Ekonomska Politika 1748:19–22 (30 September 1985).

______. (1986) Svojina. Beograd: Centar za filozofiju i društvenu teoriju. (Reprinted 1988) Beograd: Naučna Knjiga.

Gandhi, M. K. (1939) Hind Swaraj or Indian Home Rule. Ahmedabad: Navajivan Publishing House.

Geertz, Clifford. (1983) "Common Sense as a Cultural System." In C. Geertz, Local Knowledge. New York: Basic Books.

Gibbs, James. (1963) "The Kpelle Moot." Africa 33:1–10.

Gligorov, Kiro. (1977) "Report of the President of the SFRY Assembly, Kiro Gligorov, Made in Connection with the Adoption of the Associated Labour Act." In The Associated Labour Act. Ljubljana: Dopisna Delevska Univerza.

Gluckman, Max. (1967[1955]) The Judicial Process among the Barotse of Northern Rhodesia (Zambia). Manchester: Manchester University Press.

Goldberg, Stephan, Eric Green, and Frank Sander. (1985) Dispute Resolution. Boston: Little, Brown.

Gorupić, Drago. (1982) "The Basic Organization of Associated Labour." In R. Lang, G. Macesich, and D. Vojnić, eds., Essays on the Political Economy of Yugoslavia. Zagreb: Informator.

Greenhouse, Carol. (1985a) "Interpreting American Litigiousness." Paper presented at the Wenner-Gren international symposium on "Ethnohistorical Models for the Evolution of Law in Specific Societies," Bellagio, Italy, August 10–18.

______. (1985b) "Mediation: A Comparative Approach." Man 20:90–114.

Gulliver, Philip. (1969) "Dispute Settlement without Courts: The Ndendeuli of Tanzania." In L. Nader, ed., Law in Culture and Society. Chicago: Aldine.

Habermas, Jürgen. (1979) Communication and the Evolution of Society. Boston: Beacon Press.

Halpern, Joel. (1983) "Research and Policy: The Case of American Anthropological Work in Eastern Europe." East European Anthropology Group Newsletter 2(2):7–10 (Spring 1983).

Hann, Chris. (1987) "The Politics of Anthropology in Socialist Eastern Europe." In Anthony Jackson, ed., Anthropology at Home. London: Tavistock.

Haraszti, Miklos. (1978) A Worker in a Worker's State. New York: Universe Books.

Harrington, Christine. (1982) "Delegalization Reform Movements: A Historical Analysis." In R. Abel, ed., The Politics of Informal Justice, vol. 1, pp. 35–71.

______. (1984) "The Politics of Participation and Nonparticipation in Dispute Processes." Law & Policy 6:203–230.

______. (1985) Shadow Justice: The Ideology and Institutionalization of Alternatives to Court. Westport, CT: Greenwood Press.

Hart, H. L. A. (1983[1958]) "Positivism and the Separation of Law and Morals." In H. L. A. Hart, Essays in Jurisprudence and Philosophy. Oxford: Clarendon Press.

______. (1961) The Concept of Law. Oxford: Oxford University Press.

Hayden, Robert. (1981) "No One is Stronger than the Caste"—Arguing Dispute Cases in an Indian Caste Panchayat. Unpublished Ph.D. dissertation, Department of Anthropology, State University of New York at Buffalo.

______. (1983) "Excommunication as Everyday Event and Ultimate Sanction: The Nature of Suspension from an Indian Caste." Journal of Asian Studies 42:291–307.

______. (1984a) "A Note on Caste Panchayats and Government Courts in India: Different Kinds of Stages for Different Kinds of Performances." Journal of Legal Pluralism 22:43–52.

______. (1984b) "Rules, Processes and Interpretations: Geertz, Comaroff and Roberts." American Bar Foundation Research Journal 1984:469–478.

______. (1987) "Turn-Taking, Overlap and the Task at Hand: Ordering Speaking Turns in Legal Settings." American Ethnologist 14:251–270.

______. (1989a) "Social Theory and Legal Practice: Intuition, Discourse and Legal Scholarship." Northwestern University Law Review 83:801–812.

______. (1989b) "The Cultural Logic of a Political Crisis: Common Sense, Hegemony and the Great American Liability Insurance Famine of 1986." University of Wisconsin Law School, Disputes Processing Research Program, Working Paper Series 9, Paper no. 8 (March 1989).

______. (1989c) "Using a Microscope to Scan the Horizon." Slavic Review 48:275–279.

______. (1990) Constitutional Events in Yugoslavia, 1988–90: The Confederalization of a Federation? Manuscript.

Hazard, John. (1962) "Furniture Arrangement as a Symbol of Judicial Roles." Et cetera 19:181.

———. (1984) "Socialism and Federation." Michigan Law Review 82:1182–1194.

Helsinki Watch. (1985) Ten Years Later: Violations of the Helsinki Accords. New York: U.S. Helsinki Watch Committee.

Henry, Stuart. (1983) Private Justice. London: Routledge & Kegan Paul.

———. (1985) Community Justice, Capitalist Society and Human Agency: The Dialectics of Collective Law in the Cooperative. Law & Society Review 19:303–327.

Huszar, Tibor. (1978) "White-Collar Workers, Intellectuals, Graduates in Hungary." In T. Huszar, K. Kulcsar, and S. Szalai, eds., Hungarian Society and Marxist Sociology in the Nineteen-Seventies. Budapest: Corvina Press.

ILO (International Labour Office). (1985) The Trade Union Situation and Industrial Relations in Yugoslavia. Geneva: ILO.

Inden, Ronald. (1986) "Orientalist Constructions of India." Modern Asian Studies 20:1–46.

Isaacman, Barbara, and Allen Isaacman. (1982) "A Socialist Legal System in the Making: Mozambique Before and After Independence." In R. Abel, ed., The Politics of Informal Justice, vol. 2. New York: Academic Press.

Jacobs, Herbert. (1972) Justice in America: Courts, Lawyers and the Judicial Process (2d ed.). Boston: Little, Brown.

———. (1978) Justice in America: Courts, Lawyers and the Judicial Process (3d ed.). Boston: Little, Brown.

Jambrek, Peter. (1983) "Compatibility Between Self-Government and Courts: The Case of Judicial Reforms in Yugoslavia." In M. Cain and K. Kulcsar, eds., Disputes and the Law. Budapest: Akademiai Kiado.

———, and Patricia Taylor. (1987) "Modes of Community Involvement of Legal Occupations in Yugoslavia." In D. Kalogeropoulos and J. Kurczewski, eds., Lawyers and Community Involvement. Budapest: Hungarian Academy of Sciences.

Johnson, Earl, Valerie Kantor, and Elizabeth Schwartz. (1977) Outside the Courts: A Survey of Diversion Alternatives in Civil Cases. Williamsburg: National Center for State Courts.

Johnson, Earl, and Elizabeth Schwartz. (1978) A Preliminary Analysis of Alternative Strategies for Processing Civil Disputes. Washington, DC: U.S. Department of Justice.

Journal of Legal Pluralism. (1984) Special Issue on Alternative Dispute Resolution in the Law Curriculum.

Jovanović, Vladimir. (1981) "The Sources of Self-Management Law." Yugoslav Law 1981(1):15–32.

Jugoslovenski Pregled. (1980) Constitutional System of Yugoslavia. Beograd: Jugoslovenski Pregled.

Kanowitz, Leo. (1985) Cases and Materials on Alternative Dispute Resolution. St. Paul, MN: West Publishing Co.

Kelsen, Hans. (1954) The Communist Theory of Law. New York: Praeger.

Kidder, Robert. (1987) "Finding Our Voice in Japan: Upham's Law and Social Change in Japan." Law & Social Inquiry 13:407–412.

Klare, Karl. (1981) "Labor Law as Ideology: Toward a New Historiography of Collective Bargaining." Industrial Relations Law Journal 4:450–482.

Knapp, Victor. (1975) "Socialist Countries." In Property and Trust: International Encyclopedia of Comparative Law, vol. 6, ch. 2. The Hague: Mouton.

______. (1975a) "State Arbitration in Socialist Countries." International Encyclopedia of Comparative Law, vol. 16, ch. 13. The Hague: Mouton.

Konečni, Vladimir, and Ebbe Ebbesen. (1979) "External Validity of Research in Legal Psychology." Law and Human Behavior 3:39–70.

Korać, Ljubiša. (1981) "Sudovi Udruženog Rada Danas i Sutra: Prilog Raspravi o Mogućim Izmenjama i Dopunama Saveznog Zakona o Sudovima Udruženog Rada." Sudska Praksa 1(#12):7–14.

Koštunica, Vojislav, and Kosta Čavoški. (1983) Stranački Pluralizm ili Monizam. Beograd: Univerzitet u Beogradu, Institut društvenih nauka, Centar za filozofiju i društvenu teoriju.

______. (1985) Party Pluralism or Monism. New York: Columbia University Press.

Kuhar, Slavko, and Milenko Jovanović. (1971) "The Judicial System." Yugoslav Survey 12(3):19–40.

Kuhn, Thomas. (1962) The Structure of Scientific Revolutions. Chicago: University of Chicago Press.

Kulcsar, Kalman. (1982) People's Assessors in the Courts. Budapest: Akademia Kiado.

______. (1984) Contemporary Hungarian Society. Budapest(?): Corvina Kiado.

Kurcewski, Jacek, and Kazimierz Frieske. (1977) "Some Problems in the Legal Regulation of the Activities of Economic Institutions." Law & Society Review 11:489–505.

______. (1978) "The Social Conciliatory Commissions in Poland." In M. Cappelletti, ed., Access to Justice, vol. 2, pp. 153–427. Milan: Giuffre.

Laitin, David. (1986) Hegemony and Culture. Chicago: University of Chicago Press.

Lapenna, Ivo. (1964) State and Law: Soviet and Yugoslav Theory. New Haven: Yale University Press.

Lawson, Frederick. (1975) "Common Law." In Property and Trust: International Encyclopedia of Comparative Law, vol. 6, ch. 2. The Hague: Mouton.

Lijphart, Arend. (1971) "Comparative Politics and the Comparative Method." American Political Science Review 65:682–693.

Llewellyn, Karl, and E. Adamson Hoebel. (1941) The Cheyenne Way. Norman: University of Oklahoma Press.

Los, Maria. (1978) "Access to the Civil Justice System in Poland." In M. Cappelletti, ed., Access to Justice, vol. 1. Milan: Giuffre.

Lukić, Radomir. (1982) Sociologija Morala. Beograd: Naučna Knjiga.

______. (1985) Uvod u Pravo. Beograd: Naučna Knjiga.

Macaulay, Stewart. (1963) "Non-Contractual Relations in Business: A Preliminary Study." American Sociological Review 28:55–67.

Madison, James. (1984) Notes of Debates in the Federal Convention of 1787 (rev. ed.). Athens, Ohio: Ohio University Press.

Mandić, Milisav. (1978) "Courts of Associated Labour." Yugoslav Survey 29(#2):71–82.

Marcus, George, and Michael Fischer. (1986) Anthropology as Cultural Critique: An Experimental Moment in the Human Sciences. Chicago: University of Chicago Press.

Markovits, Inga. (1982) "Law or Order—Constitutionalism and Legality in Eastern Europe." Stanford Law Review 34:513–613.

______. (1984) "Social Courts in East Germany." Paper presented at the annual meeting of the Law & Society Association, Boston, MA, June 7–10.

Martin, Peter. (1985) "Of Law and the River, and of Nihilism and Academic Freedom." Journal of Legal Education 35:1–26.

Mather, Lynn. (1977) "Ethnography and the Study of Trial Courts." In John Gardiner, ed., Public Law and Public Policy. New York: Praeger.

______. (1979) Plea Bargaining or Trial? The Process of Criminal Case Disposition. Lexington, MA: Lexington Books.

______, and Barbara Yngvesson. (1980) "Language, Audience and the Transformation of Disputes." Law & Society Review 15:775–821.

Matović, Ivan. (1974) "Sudovi Udruženog Rada kao Instrument Samoupravnog Rješavanja Sporova iz Društveno-ekonomskih i Drugih Samoupravnih Odnosa u Udruženom Radu." Naša Zakonitost 28:949–974.

Mayr, Ernst. (1965) Animal Species and Evolution. Cambridge: The Belknap Press.

McEwan, Craig, and Richard Maiman. (1984) "Mediation in Small Claims Court: Achieving Compliance through Consent." Law & Society Review 18:11–49.

McGillis, Daniel, and Joan Mullen. (1977) Neighborhood Justice Centers: An Analysis of Potential Models. Washington, DC: U.S. Department of Justice.

Merry, Sally. (1982) "The Social Organization of Mediation in Nonindustrial Societies: Implications for Community Justice in America." In R. Abel, ed., The Politics of Informal Justice, vol. 2, pp. 17–45. New York: Academic Press.

______. (1987) "Disputing Without Culture." Harvard Law Review 100:2057–2073.

______, and Susan Silbey. (1984) "What Do Plaintiffs Want? Reexamining the Concept of Dispute." Justice System Journal 9:151–178.

Merryman, John. (1969) The Civil Law Tradition. Stanford: Stanford University Press.

Meschievitz, Catherine. (1986) Civil Litigation and Judicial Policy in the Madras Presidency, 1800–1843. Unpublished doctoral dissertation, Department of History, University of Wisconsin, Madison.

______. (1987) "Panchayat Justice: State-Sponsored Informal Courts in 19th and 20th Century India." University of Wisconsin Law School, Disputes Processing Research Program, Working Paper Series 8, no. 1.

______, and Marc Galanter. (1982) "In Search of Nyaya Panchayats: The Politics of a Moribund Institution." In R. Abel, ed., The Politics of Informal Justice, vol. 2, pp. 47–80. New York: Academic Press.

Messick, Brinkley. (1988) "Kissing Hands and Knees: Hegemony and Hierarchy in Shari'a Discourse." Law & Society Review 22:637–659.

Michelman, Frank. (1986) "Forward: Traces of Self-Government." Harvard Law Review 100:4–77.

Miles-Jašarević, Maja. (1978) "Pravda u Radničkom Kombinezom." Start (Zagreb), March 8, pp. 19–22.

Milošević, Nikša. (1985) "Mirovna Vjeća u Organizacijam Udruženog Rada." Privreda i Prava 24:183–187.

Minear, Richard. (1980) "Orientalism and the Study of Japan." Journal of Asian Studies 39:507–517.

Mnookin, Robert, and Lewis Kornhauser. (1979) "Bargaining in the Shadow of the Law: The Case of Divorce." Yale Law Journal 88:950–997.

Moore, Erin. (1985) Conflict and Compromise: Justice in an Indian Village. Lanham, MD: University Press of America.

Moore, Sally F. (1977) "Individual Interests and Organizational Structures: Dispute Settlements as 'Events of Articulation.'" In Ian Hamnett, ed., Social Anthropology and Law. London: Academic Press.

______. (1978) Law as Process. London: Routledge and Kegan Paul.

______. (1988) "Theories of Force and the Force of Theory." Paper presented at the annual meeting of the American Anthropological Association, Phoenix, AZ, 17–20 November 1988.

Motyl, Alexander. (1989) "'Sovietology in One Country' or Comparative Nationality Studies?" Slavic Review 48:83–88.

Murphey, Rhoads. (1988) "Presidential Address: Toward the Complete Asianist." Journal of Asian Studies 47:747–755.

Musa, Krešimir. (1982) Arbitraža u Organizacijama Udruženog Rada: Samoupravni Sud. Zagreb: Informator.

Nader, Laura. (1969) "Styles of Court Procedure: To Make the Balance." In L. Nader, ed., Law in Culture and Society. Chicago: Aldine.

______. (1984) "From Disputing to Complaining." In D. Black, ed., Toward a General Theory of Social Control. New York: Academic Press.

______, and Harry Todd. (1978) "Introduction: The Disputing Process." In L. Nader and H. Todd, eds., The Disputing Process: Law in Ten Societies. New York: Columbia University Press.

Narodna Skupština FNRJ. (1946) Ustavotvorni Odbori. Beograd: Narodna Skupština FNRJ.

Naroll, Raoul. (1962) Data Quality Control. New York: Free Press.

______. (1966) "Scientific Comparative Politics and International Relations." In R. B. Farrell, ed., Approaches to Comparative and International Politics. Evanston, IL: Northwestern University Press.

______. (1970) "Data Quality Control in Cross-Cultural Surveys." In R. Naroll and R. Cohen, eds., A Handbook of Method in Cultural Anthropology. New York: Columbia University Press.

Newman, Donald. (1966) Conviction: The Determination of Guilt or Innocence without Trial. Boston: Little, Brown.

Nikolić, Aleksandar, and Milan Petrović. (1980) Samoupravno Pravo. Beograd: Službeni list SFRJ.

O'Barr, William. (1982) Linguistic Evidence: Language, Power and Strategy in the Courtroom. New York: Academic Press.

Osakwe, Christopher. (1987) "Introduction: The Greening of Socialist Law as an Academic Discipline." Tulane Law Review 61:1257–1306.

Pantović, Miomir. (1985) Primena Zakona o Parničnom Postupku pred Sudovima Udruženog Rada. Beograd: Dunav.

Pašić, Najdan. (1978) "Ključne Institucije, Odnosi i Kategorije Socialističkog Samoupravljanja." In N. Pašić, ed., Socijalističko Samoupravljanje u Jugoslaviji. Beograd: Radnička Štampa.

______, and Stanislav Grozdanić. (1978) "Razvoj Samoupravljanja u Jugoslaviji." In N. Pašić, ed., Socijalističko Samoupravljanje u Jugoslaviji. Beograd: Radnička Štampa.

Pavćnik, Marijan. (1984) "Self-Management General Acts (The Self-Management Law) as a Source of Law." Yugoslav Law 1984(2):137–166.

Pearson, Jessica. (1982) "An Evaluation of Alternatives to Court Adjudication." Justice System Journal 7:420–444.

Perović, Mirko. (1980) Pravosudni Sistem Jugoslavije. Beograd: Partizanska Knjiga.

Pletsch, Carl. (1981) "The Three Worlds, or the Division of Social Scientific Labor, circa 1950–1975." Comparative Studies in Society and History 23:565–590.

Polan, Anthony. (1984) Lenin and the End of Politics. Berkeley: University of California Press.

Prasnikar, Janez, and Jan Svejnar. (1988) "Economic Behavior of Yugoslav Enterprises." Advances in the Economic Analysis of Participatory and Labor Managed Firms 3:237–311.

Rajović, Veroljub. (1978) Društvena Zaštita Društvene Svojine i Samoupravnih Prava. Beograd: Privredna Štampa.

———. (1979) Sudovi Udruženog Rada (2d ed.). Beograd: Službeni List SFRJ.

Rakić-Vodinelić, Vesna. (1982) "Protection of Diffuse, Fragmentary and Collective Interests in the Yugoslav Court Procedures." Yugoslav Law 1982(3):43–60.

Ramundo, Bernard. (1965) "The Comrades' Court: Molder and Keeper of Socialist Morality." George Washington Law Review 33:692–727.

Ray, Larry, ed. (1983) Dispute Resolution Program Directory. Washington, DC: American Bar Association, Special Committee on Alternative Dispute Resolution.

Ribičič, Ciril, and Zdravko Tomac. (1989) Federalizam po Mjeri Budućnosti. Zagreb: Globus.

Richert, J. (1983) West German Lay Judges: Recruitment and Representativeness. Tampa: University Presses of Florida.

Robinson, Gertrude. (1977) Tito's Maverick Media: The Politics of Mass Communication in Yugoslavia. Urbana: University of Illinois Press.

Rosen, Lawrence. (1980–81) "Equity and Discretion in a Modern Islamic Legal System." Law & Society Review 15:217–245.

Roth, Guenther. (1968) "Introduction." In M. Weber, Economy and Society, pp. xxvii–civ. New York: Bedminster Press.

Rudolph, Lloyd, and Susanne Rudolph. (1965) "Barristers and Brahmans in India: Legal Cultures and Social Change." Comparative Studies in Society and History 8:24–49.

———. (1967) The Modernity of Tradition. Chicago: University of Chicago Press.

Rusinow, Dennison. (1978) The Yugoslav Experiment, 1948–1974. Berkeley: University of California Press.

———, ed. (1988) Yugoslavia: A Fractured Federalism. Washington, DC: The Wilson Center.

Sachs, Albie. (1985) "The Two Dimensions of Socialist Legality: Recent Experience in Mozambique." International Journal of the Sociology of Law 13:133–146.

Said, Edward. (1978) Orientalism. New York: Vintage.

Salas, Luis. (1983) "The Emergence and Decline of the Cuban Popular Tribunals." Law & Society Review 17:587–612.

Sander, Frank. (1976) "Varieties of Dispute Processing." Federal Rules Decisions 76:111–133.

Sarat, Austin, and Susan Silbey. (1988) "The Pull of the Policy Audience." Law & Policy 10:97–166.

Šarkić, Nejbojša. (1986) Izveršenje odluka samoupravnih sudova, sa posebnim osvrtom na izvršenje odluka sudova udruženog rada. Ph.D. dissertation, Faculty of Law, University of Belgrade.

Scaglion, Richard. (1976) Seasonal Patterns in Western Abelam Conflict Management Practices. Ph.D. dissertation, Department of Anthropology, University of Pittsburgh.

Schulhofer, Stephan. (1984) "Is Plea Bargaining Inevitable?" Harvard Law Review 97:1037–1107.

Secretariat of the Federal Assembly [Yugoslavia] Information Service. (1969) The Constitution of the Socialist Federal Republic of Yugoslavia: Constitutional Amendments. Novi Sad: Prosveta.

Secretariat of Information of the Federal Executive Council [Yugoslavia]. (1971) Constitutional Amendments XX–XLII. Novi Sad: Prosveta.

Seroka, James. (1984) "The Policy-Making Roles of the Yugoslav Federal Assembly: Changes, Trends and Implications." Western Political Quarterly 37:363.

Silbey, Susan, and Austin Sarat. (1987) "Critical Traditions in Law and Society Research." Law & Society Review 21:165–174.

Simic, Andrei. (1976) "Acculturation to Urban Life in Serbia." In B. L. Faber, ed., The Social Structure of Eastern Europe, pp. 331–352. New York: Praeger.

Singleton, Fred. (1985) A Short History of the Yugoslav Peoples. Cambridge: Cambridge University Press.

Snyder, Francis. (1981) "Anthropology, Dispute Processes and Law." British Journal of Law and Society 8:141.

Snyder, Frederick. (1980) "Soviet Union Visit Yields Dispute Settlement Insight." Dispute Resolution 5:11.

Sofronić, Zlatomir, ed. (1974) Ustav SFRJ; Ustavi Socialističkih Republika i Pokrajna. Beograd: Prosveta.

Sparer, Ed. (1984) "Fundamental Human Rights, Legal Entitlements, and the Social Struggle: A Friendly Critique of the Critical Legal Studies Movement." Stanford Law Review 36.

Srzentić, Nikola. (1984) The Constitutional Judiciary in Yugoslavia. Beograd: Jugoslovenski Pregled.

Stanković, Gordana. (1988) "Samoupravni Sudovi i Ustavne Promene." Pravni Život 38:888–897.

Starr, June, and Barbara Yngvesson. (1975) "Scarcity and Disputing: Zeroing-In on Compromise Decisions." American Ethnologist 2:553–566.

Steele, Eric. (1981) "The Historical Context of Small Claims Courts." American Bar Foundation Research Journal 1981:296–376.

Stephan, Paul. (1984) "Comrades' Courts and Labor Discipline Since Brezhnev." Paper presented at the annual meeting of the Law & Society Association, Boston, MA, June 7–10.

Stojanović, Ljubisav. (1987) "Courts of Associated Labor." Yugoslav Survey, 1987(2):25–42.

Strempel, Dieter. (1983) "Alternatives Within the Civil Justice System: Report on Stock-Taking and Research Projects in the Federal Republic of Germany, Ministry of Justice." University of Wisconsin Disputes Processing Research Group Working Paper 1983–84. Madison: University of Wisconsin Law School.

Sunstein, Cass. (1985) "Interest Groups in American Public Law." Stanford Law Review 38:29–87.

Supek, Rudi. (1973) "The Statist and Self-managing Models of Socialism." In A. Barton, B. Denitch, and C. Kadushin, eds., Opinion-Making Elites in Yugoslavia, pp. 295–315. New York: Praeger.

———. (1978) "Participation and Industrial Democracy." In J. Obradović and W. Dunn, eds., Workers' Self-Management and Organizational Power in Yugoslavia. Pittsburgh: University of Pittsburgh.

Szelenyi, Ivan. (1976) "The Housing System and Social Structure in Hungary." In B. L. Faber, ed., The Social Structure of Eastern Europe, pp. 301–330. New York: Praeger.

Thomas, Colin. (1982) "Migration and Urban Growth in Yugoslavia." East European Quarterly 16:192–216.

Tiruchelvam, Neelan. (1984) The Ideology of Popular Justice in Sri Lanka: A Socio-Legal Inquiry. Delhi: Vikas.

Tomasic, Roman. (1982) "Mediation as an Alternative to Adjudication: Rhetoric and Reality in the Neighborhood Justice Movement." In R. Tomasic and M. Feeley, eds., Neighborhood Justice: Assessment of an Emerging Idea, pp. 215–248. New York: Longman.

———, and Malcom Feeley. (1982) Neighborhood Justice: Assessment of an Emerging Idea. New York: Longman.

Trajković, Josip. (1980) "Courts of Law." Yugoslav Survey 21:18–35.

Trajkovski, T. (1978) "The Social Attorney of Self-Management." Yugoslav Survey 29(4):23–30.

Trifunović, Miodrag. (1975) "Sudovi udruženog rada." Arhiv za pravne i društvene nauke 1975 (1):17–27.

Trubek, David. (1980–81) "The Construction and Deconstruction of a Disputes-Focussed Approach: An Afterword." Law & Society Review 15:727–747.

———. (1984) "Where the Action Is: Critical Legal Studies and Empiricism." Stanford Law Review 36:575.

———. (1986) "Max Weber's Tragic Modernism and the Study of Law in Society." Law & Society Review 20:573–598.

———, and John Esser. (1989) "Critical Empiricism in American Legal Studies: Paradox, Program or Pandora's Box?" Law & Social Inquiry 14:3–52.

Tushnet, Mark. (1984) "An Essay on Rights." Texas Law Review 62:1363–1403.

Twining, William. (1964) The Place of Customary Law in the National Legal Systems of East Africa. Chicago: University of Chicago Law School.

Unger, Roberto. (1986) The Critical Legal Studies Movement. Cambridge: Harvard University Press.

Union of Jurists' Federations of Yugoslavia. (1960) The Constitution of the Federal People's Republic of Yugoslavia [1953/54]. Beograd: Union of Jurists' Associations of Yugoslavia.

U.S. Department of Justice. (1974) An Exemplary Project: Citizen Dispute Settlement: The Night Prosecutor Program of Columbus, Ohio. Washington, DC: U.S. Department of Justice.

U.S. Department of State, Office of Research and Intelligence. (1946) The Constitution of the Federative Peoples' Republic of Yugoslavia (Publication No. 3725, April 10, 1946). Washington, DC.

Utz, Pamela. (1978) Settling the Facts: Discretion and Negotiation in Criminal Court. Lexington, MA: Lexington Books.
Van Doren, John. (1972) "Ownership of Yugoslav Social Property and United States Industrial Property—A Comparison." Rutgers Law Review 26:73–108.
Van Velsen, J. (1969) "Procedural Informality, Reconciliation and False Comparisons." In M. Gluckman, ed., Ideas and Procedures in African Customary Law, pp. 137–152. London: Oxford University Press.
Vidmar, Neil. (1984) "The Small Claims Court: A Reconceptualization of Disputes and an Empirical Investigation." Law & Society Review 18:515–550.
Vukičević, Borivoje, ed. (1985) Deset Godina Osnovnog Suda Udruženog Rada u Požarevcu, 1975–1985. Požarevac: Osnovni Sud Udruženog Rad.
Washbrook, David. (1981) "Law, State and Agrarian Society in Colonial India." Modern Asian Studies 15:649–721.
Yngvesson, Barbara. (1984) "What Is a Dispute About? The Political Interpretation of Social Control." In D. Black, ed., Toward a General Theory of Social Control, vol. 2. New York: Academic Press.
______. (1985) "Legal Ideology and Community Justice in the Clerk's Office." Legal Studies Forum 9:71–88.
______. (1988) "Disputing Alternatives: Settlement as Science and Politics." Law & Social Inquiry 13:113–132.
Zukin, Sharon. (1981) "The Representation of Working-Class Interests in Socialist Society: Yugoslav Labor Unions." Politics & Society 10:281–316.
Zvekić, Uglješa. (1983) Profesija Sudija: Sociološka Analiza. Ph.D. dissertation, Faculty of Law, University of Belgrade.

Index

University of Pennsylvania Press
Law in Social Context Series

Series Editors

Keith Hawkins, Oxford University, Centre for Socio-Legal Studies
John M. Thomas, State University of New York at Buffalo, School of Management

Richard Lempert and Joseph Sanders. *An Invitation to Law and Social Science: Desert, Disputes and Distribution*. 1986.
Joseph Rees. *Reforming the Workplace: A Study of Self-Regulation in Occupational Safety*. 1988.
Jeffrey A. Roth, John T. Scholz, and Ann Dryden Witte, eds. *Taxpayer Compliance Volume 1: An Agenda for Research*. 1989.
Jeffrey A. Roth and John T. Scholz, eds. *Taxpayer Compliance Volume 2: Social Science Perspectives*. 1989.
Joel F. Handler. *Law and the Search for Community*. 1990.
Robert M. Hayden. *Social Courts in Theory and Practice: Yugslav Workers' Courts in Comparative Perspective*. 1990.

This book was set in Baskerville and Eras typefaces. Baskerville was designed by John Baskerville at his private press in Birmingham, England, in the eighteenth century. The first typeface to depart from oldstyle typeface design, Baskerville has more variation between thick and thin strokes. In an effort to insure that the thick and thin strokes of his typeface reproduced well on paper, John Baskerville developed the first wove paper, the surface of which was much smoother than the laid paper of the time. The development of wove paper was partly responsible for the introduction of typefaces classified as modern, which have even more contrast between thick and thin strokes.

Eras was designed in 1969 by Studio Hollenstein in Paris for the Wagner Typefoundry. A contemporary script-like version of a sans-serif typeface, the letters of Eras have a monotone stroke and are slightly inclined.